BY BARBARA DEMICK

EAT THE BUDDHA
NOTHING TO ENVY
LOGAVINA STREET

LOGAVINA STREET

LOGAVINA STREET

LIFE AND DEATH IN A
SARAJEVO NEIGHBORHOOD

BARBARA DEMICK

RANDOM HOUSE
NEW YORK

2012 Trade Paperback Edition

Copyright © 1996, 2012 by Barbara Demick

All rights reserved.

Published in the United States by Random House, an imprint and division of Penguin Random House LLC, New York.

RANDOM HOUSE and the HOUSE colophon are registered trademarks of Penguin Random House LLC.

Originally published in hardcover and in different form in the United States by Andrews McMeel, a Universal Press Syndicate Company, in 1996.

Photographs by John Costello

Library of Congress Cataloging-in-Publication Data
Demick, Barbara.
Logavina Street : life and death in a Sarajevo neighborhood / by Barbara Demick.—Spiegel & Grau trade pbk. ed.
p. cm.
"Originally published in hardcover in the United States by Andrews McMeel . . . in 1996"—T.p. verso.
Includes bibliographical references.
ISBN 978-0-8129-8276-3
eISBN 978-0-679-64412-5
1. Sarajevo (Bosnia and Hercegovina)—History—Siege, 1992–1996—Personal narratives.   2. Yugoslav War, 1991–1995—Personal narratives, Bosnian.   3. Sarajevo (Bosnia and Hercegovina)—Biography.
4. Sarajevo (Bosnia and Hercegovina)—Social conditions—20th century.   5. Neighborhoods—Bosnia and Hercegovina—Sarajevo—History—20th century.   6. War and society—Bosnia and Hercegovina—Sarajevo—History—20th century.   7. Civilians in war—Bosnia and Hercegovina—Sarajevo—History—20th century.   8. Civilian war casualties—Bosnia and Hercegovina—Sarajevo—History—20th century.
9. Demick, Barbara—Travel—Bosnia and Hercegovina—Sarajevo.   I. Title.
DR1313.32.S27D46 2012
949.703—dc23
2011048307

randomhousebooks.com

Book design by Liz Cosgrove

146122990

Dedicated to
Elizabeth Neuffer (1956–2003)

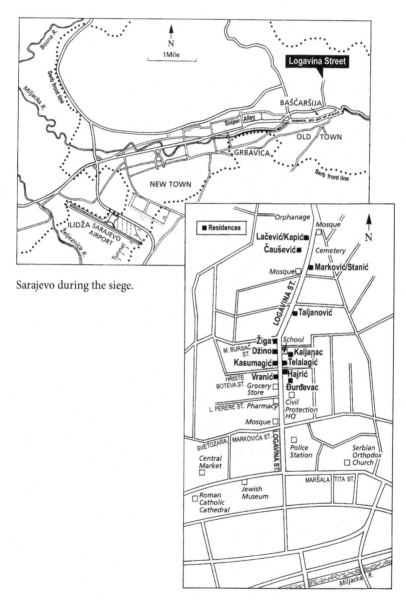

Sarajevo during the siege.

The families of Logavina Street.

Bosnia partitioned: The Dayton peace accord in 1995 ended the war by partitioning Bosnia into a Serb Republic and a federation of Muslims and Croats.

PREFACE

In 1991, the year that the Soviet Union broke up, a nationalist revival was sweeping Eastern Europe. It found its most pernicious expression in the Socialist Federal Republic of Yugoslavia, a country patched together in 1943 out of six republics. Slovenia, the richest and most westernized, extricated itself after only a ten-day war. Croatia's war was longer and deadlier. The Yugoslav National Army, dominated by Serbs, put up more of a fight to hold on to the boomerang-shaped republic that included most of the Adriatic coastline. The savagery reached its height the following year when Bosnia declared its independence from the country that had been collapsing around it. Bosnia was the most ethnically diverse of the republics, and its leaders proposed that it would be in effect a mini-Yugoslavia of Serbs, Croats, and Muslims living together. Nationalists in the Serb population wanted to remain with Serbia and formed a breakaway republic, the Republika Srpska. With the tacit support of Serbian president Slobodan Milošević, they commandeered much of the weaponry of the disbanding Yugoslav National Army and launched a campaign to erase the Muslim presence on the lands they claimed for their own. Concentration camps and mass graves returned to Europe for the first time since World War II. The beautiful city of Sarajevo, with its mosques, synagogues, Orthodox and Catholic churches, was besieged for three and a half years, its food and electric supplies cut off, its civilian population relentlessly bombarded.

Given our experiences of the past two decades—the September 11 attacks, the wars in Iraq and Afghanistan—it is hard to imagine how shocked the world was by the brutality in Bosnia.

The early '90s were a time of giddy optimism. A celebratory mood followed the end of the Cold War. The first Persian Gulf War had been waged and won. The Berlin Wall was gone. Liberal democratic values had triumphed, and we thought we could close the door on the evils of the twentieth century. People were talking about "peace dividend" and "new world order." Who would have guessed that the term *ethnic cleansing* would instead enter the popular lexicon?

In 1993 I accepted an assignment from my newspaper, *The Philadelphia Inquirer,* to report on Eastern Europe while based in Berlin. My background was in investigative and financial reporting (I had recently covered the issue of campaign finance for the 1992 U.S. presidential race, in which Bill Clinton was elected). My focus in Berlin was supposed to be on the reshaping of the region's economy, post–Cold War. As for that nasty little war going on in the former Yugoslavia, a colleague assured me, "It will be over by the time you get there."

Of course it wasn't. And during my stint in Eastern Europe, I never wrote an economic story. The war in Bosnia subsumed my entire four years in Eastern Europe, and I lived less in Berlin than in Sarajevo.

I first came to Sarajevo in January 1994 on a C-130 cargo plane from Split, on the Croatian coast, that was part of the UN airlift bringing aid into the besieged city. When we arrived, we sprinted to the terminal, bags flung over our shoulders, because the airport was under constant fire from Bosnian Serb gunners. We rode downtown in an armored personnel carrier. Like the rest of the press corps, I was staying in the Holiday Inn, its mustard-colored glass façade on the south side blown away by mortar fire from the Serb lines just across the river, less than a mile away.

Luckily, my room faced north. But there were bullet holes and shrapnel in the wall, around which somebody had drawn circles on the wallpaper and written down the dates. It was not an encouraging sign.

A whole generation of war correspondents cut their teeth covering Bosnia, watching from the ground up as a civilian population was bombed and besieged. It was so difficult to get in and out of Sarajevo that a huge press corps simply moved in and became ourselves part of the story. I experienced the siege with the Sarajevans. True, we had electricity, some food, and occasional running water and many of us drove around in armored cars, but we were as vulnerable as anybody to the constant mortar fire. In this environment, the line between journalist and subject blurred.

From the outside, the conflict seemed very complicated—ancient Balkan hatreds, geopolitical fault lines, and all that stuff—but when you were actually there, it was simple. Civilians were trapped inside the city; people with guns were shooting at them—and us. The Sarajevans were impressive. Well into the war, well past the point that brutality should have engendered hatred, when idealism should have been shattered, most Sarajevans still believed they could preserve a multicultural space in their city.

Sarajevo became a cause and a cri de guerre. In the Western world, its very name—like Darfur or Dunkirk—elicited knowing and downcast looks. Luciano Pavarotti organized humanitarian concerts; U2's Bono composed the song "Miss Sarajevo" and visited at the end of the war. The writer Susan Sontag visited Sarajevo when the war was at its height and directed a production of *Waiting for Godot*. She later compared Sarajevo to the Spanish Civil War, calling both "emblematic events" that seemed to "sum up the principal opposing forces of one's time."[1]

When I arrived, an "empathy fatigue"—as they called it in the humanitarian aid business—had settled over Bosnia. Readers were numbed to the suffering of a people whose names they couldn't pronounce in a place they'd never been. To bring home the reality of the war, my editors suggested that, with staff photographer John Costello, I pick a street in Sarajevo and profile the people living there, describing their lives during the war.

I knew the street I wanted to write about the first time I walked up it. Even battered by war, it was a beautiful street, rising uphill at a perfect perpendicular angle from the main thoroughfare, three white minarets piercing the sky above red rooftops. At the first house I visited, a friendly couple guided me through their garden into a small low room protected from the bombing, and served me a delicious *filjan* of perfect coffee. There was a problem though—the name was Kaukčije Abdulah Efendije Street. It would hardly roll off the tongue of my readers, or make them think of the streets where they grew up.

I explained this to my gracious hosts. "But no," the woman of the house told me, "that was a name picked by the Communists. They changed the name back last year. It's called Logavina Street."

I spent the better part of two years on Logavina Street, knocking on doors, drinking the coffee of people who could barely afford it, hearing their tragedies. Their stories formed the basis of a series of articles and later were woven into a book. In early 1995, after a cease-fire made the city a little safer, I moved out of the Holiday Inn into an apartment around the corner from Logavina; later I rented a room in the house of the first couple I met, Jela and Zijo Džino.

The war ended in 1995. After more than a hundred thousand deaths and a massacre in which eight thousand unarmed Muslim men were murdered in the town of Srebrenica, NATO finally intervened in August with air strikes against the Serbs. Much of the initiative came from Bill Clinton, who—although he declared "Never again" at the 1993 dedication of the U.S. Holocaust Memorial Museum in Washington—had dithered for years as the Bosnians were slaughtered. Later that year, a peace deal was signed in Dayton, Ohio, that essentially partitioned Bosnia in two under a weak central government. Clinton's words at the signing reflected the can-do spirit of the time. "We cannot stop all wars for all time but we can stop some wars. We cannot save all women and all children but we can save many of them. We can't do everything but we must do what we can."

Today, all six republics are separate countries—Serbia, Croatia, Macedonia, Montenegro, and Slovenia, as well as Bosnia, although Bosnia is partitioned into separate republics, one for Serbs, one for Croats and Muslims. Kosovo, which is largely Albanian, broke off in 2008, although Serbia has not recognized its independence. The region is more or less at peace, with the exception of occasional skirmishes in Kosovo, where international peacekeepers are still present. The Balkans are considered, as political economist Gerald Knaus wrote in the recently published *Can Intervention Work?*, which he co-authored with Rory Stewart, "the crucible for the emergence of twenty-first-century doctrines of humanitarian intervention, for the modern principle of 'the responsibility to protect,' and for liberal imperialism."[2]

As quickly as Bosnia had made its way into the world's headlines, it disappeared. Every so often a war criminal is arrested— the most important being Bosnian Serb general Ratko Mladić in May 2011. But Bosnia is largely forgotten, its tragedies buried by news about Rwanda, Somalia, September 11. The wars in Iraq and Afghanistan gave intervention a bad name and made foreign policy makers less confident of their ability to build democratic, pluralistic societies abroad. The can-do American idealism that characterized the Clinton administration's intervention in Bosnia long ago fizzled (notwithstanding the relative success of Libya). People don't talk as much about multiculturalism as they did in the 1990s. Perhaps we are less idealistic about ethnic relations or feel we don't have the luxury of worrying about the finer points of civilization when the world is in crisis. A younger generation is coming of age, too young to remember what Bosnia was about or why many of us believed it was a cause worth fighting for. The book *Logavina Street* was originally published in 1996, a year after the war ended. After Bosnia, I left my post in Eastern Europe to cover the Middle East, then Korea, and now China. I'm more cynical now, and less easily shocked by human suffering. In republishing the book, I've made some editorial changes to smooth out the writing but have resisted the temptation to change sections that now strike me as a little naïve. I wanted to preserve the innocence of the time. It is more authentic for the reader to experience it as it was for me in the 1990s, and to share the sense of outrage I felt as a novice foreign correspondent covering Bosnia.

CONTENTS

THE PEOPLE OF LOGAVINA STREET
(AS OF 1994)

SUADA ČAUŠEVIĆ and her husband, ADNAN, live in a basement apartment with their daughter, LEJLA.

JOVAN DIVJAK is the second-ranking general in the Bosnian Army. A Serb, he was born in Belgrade and now lives in an apartment near the foot of Logavina Street.

MILUTIN ĐURĐEVAC, an elderly Serb, was a prominent executive before the war. He and his wife, CVIJETA, live in a large apartment building at the lower end of Logavina.

ZIJO and JELA DŽINO. Zijo is a craftsman who makes silver-inlaid jewelry and pipes for smoking. They live in a house that has been in the family for hundreds of years.

SUAD and BUBA HAJRIĆ are another of the old Logavina families.

EKREM and MINKA KALJANAC. Ekrem is a police officer, and his wife works in a restaurant. They have two young sons.

SELMA and MIRZA KAPIĆ, fourteen and eleven years old at the beginning of the war, are refugees from Derventa in northern Bosnia. They live with the Lačević family.

FUAD KASUMAGIĆ is a jeweler and cousin of Zijo Džino's. He lives next door to the Džinos.

DELILA LAČEVIĆ, a teenager, lives in an old house across from the Logavina Street cemetery, at the top of the hill. Her uncle and aunt, MUSTAFA and ŠAĆIRA LAČEVIĆ, and their daughters, LANA and MAŠA, share the house along with their refugee cousins from Derventa.

MLADEN MARKOVIĆ is a soldier in the Bosnian Army. He is Serb. His wife, VERONIKA, and young son live in Germany.

KIRA PRGOVSKI is a nurse who lives downstairs from the Kaljanacs.

DESA STANIĆ, an ethnic Serb married to an ethnic Croatian, who was killed serving in the Bosnian Army; lives with her two children on the upper part of Logavina Street.

ESAD TALJANOVIĆ is a dentist who runs a private practice out of an old family house next to the Razija Omanović school. His wife, ŠAĆIRA, is a nurse; they have two children.

KASEMA TELALAGIĆ is a doctor. Her husband, DINO, owns an auto body shop attached to their house.

SEAD and VETKA VRANIĆ live in a pink mansion, the biggest house on Logavina. They have a son, TARIK, in the Bosnian Army.

ALIJA ŽIGA runs a small mosque next door to his apartment, and across from the cemetery.

INTRODUCTION

DELILA LAČEVIĆ WOULD later say that the shrapnel in her body had been itching all day. She was only nineteen years old but she had an ancient's sensibility for danger. It was just past noon, February 5, 1994, and we were standing outside an apartment building on Logavina Street when we heard the thud. It was a dull thud, no more startling than a taxi honking its horn a block away. With the blithe ignorance of a new-comer, I wasn't overly alarmed, but Delila instantly tensed, the color draining from her face.

"That sounded like it was the market," she said darkly. How did she know? I had arrived from New York two weeks earlier to discover that Sarajevo was an even noisier city. It had a strange urban clamor. Some sounds signaled imminent danger.

Delila had become an expert in matters of mortar shells. She knew an incoming whistle from an outgoing one, and could tell you the shell's caliber from the resonance of the thud. She'd developed the knowledge after her own close encounter with a mortar shell, during the second year of the war, a horrific incident in which her parents were killed. Although barely a year had passed, Delila was funny and gregarious—with the animated manner of an actress—and she took me under her wing as soon as I arrived. I was writing a series of stories for *The Philadelphia Inquirer* about the street where Delila lived—Logavina Street—and she immediately volunteered to introduce me to her neighbors.

On the Saturday afternoon when we heard the thud, Delila wanted to buy cigarettes at the outdoor market, and I was impatient to snag a couple of onions before all of the goods ran out. But she persuaded me to meet just one more neighbor before heading downtown.

So it happened that Delila and I were standing on the concrete stoop of an apartment building on Logavina, instead of shopping at the market, when we heard it. Delila insisted on running home, but my driver and I decided to go on without her, down the steep hill of Logavina Street, making a right turn onto Sarajevo's main street, Maršala Tita, into chaos.

We were blocked by a cordon of police but could hear a steady wail coming from the market. Cars screeched past with their hatchbacks lifted to carry as many bodies as possible. Through the three-inch-thick windshield of my bulletproof car, it was hard to tell whether the wounded were dead or alive. My driver murmured, *"Granata,"* mortar shell, and knowing that one shell was often followed by another, he took off in the direction of the Holiday Inn. We picked up *Inquirer* photographer John Costello and returned to the market a few minutes later.

By the time we got back, the market was eerily quiet, just a handful of tense policemen with Kalashnikov rifles standing about. The bodies had been removed, but not the remains. A man was carting off a black lace-up boot with a foot still in it.

We wandered among the tables looking at what was left: shopping bags dropped in terror, a schoolchild's blue knapsack with little brown apples spilling out—treasures in a city where no scrap of food was wasted.

It was an uncommonly pretty day for February—which had drawn a large crowd to the market—and sunlight glinted off the pools of blood. You could see where the victims had been dragged away, by the streaks that looked like red paint spread by a roller. Much of the merchandise still sat undisturbed—little piles of potatoes and, yes, onions, stacked neatly as cannonballs. A reporter I knew spotted a man's severed head, which had landed upright on a table, like a cabbage proffered for sale.

We returned to Logavina Street the next day and found Delila at home, pale and subdued. She told me she had burst into tears after she'd heard the news. "I cried like it happened to me, as if it was my own parents all over again," she said.

Sixty-eight people died that day at the market. A single 120-millimeter mortar shell had done the damage. It was the same weapon that Delila had encountered the year before, and just another dose of punishment for the people of Sarajevo who refused to surrender to the Bosnian Serbs, who had formed their own army with support and equipment from Belgrade. It was the deadliest single incident in the Bosnian war up to that time. But, after twenty-two months of siege, it was just another in a succession of very, very bad days.

Logavina Street is a six-block-long history lesson. To know Logavina is to know Sarajevo, and to understand what this city once was, and what it has become. To know Logavina is to witness the strength and ingenuity that ordinary people can muster in order to survive. Here, as elsewhere, the war had turned everything upside down. It had turned rich men into paupers, and light into darkness.

Before the war, residents of Logavina Street looked forward to clear, bright days. Now they waited for fog and rain, which obscured them from the snipers' view. Before the war, the best homes on Logavina faced south and offered unobstructed views of lovely Mount Trebević, the site of the toboggan and bobsled competitions in the 1984 Winter Olympics. Now, the mountain and former ski chalets were occupied by Bosnian Serbs, their artillery guns pointing toward Sarajevo.

Esad Taljanović, a dentist, lived in one of Logavina Street's nicer houses, which had a playroom with a big bay window overlooking the mountain. He kept the room locked to prevent his children from playing there. "What else can I do?" he demanded with an angry, helpless shrug. "How do I explain to my babies that there are people up there who want to kill them? How do I explain that to anyone?"

In 1993, Esad's father was killed by a shell while he napped in an armchair near a window. "My father died in my arms," he remembered. "All I could think at the time was, Thank God it was him and not one of the kids."

On the day of the market massacre, Zijo Džino, a gentle man of fifty-nine whom I'd met two weeks earlier, was in a blind rage. "This isn't a war, this is murder. If they were normal people, they would go out on the front lines and fight, not throw bombs at civilians."

Everybody I met on Logavina Street had a tale to tell about a relative, a friend, or a neighbor killed. The deaths were tragic, unexpected. A six-year-old boy was killed when he rushed to the window to gawk at mortars crashing in the backyard. His mother had been taking a bath and wasn't quick enough to pull him to safety. A woman stepped out of her house to take out the rubbish just as a mortar landed outside her door.

By late 1995, the Bosnian Institute of Public Health had logged more than 10,000 deaths and 61,000 injuries, in a city with a wartime population of about 360,000. Your chances of death or serious injury were about one in five. On Logavina Street, which was somewhat safer than other neighborhoods, 14 people had been killed and more than 40 wounded. A residential street of single-family homes and small apartment buildings, it is home to about 240 families—roughly 700 people in all.

Logavina is one of the oldest streets in Sarajevo, named for the Logavije family, rich Muslim landowners who settled there in the sixteenth century. It originates in the medieval heart of old Sarajevo and wends its way northward, up to the hills above the city. Steep as any San Francisco street, Logavina is a breathless climb upward and a death-defying descent for children on wooden sleds in the snowy winters.

The residents were predominantly Muslim, though not exclusively. Nobody on the street missed an opportunity to point out that Serbs still lived there, the same as anyone else. "We have lived here among the Muslims for forty-three years," Milutin Đurđevac, an elderly Serb, told me. "Those same fanatics up there are shooting at me. I feel more uncomfortable by the fact that I'm here, where I can get shot or shelled, than I am from being a Serb in Sarajevo."

There are three mosques on Logavina, their white minarets jutting into the distinctive Sarajevo skyline. Within a few blocks are Sarajevo's old Orthodox church, the Roman Catholic cathedral, and a Jewish museum.

The architecture bears witness to the empires that have occupied Bosnia over the centuries. Near the foot of Logavina Street is the Baščaršija, the historic Turkish market district made up of cobblestoned alleyways flanked by coppersmiths and tiny coffee shops. It is the legacy of the Ottoman Turks, who conquered Bosnia in 1463, bringing the Islamic faith with them.

Farther up the street are a few of the grander homes in Sarajevo, haughty buildings painted in pinks and yellows with ornate detailing typical of the Austro-Hungarian Empire, which ruled Bosnia before World War I. Then, in drabber tones, come the concrete apartment buildings, bearing the unmistakable stamp of Yugoslavia's Communist era.

Logavina was traditionally one of the better addresses in Sarajevo, home to the merchant and landowning class, but after World War II, when Marshal Tito came to power, many of the larger homes were confiscated and demolished. The Communists changed the name of the street to Kaukčije Abdulah Efendije, after a nineteenth-century Bosnian patriot who was executed for his resistance to the Austrian empire. The name never stuck—residents always preferred the shorter Logavina. It was officially changed back in 1993, although the city was too broke to buy new street signs.

When John Costello and I arrived in Sarajevo during the second winter of the war, the street was being rearranged by yet another would-be occupation force: the Bosnian Serbs. The city had weathered ninety-three straight weeks of shelling and looked like the set of a post-nuclear-holocaust science fiction film.

The shops on Logavina Street were all closed. Stray dogs prowled for food, growling at pedestrians. Many were household pets let loose by their owners for lack of food. At the intersection of Logavina and Maršala Tita, we peered into the ghostly remains of the Caffe Elvis with its shattered windows and empty sun patio. Heading up Logavina, we passed the Bozadžijina mosque behind a padlocked gate, garbage piled high out front, part of its minaret blasted away.

Not one of the seventy buildings on Logavina Street had been spared from the shelling. Shrapnel had pocked every façade. Red plastic tarpaulins were draped over partially destroyed roofs. Where there had once been windows, now there was thin plastic sheeting. The cars were riddled with bullet holes—their tires and upholstery had been stripped to burn for fuel. With gasoline prices at $100 a gallon, hardly anybody drove anymore. Traffic was made up mostly of UN trucks and tanks.

As we climbed farther up Logavina the pedestrian traffic began to thin out, too. A hand-lettered sign at an intersection warned *pazi snajper!*—"Caution Sniper!" There was a peculiar spiraling imprint in the middle of the road, as though a monstrous animal had stepped in wet pavement. An old woman spit at it. Later, we learned it was the scar of a 120-millimeter mortar shell—they called them pawprints—and that the superstitious believed spitting on them would ward off more bad luck.

This was an exposed area, next to a large Muslim cemetery where Delila's parents were buried, not twenty feet from her house. Delila rarely visited their graves because of snipers. "I put artificial flowers on their graves a couple of days ago, but they blew away. I'm frightened to go back there now," she had told me.

It was a scary time in Sarajevo. In daylight, it was too dangerous to go outside within view of the snipers. By night, a terrifying perversion of a sound and light show. The sound alone was maddening. Sarajevo's peculiar topography, being situated in a valley, amplified the sounds of shelling from the hillside so the entire city resonated like a giant kettledrum. Without working streetlights, the city became a void of darkness, pierced by the streaks of tracer bullets and a glow from the frequently erupting fires. It smelled bad, too, with the acrid odor of stoves consuming shoes, plastic, and other random objects, burned by Sarajevans desperate to stay warm.

Since April 1992, militant Serb nationalists had held Sarajevo hostage in retaliation for Bosnia's secession from Serb-dominated Yugoslavia. The Bosnian capital was in an indefensible position, encircled by mountains. Entrenched high in the hills, the Serbs were able to isolate Sarajevo as easily as a child trapping an insect in a jar. This was medieval siege warfare, adapted for the twentieth century. The Serbs cut off food, fuel, and running water, along with the modern amenities: electricity, telephones, and mail.

Suada Čaušević, a neighbor of Delila's, explained the incredible shock of living under primitive siege conditions in the modern world. Like everybody else, she used a car battery to watch television and could pick up broadcasts from Belgrade—a hundred miles away. "I saw a pizza advertised on Belgrade television. Can you believe it? A pizza? I don't have anything to give my daughter but beans and rice. I feel like screaming!"

Suada was five months pregnant with her second child when we met, and she weighed barely a hundred pounds. She had nearly miscarried twice but was too frightened to leave her basement apartment to visit the doctor. "We live like little birds in a cage."

With good reason, life in Sarajevo had burrowed underground. If people weren't hiding in a bomb shelter, they sought out the safest corner of their own homes and set up camp. Kasema Telalagić, a thirty-seven-year-old doctor, lived in a claustrophobic laundry room with her husband, two children, and mother-in-law.

"This is how doctors live now in Sarajevo," Kasema said with a laugh. Upstairs, she had a four-poster bed, velvet-covered dining room chairs and sofa, antique paintings, and a gourmet kitchen with a mixer, juicer, microwave, and espresso machine. As we sat in the laundry room under the sandbags protecting the single window, she pulled out a photo album to show us pictures of the rest of her house.

Everybody was anxious to explain that they hadn't always lived like barbarians. Usually within minutes of meeting us, they pulled out their fading snapshots of vacations spent skiing in Switzerland or sunning on the Mediterranean. They showed off the fashionable clothes they once wore—usually imported from Italy. Sarajevans were sophisticated travelers, and many had worked abroad.

Suad and Buba Hajrić, a couple in their fifties, rigged their video recorder and television to a car battery to show us their weekend house, about two miles up the hill from Logavina Street. Suad had spent nearly $300,000 building the place himself. The house sat on what became the front lines and was annihilated within weeks of the war's beginning.

They popped in another videotape. This one showed their twenty-one-year-old son, an only child, in San Diego. He had been critically wounded in the legs fighting for the Bosnian Army and was lucky enough to be evacuated. They had no idea when, if ever, they might see him again.

"This street has been through a lot of hard times," said Suad Hajrić. He pointed out the spot in the backyard where his father had been killed in 1943, when Allied troops bombed a school next door that had been taken over by the Nazis. "A lot of terrible things happened during World War II, but nothing so terrible as this. All of that war, the trams kept running. We've had no public transportation here for almost two years."

Sarajevans were especially prone to morbid reflection the week after the market massacre. The bombing happened on the ten-year anniversary of the Sarajevo Winter Olympics, the most glorious event in the city's modern history. As they buried the market victims in a former training field next to Zetra Olympic Hall, the television was broadcasting live the opening ceremonies of the 1994 Winter Olympics from Lillehammer, Norway.

Jela Džino could still remember what she had cooked ten years earlier, for the foreign visitors who flocked to Sarajevo—Dalmatian fish stews and grilled meats. Her daughter, Alma, had been a guide for the German Olympic team during the Sarajevo games and had brought a parade of foreigners to taste her mother's famous cooking. Jela pulled a stash of Olympic memorabilia out of a closet: ski hats, scarves, posters, a special edition of a Japanese magazine on Sarajevo. There was a picture of Alma, blond and smiling, on her skis. Alma had fled Sarajevo at the beginning of the war, moving to Johannesburg. Jela and her husband, Zijo, had not heard anything from her and their granddaughter for seven months.

"It is fate. How terrible it is," moaned Jela, tears welling in her eyes. "My Alma, she is so pretty. She speaks fluent German. Germans always ask her, 'What part of Germany are you from?'"

Fuad Kasumagić, a cousin of the Džinos' who lived next door, remembered the morning of February 9, 1984, with excruciating clarity. The night before, he had been invited to an Olympic opening ceremony reception with some friends from Slovenia, in the northwest of what was then Yugoslavia.

"It had been a year without snow. The Slovenes were very

jealous that we had the Olympics, not them, and were teasing us about the weather. But then, it snowed heavily overnight after the opening ceremony. We woke up and the city was blanketed with snow, beautiful white snow. It was like choreography, executed perfectly. . . . Every Sarajevan had great memories of the Olympics. We were all pretty rich. We lived well. Yugoslavia was Yugoslavia. The Slovenes, the Serbs, the Croats, they all came here and felt at home. The city was crowded with people, laughing, smiling."

Fuad's eyes misted as he spoke, and he removed his glasses to wipe them.

In *Survival in Auschwitz,* Primo Levi wrote that he and others interned in the most infamous Nazi concentration camps never lost their ability to experience joy. "Sooner or later in life, everyone discovers that perfect happiness is unrealizable, but there are few who pause to consider the antithesis: that perfect unhappiness is equally unobtainable. . . . Our ever-insufficient knowledge of the future opposes it and this is called in the one instance hope."[1]

Sarajevans had learned to extract small doses of pleasure from a well of misery. Kasema Telalagić described optimism as her most precious asset for survival. "I have to think things will get better or else I can't go on."

Joy was never completely extinguished on Logavina Street. There was a soccer team with members who managed to stay in shape, even if it meant doing calisthenics in the bomb shelter. After the lights went out and the schools closed, children on wooden sleds careened down Logavina Street with maniacal disregard for their safety.

"You can't stop life," Kasema said. "My thirteen-year-old son, he tells me, 'I want to play. What will happen, will happen. That is destiny.' It is hard to argue with him."

If every day was an ordeal, every night was a celebration of survival. There were simple pleasures. If it was too dangerous to go out by daylight, night provided some cover from the snipers. Sarajevans strolled by night—they quickly learned to navigate through the darkness. Without electricity, the stars twinkled brighter in Sarajevo than in any other city I had visited. There was a manic quality to the way people laughed, and to the way they relished a cup of coffee.

They learned to live for the moment; sudden death taught them there might be few moments left.

"Today, if you give me a pack of cigarettes, I'll smoke them all at once because I don't know if I'll be here tomorrow," Delila Lačević explained.

Sead Vranić, a proud, impecunious man of fifty-six, took us on a room-by-room tour of his house, pointing out the priceless antiques he had refused to sell. His was the biggest house on Logavina Street, an imposing pink mansion that his grandfather had built in 1925. It had been one of the first homes in Sarajevo with radiators and steam heat. By the time I met the Vranićs, the family fortune was long gone, the radiators stone cold. Sead's wife, Vetka, was urging him to burn a collection of ten thousand sports magazines. "I know people in Sarajevo are burning books," he said, "but some things are sacred."

Instead, they were burning leaves and branches from the rose garden. They had set up a makeshift aluminum stove in the middle of the living room where they slept, cooked, and heated the water for washing. As we talked, Vetka boiled rosehip tea from the garden and apologized that they could not afford coffee.

"This war has sent us back not to the Middle Ages, but to the stone ages," Sead said. "We have eaten nothing but rice and beans for the last three months and yet we have survived. Out of spite, we will survive to show that we are stronger than they are."

Watching Sead and Vetka tend the stove, it struck me that their ordeal was just as daunting as adventure tales about people who are trapped for days in avalanches, or about plane crash survivors who are stuck on desert islands. Sead and Vetka were ordinary people—not particularly heroic in disposition or in physical strength—yet by simply holding out, they had withstood one of the most extreme endurance tests of the late twentieth century.

As though she were reading my thoughts, Vetka Vranić looked up from the stove and asked point-blank: "How do you think you Americans would survive in conditions like this? Do you think you would have survived?"

I couldn't honestly say.

LOGAVINA STREET

1

DENIAL

A PLAQUE IDENTIFIES a mustard-yellow house on Logavina Street as the residence and office of Esad Taljanović,
stomatolog—dentist. You enter into a formal dining room
dominated by a well-polished mahogany table, which is invariably spread with a lace cloth and, in summer, dressed with
fresh-cut flowers in a crystal vase. It looks as though the
Taljanovićs are expecting guests for tea and scones.

At almost any hour, Šaćira Taljanović, Esad's wife, answers
the door with a fresh coating of pink lipstick, her blond hair
brushed back behind a velvet headband.

Esad is a tall, fit man with a confident, white grin, as befits
his profession. Whether speaking to a gape-mouthed patient
or sitting around the dining room table, he is happy to ex-
pound his many theories of politics and culture. But Esad is
also willing to admit when he is wrong, and he was dead wrong
during the winter of 1991–92, when he declared to anyone
who would listen: There will be no war in Sarajevo.

As far as Esad and many of his friends were concerned, war
was something you watched on television. Something the old

folks reminisced about. Well past the point when they should have known better, Sarajevans found it simply inconceivable that their country would succumb to the lunacy of war.

Throughout the last half of 1991, large swaths of Croatia were in flames. Esad and Šaćira followed developments in the Croatian war from the comfort of their living room, watching the nightly news and reading the papers every morning. As educated people, they naturally were concerned, especially when the architectural jewel of Dubrovnik was attacked. Like so many other Sarajevo families, the Taljanovićs spent summer weekends on the sun-baked beaches of the Adriatic around Dubrovnik. What would become of their summer home? Would they need to cancel their vacations?

The Taljanovićs were not indifferent to human suffering. They were among the first to donate canned goods when a humanitarian organization started a collection for the children of besieged Dubrovnik.

"I can understand how it is that you Americans don't care anything about Bosnia," Esad told me gently, as we sat around his still-glossy dining room table in the summer of 1995, three years after war had come to Bosnia. "Here all this shelling was going on a couple of hundred kilometers from here and we were watching like it was happening in the Congo. We were so naïve."

Most Sarajevans had come of age in a united Yugoslavia, and their naïveté was bred from a lifestyle of creature comforts. Yugoslavia was way off the charts of the Eastern bloc nations, with a living standard approximating that in Western Europe. In ten years of practicing dentistry, Esad and his family had acquired just about every home appliance, from his fax machine to the Cuisinart that Šaćira used to whip up gourmet meals. Although his brother, who was living in Michigan, would regularly send videotapes to show off the American swimming pools and supermarkets, Esad was not envious. He grimaced when he watched the videos. To his eye, Americans looked overweight, unhappy, and alienated from each other and their families.

In Sarajevo, he had everything he could possibly want, with his parents living right downstairs. Practically in his backyard, he had powdery ski slopes that were among the best in Europe and that had made Sarajevo the site of the 1984 Winter Olympics. The clear, turquoise waters of the Adriatic were less than a three-hour drive away. Sarajevo, a city of almost 500,000, had a fine university and medical school for his children when the time came.

As Esad Taljanović appraised things, Sarajevo represented the apotheosis of late-twentieth-century civilization, and civilized people did not murder one another. War was out of the question.

Across Logavina Street, behind a red gate, Zijo and Jela Džino could usually be found in their garden. A spry man of nearly sixty, Zijo was filled with kinetic energy. Jela was broad, but also quick, prone to fits of tears or laughter.

Jela was a worrier, and she had plenty of fodder: the tight pensions she and her husband received as recently retired factory workers; her daughter, who was in the process of moving her family to South Africa; her son, who was working for pocket money in a café and couldn't decide on a career.

Still, the possibility of an ethnic war in Bosnia seemed preposterous to Jela, even though post-Communist Yugoslavia was disintegrating along bloodlines: Serbs and Croats had been locked in battle since mid-1991 over Croatia's declaration of independence from Yugoslavia. Her own family typi-

fied something that Bosnian president Alija Izetbegović liked
to say—that any attempt to divide the ethnic groups of Bosnia
would be "like trying to separate cornmeal and flour after they
were stirred in the same bowl."[1]

Zijo was a Muslim from an old Sarajevo family that had
lived in the same house for two centuries. Jela was a Catholic
from Šibenik, on the Croatian coast. They had met in 1956
when Zijo was vacationing at a seaside motel. Jela was working
there as a waitress. He thought she looked like an actress. She
thought he was too skinny, and brought him extra portions of
dinner.

When they married, nobody in their respective families
raised objections about religious differences between the two,
who were so madly in love. A quarter century later, when their
daughter, Alma, fell for a nice Sarajevo boy from an Orthodox
Serb family, it was no different. Zijo says with a laugh that he
thought fleetingly about objecting before realizing "I didn't
have much ground for complaint, since I had married a Catholic."

About one-third of the marriages in Sarajevo were similarly mixed. Mostly, it meant families had more holidays to
celebrate: the Catholic and Orthodox Christmases, the Muslim holiday of Bajram in the spring. For all the blather about
ethnicity, everyone traced their roots to the same Slavic stock,
and they were virtually indistinguishable in appearance.

Zijo and Jela believed in God but were not concerned with
specifics. Zijo disregarded the Islamic prohibitions on pork
and alcohol and Jela only attended Christmas Eve mass—which,
for that matter, many of her Muslim and Orthodox neighbors
also attended. Pre-war tourist brochures boasted of Sarajevo's
historic mosques, Roman Catholic cathedrals, and Serbian
Orthodox churches with the same multicultural pride that

New Yorkers apply to their ethnic restaurants. Sarajevans' tradition of religious tolerance dated back to the late fifteenth century, when Sarajevo had welcomed Sephardic Jews who were fleeing the Spanish Inquisition. Zijo's own father had hidden Jews in a tucked-away room of their Logavina Street house during World War II, even though they lived directly across the street from the Nazi headquarters.

People like the Džinos scoffed when they listened to speeches by Radovan Karadžić, who led the militant faction of Serbs in the Bosnian parliament. Karadžić was making menacing threats about what would happen if Bosnia, still a Yugoslav republic, should follow Croatia and secede. He claimed that it would put Bosnia on a "highway of hell and suffering" that might lead the "Muslim people into annihilation," in his October 1991 speech before parliament.[2]

Karadžić, a psychiatrist at Sarajevo's main medical center, Koševo Hospital, was known around town as a goofball. He was an amateur poet and grafter—always obliging if you needed a medical excuse from work or the army if you slipped him some cash. He had served jail time in 1985 for misusing public funds. Nobody could take him seriously.

Moreover, Izetbegović seemed to be bending over backward to accommodate the increasingly militant Serbs. "It takes two sides to have a war and we will not fight," Izetbegović declared in early 1992.[3]

Jela was reassured by Izetbegović's speech. She and Zijo went on drinking coffee in their garden. They weren't worried. But the truth was that Bosnia was being boxed into a smaller and smaller space, with fewer ways to dodge the impending war.

On June 25, 1991, Croatia and Slovenia declared their full independence from Yugoslavia. Macedonia, another Yugoslav republic, was also stumbling toward independence. That left Bosnia isolated in a stripped-down Yugoslavia—dominated by the biggest republic, Serbia. If Bosnia remained part of Yugoslavia, it would be subjugated under the stridently nationalist Serb president, Slobodan Milošević.

Some Croat politicians suggested that Bosnia form a federation with Croatia. The Bosnians were sure that joining Croatia would trigger a revolt by the Bosnian Serbs, who feared being cut off from Serbia, and outside intervention by the Serb-dominated Yugoslav National Army. Those who had watched coverage of the bombardment of Dubrovnik were terrified of the possible outcome. Other European diplomats suggested carving up Bosnia, but that posed a logistical nightmare since Bosnia was the most ethnically diverse of the six Yugoslav republics. A 1990 census showed that 44 percent of the Bosnian population was Muslim, 31 percent Orthodox, and 17 percent Catholic. With the bloodlines slicing through towns and families like the Džinos, there was no way to split Bosnia into ethnic enclaves without displacing hundreds of thousands of people.

It seemed that the best—if not the only—plausible course of action was for Bosnians to opt for independence. If Marshal Tito's ethnically diverse Yugoslavia could no longer exist, Bosnia would be the one republic to live out the vision of all religions living together peacefully.

So Bosnia toddled ahead with halting baby steps toward nationhood, unaware of the forces assembling to shoot it down. Over the weekend of February 29–March 1, 1992, voters answered a referendum question: "Are you in favor of a sovereign and independent Bosnia-Herzegovina, a state of equal citizens . . . of Muslims, Serbs, Croats and others who live in it?"

The response to the referendum was a nearly unanimous "yes," although only 64 percent of eligible voters participated. Karadžić had declared a boycott of the election, and in many Serb-controlled districts voting was not permitted to take place.

Ekrem and Minka Kaljanac were decidedly apathetic about politics. They lived on the second floor of a small, nondescript apartment house on Logavina Street and had their hands full, raising two rambunctious boys. Ekrem moonlighted at various jobs to make ends meet.

Ekrem and Minka, having come of age under Communism, were deeply distrustful of politicians and hadn't bothered to vote in 1990 when Bosnia held its first free parliamentary elections. But on the day of the referendum, they were among the first to vote. "I voted because I didn't want war. I thought by voting for an independent Bosnia we would be showing that we all wanted to live together," Minka explained.

A few days after the referendum, Serb militants blocked the roads in and out of Sarajevo. Five student demonstrators were killed removing the barricades. But that would be the last of the violence, Ekrem was convinced. "I was positive about the cohesion of Sarajevo. Positive. I was certain it couldn't happen here," he said.

Ekrem and Minka are not easily fooled. Although neither is a university graduate, they are acute observers of their environment. They are street-smart. Minka is a thin, shy redhead. Her good looks are only marred by the ravages that war has taken on her teeth. Ekrem has a taut carriage and darting blue eyes, always challenging you with a measure of suspicion. He later became a cop.

Ekrem's unwavering confidence in Bosnia's future suffered

its first blow on a business trip to Belgrade, where he was installing a heating system. Ekrem was driving home at 5 A.M., in heavy rain, when he found himself rerouted onto a back road by an unexpected police checkpoint. The road led him into the mountains, and he was surprised to see cadres of soldiers conducting some sort of training in the hills. They seemed to be part of the Yugoslav National Army, but many of the soldiers had longish hair and beards, not the usual close-cropped military cuts.

A commander ordered Ekrem to speed up and get the hell out of there. Ekrem pressed the gas pedal of his Renault to the floor in his hurry to get back to Sarajevo and tell Minka what he had seen. "We were both frightened. My skin was crawling. I knew there was something evil in the air," Minka recalled.

What Ekrem had observed, without quite comprehending its implications, was the vast military buildup in the mountains that would choke off Sarajevo from the outside world.

Karadžić's followers had declared large chunks of Bosnia "Serb Autonomous Regions" in 1991. The Serb regions had set up their own parliament and on March 27, 1992, declared a "Serb Republic." They were training "Chetniks," Serb irregular fighters. The Chetniks wore beards and patches on their jackets with a skull, eagle, and crossed swords.

At the same time, Yugoslav National Army troops were advancing from Serbia into Bosnia. Their officers claimed they were there to keep the peace if the situation got out of hand.

As March dragged on, Ekrem witnessed several other disturbing events. At Koševo Hospital, where he was doing a utility installation, he noticed that a number of his Serb colleagues were unexpectedly leaving town. One man, Grujić, said he had bought a new car in Serbia and was going to pick it up. Another coworker, Dragan, said he was going to do some work at his vacation house. Milutin announced he was off to take hunting classes for a month. He was later caught as a sniper.

Meanwhile, the foreign ministers of the European Community were planning to convene in Luxembourg, to recognize Bosnia as an independent state. They hoped it would stall the momentum that was building toward war. The meeting was scheduled for Monday, April 6.

Back in Sarajevo, it promised to be a lively weekend. Delila Lačević, seventeen, and Lana Lačević, eighteen, were off for their usual Friday night excursion to the Baščaršija, the downtown Turkish quarter laced with narrow alleys of cafés and souvenir shops. Delila, curly-haired with a mischievous grin, and Lana, tall and husky with short-cropped blond hair, were cousins and best friends. The two families—their fathers were brothers—shared a rambling old house on Logavina at the uppermost end of the street. Lana and Delila spent the evening at their favorite hangout, Alo, Alo, where they stayed out late, gossiping about boys and the latest hits on MTV.

When they arrived home they were greeted by their angry, anxious parents. There had been a shooting in Baščaršija, and someone had been killed. They were taken aback to be chastised; both were responsible girls, both planning to be doctors like Lana's mother, Šaćira. They were shocked to learn of the murder. Such incidents were rare in Sarajevo, even though the city had been the scene of one of the most famous murders of all time: the 1914 assassination of the Austro-Hungarian archduke Franz Ferdinand, which sparked World War I. The Lačević families nervously locked their front gate and went to bed.

Saturday, April 4, a policeman stopped by the Lačević house with more unsettling news. He said that Chetnik irregulars were stirring up trouble, erecting barricades around Sarajevo. Despite the palpable tension, relatives came over to the house for coffee and cakes. As Lana went to close the gate after them, at about 8 P.M., she saw beautifully eerie streaks of red light dancing in the distant hills.

"Mother, come look at what's going on!" Lana called out. She thought she was watching a fireworks display for Bajram, a Muslim holiday that began that weekend.

Šaćira Lačević yelled at her to come back inside. The lights in the hills were tracer bullets.

By Sunday morning, Sarajevans were furious about the barricades and the signs of war all around them. An impromptu peace demonstration started in Dobrinja, a high-rise suburb built for the 1984 Olympics. The numbers of demonstrators swelled, from a couple of thousand into the tens of thousands, as the throng made its way downtown to camp out in front of the Bosnian parliament building. There was a peaceful carnival atmosphere among the broad swath of Sarajevans. Communist sympathizers waved photos of Tito, while a group of teenagers carried a banner reading SEX, DRUGS AND ROCK & ROLL. They all had the same purpose, though.

"We can live together," the demonstrators chanted. *"Mi smo za mir."* "We are for peace."

Esad Taljanović watched the demonstration on television as it continued into the following day. He found himself nodding in agreement with this outpouring of support for ethnic unity.

"Let's go," Esad said, jumping up from the sofa. He and Šaćira dressed the children quickly, Amir, three, and Lejla, five. They packed a lunch and walked down Logavina to Vojvode Putnika, the main road out to the newer suburbs.

Quickly they were swallowed up in the heaving crowd,

which had swelled to 100,000. The children were afraid of the crush, so Šaćira took them home, but Esad went on. It never occurred to him that danger could lurk in this carnival-like atmosphere, with the streets so full of spontaneous good intentions.

When the first gunshots rang out, Esad didn't recognize the sound. The only other time he had heard a gunshot was on New Year's Eve. He watched in confusion as a collective shudder rippled through the crowd. Somebody yelled, *"Gore, snajper!"*—"Above, a sniper!"—and everyone started to run. "We were so unprepared, so naïve," he recalled. "I could not imagine that people would shoot on us like we were pigeons."

The shooting had come from the upper floors of the Holiday Inn. There was little doubt who was responsible. Karadžić had rented the upper floors of the hotel—another legacy of the Olympics—for the headquarters of his Serb Democratic Party. Police stormed the hotel and arrested six men, including Karadžić's personal bodyguard.

Fourteen people were killed in Sarajevo that day. April 6, 1992, would go down in the registers as the official beginning of the war.

And yet Sarajevans still were able to tap that enormous human capacity for denial that can be stretched beyond all reasonable bounds in the face of things too horrible to contemplate.

Each day of April brought escalating levels of violence, four or five deaths, a larger number of injuries. The streetlights were switched off at night to frustrate snipers. Some shopkeepers boarded up their windows and closed, but most people continued to go to work, detouring away from the broad, exposed Vojvode Putnika—already on the way to earning its nickname, Sniper Alley.

The Razija Omanović elementary school on Logavina Street closed immediately after the Holiday Inn shooting. Lana Lačević's high school made it through the first week. The students had barely settled into their desks on Friday morning when a teacher informed them that school was recessing early for the summer. The students were to return home in small groups.

"He congratulated the graduating class and told all the rest he hoped to see us again in the fall," Lana recalled. "He seemed confused and we were all confused, too. At the end of the term, you usually celebrate and tear up your books, but everybody was too surprised to do anything. From the way the teacher spoke, I had the feeling he thought it would be over in a month or two. We all did."

For the teenagers, the atmosphere was giddy, like the excitement of an unexpected day off school for snow. At night, big 120-millimeter bombs crashed into the hillsides with a quick flash and then a dull rumble like distant thunder. Sometimes the bombs landed closer, exploding on the cobblestoned streets of the Baščaršija.

Lana and her younger sister, Maša, would sneak outside along with Delila and her brother, Berin, to count the seconds between the flash and the ensuing rumble, speculating about what kind of weapon it was. It was all still far enough away from Logavina Street to be exciting.

The first shell hit Logavina Street on April 16. It sliced through the brittle wooden roof of Zijo and Jela Džino's 250-year-old house. Nobody was hurt. Esad Taljanović and Ekrem Kaljanac helped Zijo patch over the crater, as big as a washing machine. They all figured it was a fluke—there were no military targets or even government buildings on Logavina Street that would provoke such an attack.

Five days later, the next shell found Zijo and Jela drinking their morning coffee. It slammed straight into the side of the house. The shrapnel skittered across the exterior walls and burst through the kitchen window to the table where they were sitting.

"There were a lot of colors and then darkness," Zijo remembers. "I fell on the floor and hugged Jela. If we were to die, I hoped we would die together."

The explosion jolted the Taljanovićs, who lived across the street. Esad rushed to his bay window, which overlooked the Džinos' house. He later told me, "The first stupid reaction to a shell is to go to the window and look. The second stupid reaction is to run over in your slippers. Many people got wounded trying to help."

Naturally, that is exactly what Esad did. He joined a group of men who were scaling the Džinos' locked front gate, trying to reach the wounded couple inside.

By the time they got in, Jela was unconscious, lying on her stomach. Zijo was draped around his wife, trembling like a leaf. Already the ambulances in Sarajevo were too busy to be called; a neighbor took them to the hospital. Esad hurried home. Still in his slippers, his hands shaking, he began to grab blankets and to move a sofa down to the basement. It was time to prepare a bomb shelter. Undeniably, this was war.

2

ORPHANS OF WAR

THE CHILDREN LIVED on a farm, next to a forest with wild deer, pheasants, and rabbits. Then one day their parents told them they had five minutes to pack a suitcase. Selma Kapić, fourteen years old, and her brother, Mirza, eleven, were hustled into the back of a truck leaving town, without time to say a proper good-bye to their parents.

That was April 20, 1992. They have not been home since. They ended up refugees in Sarajevo, living with their cousins, the Lačevićs, on Logavina Street.

As fate would have it, they arrived on the street at the very moment the shell crashed into Jela and Zijo Džinos' kitchen. "Everybody thought, Sarajevo is the capital, nothing could happen there. We would be safe," Selma said.

Selma speaks without a trace of bitterness about what has happened. Mirza is angry. He misses his dog, a German shepherd named Mati. He regrets that he didn't have time to pack his skateboard. He often dreams that the family is back on the farm and the Chetniks are coming to get them. "In my dream, I shot them all," he says. "They were all dead."

Selma is a pretty and excruciatingly polite teenager. Her responsibility for her younger brother makes her seem a decade older than she is. Mirza is a husky boy, with the physique of a budding soccer player. He was already playing soccer of a sort—kicking a ball around in the safety of a basement bomb shelter. Soccer, Sarajevo-style.

The way that Selma and Mirza Kapić ended up stuck in besieged Sarajevo might sound like bad luck, but the place they fled was even more dangerous. They came from the northern Bosnian town of Derventa, which, in April 1992, was one of the places under threat of being "ethnically cleansed" of Muslims and Croats.

By Derventa standards, the Kapićs were rich before the war. Their ancestors had farmed the same land since the 1700s. Although the estate had been whittled down to ten acres under the Communist regime, it was lush acreage, planted with corn and wheat. The yard looked like a botanical garden. The family lived in a modern three-story house with balconies off most of the rooms, and views of the verdant countryside. They were building a swimming pool.

"It was heaven. You would have thought you were in Switzerland there," said their cousin Delila, who had often visited.

Selma and Mirza could sense trouble brewing. Derventa is close enough to the Croatian border that they could hear the dull thud of shells exploding in the border town of Slavonski Brod in 1991, during the Croatian war. By early 1992, the war was spreading. Selma remembers walking downtown with some classmates, past a Yugoslav flag. An ethnic Croat friend remarked that a Croatian flag would soon be flying in its place.

"This girl with us, she said, no, 'It will be a Serbian flag,'" Selma recalled. "I thought they were both nuts. We were all the same, just kids. We didn't pay attention to who anybody was."

Mirza was similarly walking with a group of friends when a Yugoslav army soldier jokingly pointed a gun toward the children and his comrade held up his right fist, with his thumb and first two fingers extended. In the Orthodox Church, you cross yourself with those three fingers. The sacred gesture had been corrupted into a signal of Serb nationalism.

The full blast of war reached towns like Derventa several weeks before it hit Sarajevo. Serb irregular troops were trying to wrest control of the municipal administrations, and often their method was to terrorize the Muslim population into fleeing.

By April 20, the day Selma and Mirza escaped, the Serb irregulars were ravaging their hometown. Two shells exploded within fifty yards of the Kapić house. Selma's father, Fadil Kapić, left home to buy bread and came back terrified. Several of the neighbors' houses were in flames. He had also learned that a neighbor had commandeered a truck from the shoe factory and was planning to evacuate children from Derventa.

There was no time to look for photographs, or for Mirza to find his skateboard. The family stuffed a few clothes into suitcases. Selma and Mirza scrambled into the windowless back of the truck and the door slammed behind them. They suddenly realized their mother was not coming with them. "We were really confused," Selma says. "We didn't know what was happening."

It was a nightmarish ride. There was no place to sit in the back of the truck, which was crammed full of screaming, terrified children. Shelling forced the driver to swerve off the main road, bouncing the children around like loose cargo. The driver let them off in Doboj, a nearby town, where they spent the night with cousins. Through the window, they watched helicopters evacuating the wounded from Derventa. The cousins urged Selma and Mirza not to try to travel any farther, but their father had given them careful instructions: "Go to your aunt in Sarajevo. You'll be safe there."

They all thought that Sarajevo would be spared the worst of the fighting, because Zagreb, the Croatian capital, and Slovenia's capital, Ljubljana, had escaped heavy fighting when they broke away from Yugoslavia.

At 6 A.M., Selma and Mirza boarded a train for Sarajevo. An hour outside the capital, the train stopped and someone told them that ten people had just been killed at the Sarajevo train station. Passengers began to get off, but Selma and Mirza decided to stay put and follow their father's instructions.

"That's when I got scared the most," Mirza said. "We didn't know anyone on the train. We had no idea what was going on, or what to do."

When they pulled into the station, Sarajevo was on fire. There were explosions everywhere and a sniper had the station pinned down.

Their uncle was waiting on the platform. He quickly steered them through the streets, dashing from doorway to doorway to avoid the shells. Just as they reached Logavina Street, the shell hit the Džinos' house. They ran past the Džinos' gate as neighbors tried to pull Zijo and Jela from the kitchen. They did not stop.

They kept running past the Lačević house and straight to the bomb shelter at the top of the hill. Their aunt, Šaćira, and their Lačević cousins were there taking cover.

"It was hell in Sarajevo," Selma remembered.

Later that day, April 21, Sarajevo radio proclaimed: "This is the most difficult and dramatic day in Sarajevo's long history."

Who was to know that worse days were to come?

· · ·

After April 21, Logavina residents went underground, where they remained for much of the next year.

Esad locked the door to the sunny room facing Trebević to keep the children safe. On bad days, as many as 3,500 shells rained down on the city. You could duck snipers by staying away from exposed intersections, but no one could predict where a shell might land.

No place was safe. Even Koševo Hospital, situated on a hill above the city, was an irresistible target for the Serbs. One man in the cardiac care unit was shot through the heart as he stood by a window looking at the mountains.

Jela Džino spent much of her three-month hospitalization at Koševo in the bomb shelter. The shrapnel that had flown into her kitchen had ripped off a piece of her left shin. Zijo had similar, less serious, wounds.

"The nurses would wheel us into the elevator and take us down to the basement," Jela recalled. "We'd get back to our rooms and fifteen minutes later we would have to go to the basement again."

Few of the Logavina Street houses had basements, so residents had to seek refuge elsewhere. The Razija Omanović school was a stone building that had withstood Allied bombing during World War II, when it was headquarters for the occupying Nazis. With school suspended, the basement-level kitchen was quickly put to use as a bomb shelter.

Ekrem and Minka Kaljanac's apartment home stood six feet away from the school, separated from it by an alley. They constructed a six-foot-wide staircase between the buildings, so Minka could rush home during lulls in the shelling to fix lunch for the boys, Haris, eight, and Tarik, two. Ekrem got seventy camping cots from the Boy Scouts and set them up in the school basement for the neighbors.

Despite the improvisations, the shelter was unpleasant. The toilets were upstairs and people were often too afraid to leave the basement. Instead, they urinated into bottles and left them under cots. Minka and her neighbor, Kasema Telalagić, tried to organize a chore schedule for cleaning, but not everybody cooperated. Frequent quarrels erupted over sanitation.

"It was very humid that summer and then it became very dirty. It was a very ugly period of the war," Ekrem recalls.

Like Minka, Kasema had a child who was still in diapers. Her daughter, Dženana, was not quite two when the war started. During the loudest bombardments, the frightened children suffered from diarrhea. The war had already choked off deliveries into Sarajevo, and there were no more disposable diapers anywhere in the city.

"I was trying to toilet-train Dženana in the shelter," said Kasema—an elegant woman who rarely left her house without wearing pearls. "I remember staying up all night during the shelling washing these diapers. I never liked camping, and that was a little bit what it was like. I must have said to myself a hundred times, all I want is to sleep in my own bed, in my own nightgown."

At the upper end of Logavina Street, the bomb shelter was set up in a former orphanage, a place bleaker than anything imagined by Charles Dickens. The walls were a sallow, institutional green and seemed to exude a century's misery. The building was perched, haunted-house style, atop a ridge, above a weed-strewn vacant lot. So little daylight penetrated the dank halls that you needed to navigate by a flashlight, even on the sunniest days. Built in the 1890s, the orphanage housed refugees during both world wars. It briefly functioned as a jail. Many Logavina residents thought the building was cursed with bad karma and would not go near it. Delila had grown up next door and had never been inside before the war.

The Lačevićs could not afford to be picky. Their old family homestead, built and rebuilt by previous generations, had fragile wood-and-plaster walls and the same type of brittle roof as the Džinos'. With Selma and Mirza's arrival, there were now eleven people living in the Lačević home.

On quieter evenings, the Lačevićs ate dinner at home, brushed their teeth, and retired for the night in the orphanage. The Serbs had something of a schedule—pounding the city from about 9 P.M. to 2 A.M. If the shelling abated, the Lačevićs would creep back home to sleep for a few hours in their own beds.

Over time, the Lačevićs moved more and more of their possessions to the orphanage. The radio came, and the television soon followed, so the family could watch the news. Delila, a dreamy, exuberant girl, brought romance novels, and the more studious Lana brought medical textbooks.

The girls—Selma, Delila, Lana, and Maša—turned a vacant laundry room into their clubhouse. They splattered the walls with blue and red paint and scrawled graffiti identifying their gangs: "Cool Girls" and "Devil Girls." From time to time, they would invite the boys in, switch on the transistor radio, and dance.

Even though the orphanage was a fortress compared to the Lačević home, it was not entirely safe. An exploding grenade blew a hole over the staircase and tore through to the basement, and the cascading bricks struck Selma in the head.

The place was claustrophobic. Mirza said the adults were so anxious to hear the latest turns of the war that the kids weren't allowed to make a peep when the news was on the radio or television. At night, the mattresses were laid out in such tight rows you couldn't get up without stepping on somebody.

Once Maša rolled over in her sleep and, with her knee, knocked an elderly neighbor's eyeglasses off. "She was such a nice woman. She didn't yell at me at all," Maša remembered. "She was later killed by a grenade. I still feel bad about her and the glasses."

The orphanage began to fill up. More and more refugees were filtering into Sarajevo as the Bosnian Serbs bulldozed their way through large swaths of eastern and northern Bosnia. By the end of May 1992, three-quarters of a million Bosnians were displaced from their homes. Eventually, almost half of the country's 4.3 million people would become refugees—or "internally displaced persons," as they were called by the UN High Commissioner for Refugees, since they were still living within their own country. In Sarajevo, the refugee population reached 100,000; on Logavina Street, refugees represented about one-quarter of the residents.

The refugees brought terrifying tales of their ordeals. Zulfo Fako, twenty-eight, fled from a small farming village called Ilovača in eastern Bosnia, near the town of Goražde. When the Serbs arrived, they set fire to all the houses. Those who ran out of their houses were shot; those who remained burned to death. "Where I came from, you would not think a village existed. There is nothing but the burnt ruins," he said. "It was a matter of minutes. The only ones who escaped got out right away. I left with my mother. She was sick and I carried her most of the time. She kept saying, 'Leave me and take care of yourself.' But I didn't want to do that. I'm an epileptic. I needed someone to take care of me."

Zulfo's mother died in the hospital after they reached Sarajevo. He wandered about despondently until he found his way to the orphanage on Logavina. He shared a single room on the second floor with six other men, one of whom was Dervo Karašik. Twenty-five-year-old Dervo had been living in the mock-Alpine resort of Pale, ten miles from Sarajevo. After the Holiday Inn shooting on April 6, Radovan Karadžić and the rest of the Bosnian Serb leadership skipped out of Sarajevo and set up a makeshift government for the "Republika Srpska" in a Pale tractor factory. Things soon got tough for Muslim men like Dervo. On April 14, he was rounded up with other Muslims at a market where he worked unloading produce trucks. The men were taken to a detention center in nearby Kula. Their money, watches, and wedding rings were taken away. Dervo said he was made to face the wall while he was beaten with sticks, electrical cables, and fists. He retold his story in clipped, indistinct words. Other residents in the orphanage suspected he had suffered brain damage from the beating.

The new arrivals exchanged their stories while chain-smoking and sipping tiny cups of Turkish coffee that had been prepared over camping stoves. Many of the refugees came from other parts of Sarajevo. Nermina Husić, who moved in with her strapping sixteen-year-old son, had a house less than a mile up the hill from Logavina—close enough that their destroyed roof was visible from the second floor of the orphanage. Her home had become the front line. Refugees poured in from Ilidža, a municipality within Sarajevo that had fallen to the Serb rebels. In a chilling reminder of the Nazis' anti-Jewish regulations, the new Serb authorities posted signs in City Hall and other public buildings warning: NO ADMITTANCE TO CROATS AND MUSLIMS.[1]

In Grbavica, a district of high-rise apartments across the

Miljacka River from the Holiday Inn, non-Serbs were terror-ized. Fatima Sokolović, a seamstress in her seventies who had fled to Logavina Street, told how masked men took her jew-elry, pushed her around her apartment, and stabbed her son in the shoulder with a carving knife. "They kept on insisting he was hiding weapons. It was ridiculous. He is an economist, not a soldier," she said. "The whole thing is so crazy. The whole time we lived in Grbavica, I couldn't tell you of a single conflict between the neighbors in my building."

Fatima escaped one night on foot, crossing the Bridge of Brotherhood and Unity, named for a popular slogan from the Tito years. As the front lines were sealed, the bridge became a dividing line, like the Berlin Wall—the Serbs to the south of the river, the rest to the north.

The Lačevićs listened to these stories attentively. Each story made them more concerned about the fate of Selma and Mir-za's parents.

Fadil and Mejasa Kapić had stayed behind in Derventa to try to protect their property. They telephoned several times to Sarajevo and learned that the children had arrived safely. Their calls stopped on May 2 when the central post and telephone building in downtown Sarajevo exploded into a gigantic fire-ball, streaking the night sky with yellow flashes. The explosion severed all telephone circuits into and out of the city.

Selma fretted constantly. Mirza sulked, pulling his jacket above his chin and receding like a turtle. The only news of their parents was rumors from other refugees. After Derventa fell to the Serbs the first week of July, they got a third-hand report that their parents had escaped into Croatia. Another rumor reported that they were dead.

"We heard that all our neighbors in Derventa were slaughtered," Selma said. "We had no idea what was true, what wasn't."

It was impossible to mail a letter by normal means. There was no postal service anymore. After the United Nations began an airlift in June 1992, tearful Sarajevans hung out in the lobby of the Holiday Inn, asking journalists or UN employees to carry out letters. The Red Cross carried mail, but it took several months to be delivered.

Sometimes ham radio operators could contact families, but you had to know exactly where they were in order to try. It wasn't possible to get a telephone call through to Sarajevo until 1994, and then only after hours of redialing.

Under the circumstances, almost every family on Logavina Street was cut off from a loved one.

Veronika Marković's pink lipstick still sat in a plastic cup on the shelf over the bathroom sink. Her husband could not bear to put away any of her things.

Veronika had lived on Logavina Street for almost two years. After the first burst of shells hit Sarajevo in early April 1992, Mladen Marković put his wife and their twenty-month-old son, Boris, onto a bus bound for Slovenia.

"I called my uncle in Slovenia and asked, 'Can they stay with you for fifteen days?' I was optimistic. I didn't think the war would last more than a few weeks," he said.

Mladen, a gentle, fine-featured thirty-two-year-old man, stayed behind to fight with the Bosnian Army. He spent four days a week on the front lines and then came home to his empty apartment. Sitting beside a tiny lamp fueled by vegetable oil, he composed love poems to his wife in a blue-bound notebook.

"I'll Be Faithful" was his favorite. "No other eyes for me

have the same gleam. . . . I do not want to dream of other women. I want to have fire in me for you, and only you, all the time."

Mladen had met Veronika when he was twenty and she was nineteen. They were both studying civil engineering at the university. It was love at first sight for Mladen. He used to sit behind her in the classroom, staring at her waist-length dark hair. Not knowing what to say, one day he couldn't resist temptation and he pulled her hair.

"She was irritated. She told me I was rude," Mladen recalled. Within ten days, she had dumped her boyfriend and was dating Mladen. Her parents, devout Catholics, initially disapproved of Mladen, who was from an Orthodox family, but Mladen's devotion eventually won them over, and the couple married on August 29, 1987. Their wedding dinner took place at a country restaurant tucked at the foot of Mount Igman, now on the front line.

"I saw the place on television a few days ago—there were only soldiers there—and it reminded me all over again of our wedding," Mladen said.

In the first days after the shelling began, private groups organized convoys to take civilians out of Sarajevo. Many families on Logavina Street discussed leaving. Ekrem Kaljanac wanted Minka and the boys to go, but Minka didn't want to leave her husband behind. They thought the fighting would be over quickly.

Mladen figured it would last about as long as the ten-day war that had followed Slovenia's split from Yugoslavia the previous year. "Veronika was terrified, but I thought she was being silly."

Then, it all happened in a flash. Mladen was at work that day at the city's water department. Veronika telephoned to say she had found a convoy that was leaving within the hour. He rushed to meet her at the bus station.

"I felt terrible. Veronika was crying so much, it made me feel even worse," he said. "We were trying to hold things together for Boris, but he was too young anyway to realize what was going on."

Mladen's last memory of his son is a laughing toddler in a denim jacket, waving excitedly through the bus window.

Besides the poems to his wife, Mladen composed rhymes for his son and drew pictures of "houses, rabbits, anything that wouldn't remind him of the war." In 1992, Veronika and Boris moved to Germany. Veronika had to translate Mladen's letters into German so Boris could understand.

A year after his family left, Mladen relented and gave away his son's outgrown clothing and toys to a refugee family down the street. Two years after the war began, Mladen was writing a poem in honor of his son's fifth birthday, July 30, 1994:

"We wish our son a childhood filled with colored balloons, full of joy and candy. But most of all, filled with his parents' love back in the gaiety of the family circle."

Mladen had no hope of delivering his poem in person.

After the first flurry of escapes from Sarajevo in April 1992, it became progressively more difficult to leave. Everyone was trapped where they were, on the inside or the outside. Commercial flights into Sarajevo airport were suspended the first week of April. The train that had brought Selma and Mirza into the capital on April 21 was one of the last trains to run before the station was bombed beyond recognition.

Minka Kaljanac's sister, Lala, tried to leave on three separate occasions. The first time, her husband was sick and she thought he needed her with him. The next time she backed out again, for good reason. A previous convoy had been stopped and robbed going through Pale, now controlled by the Serbs. Lala thought it was too dangerous.

The third time, Lala was absolutely convinced she would go through with it. She got to the bus station and discovered there was no gas for the buses.

"I took it as a sign. It was not my destiny to leave Sarajevo," Lala told her family.

Kasema Telalagić had a cousin who flew in from Australia the last week of March 1992 to visit her relatives in Sarajevo. It was supposed to be a three-week visit. She could not get back to Australia until January 1993, and she only managed then because she was evacuated by the United Nations.

Dervo Karašik, the refugee from Pale, made an ill-advised attempt to escape over the Sarajevo airport. The airport was at the western end of the city and had become a demilitarized zone of sorts, under UN control, by the summer of 1992. As Dervo sprinted across the runway, UN troops switched a floodlight on him. Illuminated, Dervo froze in terror and was shot by a Serb sniper. His attempt cost him a leg.

The noose around Sarajevo was tightening. The mountains loomed above the city, as oppressive as barbed-wire fences. All roads in and out of the city were impassable. Barricades were everywhere, and behind the barricades stood Serb soldiers with knives in their boots, Kalashnikov rifles propped at their sides, their bad attitudes emboldened by whiskey.

The war had made the nearest suburbs as remote as the moon. The city was hermetically sealed, a strange experiment in isolation. The siege of Sarajevo was complete. Or nearly so.

One evening in May, the kids were playing a game called Submarine in the basement of the bomb shelter. Suddenly the lightbulb flickered off. Nobody was particularly surprised, since brief blackouts were frequent during those first weeks of war.

"*Nema problema,*" Lana told the other kids. "There's no problem. Let's take a quick break. The electricity will be back on in a minute."

The lights didn't come back on that night. Or the next morning. For the rest of the war, electricity was sporadic, coming on every few days, in several-hour spurts.

At first, Sarajevans assumed the power lines had been damaged by shells. As they pondered the matter in the dark, it became clearer: their utilities had been taken prisoner of war.

The main power plant supplying Sarajevo was in Vogošća, a suburb now occupied by Serb rebels. With a flick of the switch, they could cut the juice to Sarajevo. Sarajevans made do with candles, flashlights, and gas lamps in the bomb shelter, but there was a more critical side effect to the perpetual blackout. The pumping station for the Sarajevo reservoir in Bačevo was run by electricity. No electricity meant no running water.

You could survive in the dark. You couldn't survive without water.

3

A DEATH IN THE FAMILY

Delila Lačević stares at you straight on, as though daring you to look into her wide-set brown eyes and see that she can talk about it without shedding a tear. "You may not want to hear this story," she says matter-of-factly. "But it actually makes me feel better to talk about it, so I will."

It was January 15, 1993, the first brutal winter of the war. There had been no running water on Logavina Street for months. Around the corner, a neighbor had a well, but it had run dry. The long days and nights cowering in the orphanage bomb shelter had left the Lačević family dirty and cranky. They hadn't done laundry for weeks.

Azra Lačević couldn't stand it any longer. Delila's mother, a tiny, hyperkinetic forty-three-year-old woman, was the most impatient and fearless in the family. She hated being cooped up. Even when there was shelling, Azra would volunteer to run back to the house to fetch somebody's eyeglasses or fix a lunch.

"I am going out to get some water," she announced. "Let's go to the brewery."

The brewery was across the Miljacka River from downtown Sarajevo, about a thirty-minute walk. It had long produced Sarajevsko Pivo—the local beer—but now with no malt for brewing, the plant had found a new purpose: distributing water. Azra rounded up her husband, Asim, and Delila to help. Eleven-year-old Berin begged to tag along. They were still in line with their empty canisters when the mortars came slamming into a brick wall above their heads. Delila grabbed her brother and flopped to the ground, the two lying as still as possible under a whirlwind of flying bricks and shrapnel.

"Are Mummy and Daddy okay?" Berin asked Delila after a few minutes had passed.

"Can't you see they're dead? Daddy has no head," Delila snapped back at her brother.

As she later would recount in the frigid emptiness of her parents' kitchen, "My father, he was decapitated. My mother's head was like a watermelon dropped on the floor. Berin couldn't believe it. He kept trying to wash her face. He was crying, 'Mommy, wake up. Your Bero is calling you,' but she didn't respond."

The brewery shelling left eight dead, twenty wounded. Sarajevo's daily newspaper, *Oslobođenje,* branded the day "Black Friday." It was not the first bloodbath in Sarajevo. Twenty people had been killed the previous May 27 on the Vase Miskina pedestrian mall as they queued for bread. Many Sarajevans described the horror of the breadline massacre as the moment they were forced to reckon with the reality of war.

The Lačević family thought differently, though. Until the attack on the brewery, they had persevered through nine months of war with a sense that they were somehow protected. Their belief in God and in their own righteousness—a conviction that they were upstanding citizens who should inspire no malice—blinded them to the dangers of the war.

Azra Lačević had hardly missed a day of work, even after the trams stopped running, walking an hour each way to her job as a dental assistant. "God will protect you," Azra would tell her more timid sister-in-law, Šaćira, an obstetrician and gynecologist at Koševo Hospital. "You have done so much good in this world by delivering babies. Nothing can happen to you."

On the afternoon that the group went to get water, Šaćira Lačević had remained with her husband, Mustafa, and two daughters in the safety of the shelter. They were listening to a transistor radio when they heard the news that three shells had hit the brewery. They sincerely believed that no harm could have come to their family. After thirty minutes or so passed, Mustafa ventured out to look for them.

First he stopped by Gazi Husrev Beg's mosque, a fifteenth-century landmark in the Old Town where you could sometimes fill your water buckets from the stone fountain in the courtyard. Mustafa's eyes darted eagerly, with the hope of finding his family gossiping with friends in the water line.

No luck. Mustafa proceeded to the brewery. As he approached, he could see that the road was cordoned off by soldiers. Mustafa broke into a run, crashing past a barricade. Three soldiers grabbed him. He blurted out his purpose and the soldiers let him go. "Are you a member of the Lačević family?" an officer asked in a hushed tone that pretty much told Mustafa what he needed to know.

Šaćira and the girls were standing at the doorway of the orphanage with some of the neighbors. When they saw Mustafa returning with a slow and mournful gait, his hands covering his face, they knew what had happened. "I cried and cried," Lana recalled. "I wanted to run away to the brewery to go and rescue them. My parents had to stop me."

Berin had been only lightly grazed by shrapnel along the temple, but Delila's condition was critical. Nine chunks of shrapnel had entered her body, piercing one of her lungs. Her shoulder was crushed by a tumbling brick.

It was evening by the time Šaćira and Lana made their way on foot to Koševo Hospital. At first the hospital staff didn't want to let them in. The trauma wing, where Delila was being treated, had been struck by a shell hours before. They eventually found Delila hooked up to an intravenous tube, her hair still singed and dirty with rubble. She was conscious and asked Lana to help arrange her into a more comfortable position— before posing the question: "We are best friends, Lana. We never lie to each other. Please tell me. My parents are dead, aren't they?"

"They're not dead. They'll be okay," replied Lana, following her first instinct to comfort her cousin. "They are dead. You're lying," Delila screamed back. Lana nodded sadly. Delila lowered her eyes and started to cry.

Asim and Azra Lačević were buried hastily three days later in the Vrbanjuša cemetery, across the street from 63 Logavina. Their bodies lay less than twenty feet from their front gate beneath simple pine markers inscribed with their names and the dates of each one's birth and death. The funeral lasted less than ten minutes, because the mourners feared being out too long on the exposed hillside.

The deaths left Šaćira and Mustafa in charge of six traumatized children—their own two daughters, their exiled niece and nephew from Derventa, and the newly orphaned Delila and Berin. Šaćira's younger daughter, Maša, thirteen, had a recurring nightmare that Hitler was trying to push her into a gas chamber. Berin woke up screaming after a dream in which he opened the bathroom door and saw his father standing in front of the sink, missing his head. Mirza and Selma grew silent, worrying about their own parents, whose whereabouts remained unknown. Delila was the biggest problem. The seventeen-year-old assumed an indifference to danger bordering on suicidal after the death of her parents. She would sneak out at night to see her boyfriend, Haris, a soldier in the Bosnian Army. Šaćira remembers Delila hanging laundry one day in the yard when the shelling started. "I was begging, crying, yelling at her to get in the house," Šaćira said. "She was singing a song to herself, ignoring me as though I wasn't there."

Berin was reeling from shock and confusion after the attack. He couldn't hear properly for weeks because of the explosion. He kept pointing over his shoulder, trying to explain where the shell struck. The boy was racked with guilt that he couldn't return a trolley he had borrowed from a neighbor to wheel home the water. He insisted that he go to apologize for the trolley being destroyed. All the children were obsessed with a videotape that had been made from the evening news. As soon as the electricity came on, they would run to the VCR to see the attack played out again, the mangled body parts, overturned buckets, and water canisters splattered with blood. A headless man was splayed on his back with his arms spread wide apart. It was Asim Lačević. Mustafa was there, clutching his forehead with disbelief. There was a little boy with tears streaming down his flushed round face. That was Berin.

The kids watched the tape so many times that Šaćira had to take it away from them.

As it happened, though, television played a pivotal role in the Lačevićs' destiny. Television stations in Japan, Britain,

Italy, Germany, and the United States broadcast the film of Berin at the brewery—without the more gruesome scenes—and footage from the funeral. A retired couple in Salina, Kansas, were watching and arranged to evacuate the boy so he could live with them. It all happened so quickly Berin barely had time to say good-bye. Victor Jackovich, the U.S. ambassador to Bosnia at the time, accompanied Berin on a UN flight. An ABC crew filmed the hurried good-bye in the courtyard on Logavina Street. Berin wrote Delila a letter the day he was airlifted out of Sarajevo. "I have just taken a hot shower. I ate five bananas. I watched television," Berin said in the letter written from the Frankfurt airport while he was en route to the United States.

Delila talked about Kansas incessantly. Her English grammar book and dictionary were always on the kitchen table. She would curl up on a rug-covered divan in the kitchen studying as her grandmother read the Koran. She kept an atlas open on the kitchen table with a circle drawn around Salina, Kansas.

When I first met Delila in January 1994, the kitchen was the only room in the house warm enough to sit in. It was an old house to begin with—slanty floors with bright Oriental rugs, hand-printed wallpaper curling at the edges. Plastic sheeting was taped over the broken panes of a window. A tiny aluminum stove was jerry-rigged on a stack of bricks. Berin's cat curled up to it for warmth. Delila wore a baggy maroon sweater over three layers of T-shirts. Everything hung loosely on her tall, underweight frame.

"Physically, I am in Sarajevo, but in my mind, I am in America," Delila said. "Everything that comes from America, I am interested in. I saw a television program about Bill Clinton that was great."

The retired couple in Kansas did not realize initially that

Berin had a sister still alive. After Berin's arrival, they tried to bring Delila out as well. "They know how close we are. My brother is very attached to me. He used to take my cigarettes, hide them, and say, 'I'll give you one back when you give me a kiss,'" she said.

Delila's recklessness completely vanished with the promise of emigrating to the United States. Suddenly, she was always frightened. She worried she would die before she could leave Sarajevo. She was afraid to take flowers to her parents' graves across the street. She would only go on days when fog obscured the cemetery from sniper fire. The brewery shelling had left Delila with four pieces of shrapnel in her body, and she worried that if she slipped and fell on the ice, the shrapnel would shift and hurt her.

Outside the Lačevićs' front gate, small children from the apartment next door used to sit on the stoop and play with dolls. Delila would yell at them to go back inside. "The kids hate me, but I don't care what the neighbors say. I chase them away, and tell them, 'Look, you can see Trebević like it is the palm of your hand.'"

Delila no longer disregarded the mortar shells that came crashing down from the mountain. When the shelling started, she said she could feel her shrapnel itching and she would run, not walk, to the bomb shelter, usually carrying the cat.

"I can run fast, when I'm scared. I'll tell you, Carl Lewis is nothing compared to me," she said. "When I get to America, I'm going to start running professionally."

Delila planned out her future. She wanted to eat at McDonald's and study medicine. She promised to give up her two-pack-a-day cigarette habit as soon as she got to America. ("I won't be nervous anymore, so I won't need it.")

Once she left Sarajevo, Delila declared adamantly, she

would probably never come back. Her brother had written her that his English tutor had asked if he missed Sarajevo. "He said no. If he ever came back, it would be as a tourist—and maybe not even then. I feel that way, too. I have to go somewhere where I can relax, physically, mentally. I don't know that I would ever return."

Delila's sixty-nine-year-old grandmother had been listening to Delila speak, quietly weeping. I asked if she was afraid she might never see her granddaughter again. "No," she replied, without hesitation. "I am looking forward to it. I will be happy when Delila leaves."

Delila couldn't count the days. For security reasons, people being evacuated usually had only a day or two's advance notice. So she kept her bags packed and her documents folded neatly in an envelope in the bedroom with her few precious possessions. Her grandmother had given her a farewell present, a gold four-leaf clover that she always wore around her neck.

Delila practiced her good-byes to family members. She didn't bother with her friends. "I told them that one day if I'm not around, I've either been killed or I've gone to America."

Asim and Azra Lačević were only two of Logavina Street's fatalities. The first had been May 6, 1992, exactly a month into the war. The victim was a sixty-eight-year-old retiree, Bajro Hadžić, who lived a few doors down from the Lačevićs. He, his daughter, and his son-in-law took cover in the lower level of their house when the shelling started, reasoning that anything that exploded would come through the roof. They were wrong. A mortar shell smashed into a gate across the street and the shrapnel ricocheted back into the downstairs room where they were sitting on the floor, their backs leaning up against the wall. With the efficiency of an executioner's bullet, a sliver of shrapnel entered the old man's heart and killed him instantly.

Two days later there was another gruesome tragedy. At the first intersection up from Maršala Tita Street, across from the big mosque, an elderly man died of a heart attack. A 120-millimeter mortar shell exploded in the courtyard as two neighbors were carrying out the man's body. They and the corpse were blown to unrecognizable bits.

By late 1995, fourteen people on the street had been killed and more than forty had been wounded—out of a pre-war population of about seven hundred residents. There was hardly a family on Logavina Street that had not experienced a tragedy of one sort or another. There were no homes that hadn't been hit by mortar shells. Windowpanes gradually disappeared and were replaced by opaque plastic sheeting supplied by the UN High Commissioner for Refugees. Red tarpaulins patched the gaping holes in most of the tile roofs.

Jela Džino was stunned by the devastation of Logavina Street when she emerged, on wooden crutches, from Koševo Hospital in late June 1992. Three months earlier, her house had been the only one struck by a mortar shell. Now the pockmarks of war had spread to her neighbors like a contagion. On one day alone, August 24, 1992, sixty-five mortars landed on Logavina.[1]

The Serbs let loose on the densely populated city with an array of weaponry. They used anti-aircraft guns of up to 40 millimeters to shoot at apartment buildings, trams, cars, pedestrians—"almost everything except airplanes," as one UN officer put it. They also used 120-millimeter mortar shells. The projectile was about the size of a golf bag, a chunk of fast, hot metal that splintered into thousands of shards of sharp metal—the shrapnel. It could shred the body organs of anyone standing within fifty yards. Sarajevans said that every time they went outside, they were playing Russian roulette.

Residents watched with horror as the city's landmarks went up in flames. The belle epoque Hotel Europa was transformed into a blackened cadaver. Kasema Telalagić cried. She had been married in that hotel in 1979. The National Library of Bosnia-Herzegovina, built in 1896, was gutted after being hit by incendiary bullets, anti-aircraft fire, and mortars the night of August 25. Its arabesque columns, stained-glass windows, and Hungarian marble staircases all were trashed, along with 600,000 rare books.

The fire at the library raged for over thirty hours, the yellow flames against the night sky, the wind carrying charred pages of books up to Logavina Street.

"I kept on picking up leaves of books. It was so painful. These places were part of our youth," said Esad Taljanović, the dentist, whose house was no more than a third of a mile from the library.

Serb artillery and sniper positions were scarcely one mile uphill from the Lačević house. At that distance, a 120-millimeter mortar shell could reach Logavina in about thirty seconds; a sniper on the hill could hit citizens easily if they paused in the open for less than a second. Sarajevans often said that the snipers were so close they could choose which eye to shoot you in. Some districts were even closer to the Serb battle position. In Dobrinja, an Olympic village of high-rise apartments, everyone lived within four hundred yards of the front lines. But the neighborhood around Logavina was singled out for brutal pounding, because its population was predominantly Muslim. In a tape-recorded radio transmission in 1992, Bosnian Serb commander Ratko Mladić instructed his troops to shell the Muslim districts of Sarajevo. "Shell them until they're at the edge of madness," Mladić ordered in the message, a copy of which was obtained and broadcast by the BBC.[2]

Whether or not you were killed had little to do with the degree of caution in your lifestyle. Muniba Kaninić, thirty-three, was so terrified at the start of the war that she refused to leave her apartment. On May 23, 1992, she finally ventured a few paces from the front door to take out her garbage. She was killed by a splinter of shrapnel. The wound was so small that Ekrem Kaljanac, who rushed over to help, initially believed Muniba had fainted from fear.

The same mortar fire that killed Muniba Kaninić also pulverized Esad Taljanović's white Volkswagen Golf, which had been parked outside. The dentist's kids were inconsolable. "Oh, Daddy, Bjelko is wrecked," they cried, using the family's nickname for the car. "It was a natural reaction," Esad said. "They were too young to understand that a person had died."

But Esad's children proved quick studies in the rules of survival. Just two weeks later, another burst of shells exploded around the house. Esad rushed stark naked from the bathroom out to the courtyard, looking for his son. After a frantic search, he discovered that three-year-old Amir had run into the basement at the first sound of a detonation.

Other children were less fortunate. In the apartment down the hall from the Kaljanacs, five-year-old Jasmin Teparić rushed to the window to gawk as a mortar blew apart a plum tree in the yard outside. A single piece of shrapnel flew into his head and killed him.

"His mother was one of those who never wanted to go to the bomb shelter," recalled Minka. The dead boy's father died soon afterward of a heart attack and the widowed mother moved to another neighborhood.

The five-year-old's death traumatized the Kaljanacs. The

window where the boy died was only six feet away from their own living room window.

But you can't keep your children locked in a bomb shelter forever. Two months, three months, maybe, but after that it became impossible.

After the first month of the war, Ekrem had joined the Sarajevo police department. His job required him to be out on the streets, and because of his restless personality he was thankful for the opportunity to go out and help.

On September 8, 1992, the Serbs on the mountains started shooting incendiary bullets at a cluster of wooden sheds next to Ekrem's apartment house. Ekrem rushed out to help fight the blaze. Minka screamed at him to stay home. Firefighters were easy targets for snipers.

Her instincts were right. The Serbs opened fire on the crowd with 20-millimeter anti-aircraft ordnance, designed to pierce metal. Ekrem ran to grab a disabled neighbor who was trying to make it to safety on his crutches. Just as Ekrem wrapped his arms around the man, they were hit.

The bullet exploded inside the disabled man and his guts spilled out on Ekrem. Ekrem lost the tips of two fingers on his left hand. He was in a state of shock for nearly six months, too frightened to leave his house.

The Kaljanac family was so terrorized that they would not keep a kitty litter box in their apartment. Minka figured it was better to kick the cat outside than to risk her life going out to dig sand.

4

WIZARDS OF INVENTION

THE KALJANAC FAMILY is gathered around a table laden with delicacies: roasted lamb, shish kebab, stewed mushrooms, stuffed meat pies, feta cheese, onion-and-cream spread, baklava.

The scene is from Tarik Kaljanac's first birthday party on March 17, 1991. It is on videotape. When we watched the tape almost three years later, the Kaljanacs were serving up a lunch cobbled together from humanitarian rations.

Ekrem switched off the VCR and laughed. "This is what we do when we're hungry. We watch what we used to eat on television."

There was precious little food in Sarajevo. Small rations of flour, oil, dried beans, and powdered milk were doled out by the United Nations when they began a regular airlift in June 1992. Sometimes there was sugar, but not always. Occasionally a can of meat or a tin of sardines was included.

The most eclectic item in the ration packs was supplied by the United States: high-protein biscuits left from the Vietnam War. Sarajevans eyed the dates stamped on the tins with skepticism—1967 and 1968 vintages—but they ate the biscuits just the same.

It took more than a little ingenuity to feed a family of four. Ekrem and Minka Kaljanac mined vast reservoirs of creativity to feed themselves and their boys, Haris and Tarik. Minka learned to make wiener schnitzel out of stale bread, and pâté from dried beans. She kept a notebook of her favorite "war recipes" to swap with neighbors and family. The book contained all sorts of strange culinary inventions, such as "air pie"—a pie with absolutely no filling.

Minka's downstairs neighbor, Kira Prgovski, made a cream-filled cake from the Vietnam War biscuits that didn't need to be baked. It was one of the most coveted war recipes on Logavina Street, since days without gas or electricity often stretched into months.

Recipes for ersatz coffee also were prized. In Sarajevo, coffee is considered a cultural staple—a fact not appreciated by the humanitarian organizations carrying food into the city. As a result, the only coffee available came from the black market. Sarajevans tracked its price as keenly as Wall Street watches the Dow Jones.

When the price of coffee hit $60 a pound, dried lentils were substituted for coffee beans. Sarajevans would blacken the lentils by frying them in oil, which produced a cruelly deceptive aroma of sizzling steak. The lentils were then ground in a hand-operated Balkan coffee grinder, a brass gizmo that looks like a pepper mill. They boiled the grounds, just like Turkish coffee, and served the brew up in tiny cups. It was convincing enough in appearance, though the taste resembled neither coffee nor lentil soup so much as muddy water.

In place of a refrigerator, Minka hung a wicker basket out her kitchen window. ("We usually don't have any perishables anyhow, so mostly the kids put the cat in the basket.") Ekrem rigged a stove to burn wood by punching a hole in the side for an aluminum flue. The gas supply was sufficient only for a small coil, the type used for welding metals. Minka would insert the coil in the oven or under a burner for cooking. She also used it to light cigarettes, since matches and lighters were scarce.

Still, Minka managed to serve up meals graciously. The Kaljanacs lived in a dilapidated but meticulous apartment with a large L-shaped room that functioned as the kitchen and living room. It was decorated with the Bosnian equivalent of kitsch—etchings of the Sarajevo skyline, lace doilies that were ubiquitous in every home, Russian nesting dolls, and wooden spoons that Ekrem had acquired on a business trip to Moscow.

Before meals, Minka would neatly cover the kitchen table with a crisp cloth printed with Santa Claus figures. In the flickering candlelight of a Sarajevo evening, it didn't take a hyperactive imagination to believe you were at a real dinner party.

The day I visited, when Ekrem showed me the birthday party videotape, Minka was baking *kiflice*—a Bosnian biscuit that looks like a dense croissant. "The beauty of *kiflice*," Minka explained as she bent over the oven to remove the aromatic biscuits, "is that they can be made entirely out of UN rations of flour, oil, and powdered milk.

"This is one of the things we used to eat before the war, too, although we'd usually buy them at the bakery and get them filled with something—either sweets, like jam, or else meat or cheese," Minka said.

"Honey, where's the cheese? It seems the UN forgot to bring us cheese this month," Ekrem interrupted, kidding his wife. They hadn't seen cheese for months.

"Well, maybe you ought to go to the market and buy some

cheese," Minka retorted. The market had been shelled a few days earlier and was closed.

The food that was available for purchase in Sarajevo was outrageously expensive. Minka's brother, Hikmet Hadžiha-lilović, told me how he had sunk into a weeklong depression after seeing a vendor with a single banana—the asking price was 10 German marks, about $6. "You'd have to work for two months to buy that banana," Hikmet complained. A can of Pepsi or Coca-Cola was just as much. No Yugoslav dinars were accepted on the market, only hard currency, dollars, or prefer-ably German marks.

Like everybody else, Minka had exhausted her supply of herbs and spices early in the war. There were none at the market, so she added large quantities of garlic to everything. "We use a lot of garlic, too, because it is good for your health. It keeps you from getting colds, the flu, and we have no pen-icillin here or vitamins," she said. Minka's wiener schnitzel, for example, used garlic and onions to disguise the absence of meat. The bulk of the dish was made from stale bread, but with the right seasoning it was delectable. It was a family favorite.

The Kaljanacs' improvisations kept them healthier than most Sarajevans during the war, but they were far from well fed. In the 1991 videotape, Minka had the pudgy cheeks of a new mother. Her brother, Hikmet, was a strapping, fat man, belting out a sad Serbian love song ("I cry and open my soul"), along with his plump relatives. "I weighed almost 140 kilos [308 pounds] when that video was made," said Hikmet. "I'm down to 80 [kilos, 176 pounds] now."

Minka melted down to a slip of a woman within the first months of the war. Her weight loss was accelerated by chain-smoking and incessant tension. "The Sarajevo diet," Minka would laugh, tossing her red hair in a parody of a fashion model while patting her concave belly.

Minka Kaljanac's Wiener Schnitzel

2 loaves stale bread
1 cup minced onions (if available)
5 cloves garlic
Salt and pepper (if available)
Paprika (if available)
2 tablespoons oil
Water for mixing
¼ cup flour, for dusting

Grind the bread. Mix with minced onions and garlic. Add salt, pepper, paprika, and whatever spices you can scrounge up. Add a few drops of oil and enough water to create consistency of ground meat. Flatten with rolling pin. Cut into shape of schnitzel. Dust lightly with flour. Fry with remaining oil. Makes 4 servings.

How well you lived and ate in wartime had little to do with your pre-war circumstances. The Vranić family was a stark reminder of the equalizing effect of war. Passersby would often stop and stare at their grand home at 23 Logavina Street. It was a mansion, painted a luminous pink that would have seemed garish if it weren't for the Austro-Hungarian habit of ostentation. The house was set back from the street by an apron of rose gardens and an imposing pink wall. Above a graceful loggia were two gilt-edged, embossed peacocks and a crest with the number 1925—the year the house was built.

The people inside were far less intimidating than their residence. Sead Vranić, fifty-six when I met him, wore frayed trousers several sizes too large and had a five o'clock shadow. He walked with a self-deprecating shuffle. His wife, Vetka, was a fine-featured woman with her thinning white hair tied back, and a melancholy countenance.

The Vranićs had not been rich for some decades. The impressive house was the legacy of Sead's grandfather, a wealthy merchant who had moved to Sarajevo from Montenegro to escape anti-Muslim pogroms.

Sead himself had worked seventeen years as a manufacturer's representative for one of the large Yugoslav trading companies, Galeb Omiš. But the war had severed all communications and remittances from the firm, which was headquartered in Croatia. Sead didn't get even the unemployment benefit of $1.20 a month that most Sarajevans received. So the Vranićs had less to eat than their neighbors—little more than the rations they received from the United Nations. Both Sead and Vetka were bone-thin, each having lost nearly forty pounds since the start of the war.

Vetka's sister lived in Paris and was constantly sending parcels, most of which were lost or stolen. When they did get through, the packages contained "chocolate or bonbons, the kind of things you send as gifts. She doesn't realize we need the basics, like flour, sugar, margarine," Vetka said.

Vetka tried to save up what little food they had for Tarik, their only child, who was a soldier in the Bosnian Army. "It is very tough when you have a boy at the prime of his life. He goes to the front lines hungry. He comes home hungry."

Vetka said her mother had died at the beginning of the war. "I'm glad for it. Elderly people would not survive a situation like this," she said. "She was eighty-six, half-blind and senile. She was always asking for something to eat and we had nothing to give her."

The kitchen range didn't work anymore, so Vetka cooked in the living room over a stove provided by a relief agency. It served not only for cooking, but for heat. Despite the meager rations, Vetka managed to vary their diet. She invented her own recipe for making cheese spread out of powdered milk. She was particularly proud of her french fries. "They are not really french fries since we don't have potatoes, but they are tasty," said Vetka. The fries were made of flour and cornmeal.

Vetka also got cooking hints from *Preporod*, a magazine published by the Muslim Cultural Society. In 1992, the magazine started adding war recipes as a regular feature, but Vetka said, "Most of those recipes from early in the war I can't use anymore. I don't have the ingredients."

She flipped through the magazine and scoffed at one recipe for making mayonnaise out of powdered milk, water, and mustard. "This is stupid," Vetka said. "Who has mustard anymore?"

Vetka Vranić's French Fries

1 cup flour
1 cup cornmeal
1 cup warm water
1 teaspoon yeast
Oil for frying

Mix flour and cornmeal. Mix yeast and warm water. Add enough water to flour-cornmeal mixture to make consistency of dough. Form a ball, cover with towel, and let rest in warm place for 1 hour. Flatten with a rolling pin until ¾ inch thick. Cut into fry-size slices. Fry in oil until brown.

The strategy behind the siege was to starve the city into submission. Sarajevo was like any other densely developed metropolis—completely dependent on the hinterlands for its food supply. Within days after the Serbs set up their barricades in April 1992, there was hardly anything but dandelion leaves and nettles in the produce markets. Logavina Street had boasted a huge, well-stocked supermarket before the war—the Yugoslav supermarkets were more like those of Western Europe than Poland or Hungary—but it was soon reduced to bare metal shelves and a forlorn black-and-white photograph of Tito tacked to the wall.

Sarajevans were eating pigeons by June 1992, when the United Nations wrested control of the Sarajevo airport from the Serbs and launched an airlift of food and medicine into the city. The operation quickly eclipsed the 1948 airlift into West Berlin as the largest relief effort ever mounted in Europe. Still, it was an unpredictable supply line. The Serbs installed SAM anti-aircraft missiles adjacent to the airport and could shut down the airlift on the slightest whim. The planes could never bring enough into the city, and what they managed to bring was often strange. Besides the vintage Vietnam War biscuits, Sarajevans got expensive mineral water donated from France and mounds of crude lye soap. "We had so much soap, you could build a house out of it," said Zijo Džino. "And this mineral water, nobody could figure out what we were supposed to do with it. Wash our feet?"

The most reviled item was a brand of canned meat known as ICAR that made most people sick. Veterinarians warned not to feed it to dogs and cats. "We had a dog at the police station who was eating ICAR and his hair started falling out," Ekrem Kaljanac said.

An eerie side effect of the food crisis was the appearance of packs of hungry dogs ransacking the trash bins of Logavina Street—family pets that had been abandoned. Minka, a dog lover, remembers the beautiful purebreds wandering Logavina Street—an Irish setter that would lope through the yard behind their apartment, several Dalmatians, and a distraught, starving poodle who still sported an elegant pre-war coiffure. During the first winter of the war, the Kaljanacs were given a cocker spaniel, an expensive show dog.

"The man was a Serb; his wife had been wounded and he wanted to thank Ekrem for helping him out," Minka said. "They had no food to give the dog. The dog was beautiful—we had all the pedigree papers. His name was Snoopy. But we didn't have enough food for him either. I couldn't take him out for a walk—there was too much shelling. We finally gave him away. The kids cried and cried."

The Kaljanacs got a tiny cat instead, Cicka, who was happy enough to eat the Vietnam biscuits mixed with a dash of powdered milk.

The interminable blackouts exacerbated the food crisis. Sarajevans had tried to hoard food at the first glimpses of the barricades. As bad luck would have it, the electricity went out in late May 1992, just at the start of a terrific heat wave, and almost all stores of food were lost.

Jela Džino hobbled upstairs to inspect her battered kitchen after her release from the hospital in June. A stout woman before the war, she had lost fifty-seven pounds during her three months in Koševo Hospital, and had hoped the food supply would be better at her home. All the meat in her freezer had spoiled. There still were splotches of blood and clothing on the ceiling from the shelling. "You wouldn't believe the sight of it.

And the smell," she said. Zijo and their son, Nermin, twenty-three, had cleaned up some of the mess, but not enough to satisfy Jela.

Esad Taljanović had a freezer chock-full with forty-five pounds of veal, lamb, and steaks. What could he do but host a barbecue? Esad pulled his last bags of charcoal from the basement. The dentist set up his grill on the patio, a few feet from the door to the basement bomb shelter. His mother, Adlija, stayed in the kitchen frying potatoes to go with the meat. The shelling was heavy so they interrupted their cooking marathon frequently to dash into the shelter.

"The weather was wonderful for a barbecue, but I can't say that we enjoyed it," Esad said. "We were cooking and eating just to get it over with as quickly as possible."

The big binge left them sated but anxious. Esad and Šaćira were not particularly well adapted to wartime living. The prosperity of Esad's dental practice had spoiled them with all the conveniences of modern life. Their kitchen had a microwave and food processor, two toasters, an electric juicer, and an electric barbecue—"all museum pieces now," said Esad.

Furthermore, the Taljanovićs were picky eaters. Šaćira had cooked only free-range chickens and organic eggs from the farm. She had only used fresh produce, never canned.

"When we first saw powdered milk and powdered eggs coming into Sarajevo, I said to Šaćira, 'We won't ever eat that crap,'" Esad said. "Now here we are. I don't think my children remember what a banana or an orange is anymore. We were able to get some real meat once, and one of the kids said, 'This can't be meat. Where's the can?'"

The improvisational skills that Sarajevans acquired during the summer of 1992 were only the first test of endurance. Winter descends with speed and fury in Sarajevo. The snow starts falling in October and remains well into March—the main reason Sarajevo was chosen to host the Winter Olympics. In the early months of the siege, Sarajevans couldn't conceive of spending a winter without heating oil or coal.

Few people were ready for winter. When it came, they were forced to burn their cupboards and bookshelves—and eventually the clothes and books that they contained. Ekrem Kaljanac chopped up a stack of pine wood he had purchased to panel the living room. Delila Lačević burned an armoire.

The few trees in the neighborhood vanished, chopped down in the dark of night. The city was surrounded by trees—you could look from any window up to the verdant pine forests—but it was far too dangerous to venture into the hills for firewood.

Logavina Street had a slight advantage over the newer Sarajevo neighborhoods. The old private houses were better constructed for winters without central heating than the chockablock twentieth-century high-rises. Moreover, there was an industrial gas main that supplied a shoe factory near the top of Logavina Street. Few residents had used gas heating before the war, but it took just a little tinkering to jerry-rig a home.

Ekrem's pre-war work in utility installations proved invaluable. He took lengths of garden hose and ran gas coils into his apartment and into the homes of neighbors. At best, there was enough gas for one tiny stove—usually clever aluminum gizmos distributed by humanitarian agencies that could burn just about anything.

Wherever the stove was, that was where the families slept, cooked, and bathed no matter how large their house or apartment; the other rooms were effectively refrigerators. Jela and

Zijo closed up their six-room house and moved downstairs into their utility room. Kasema Telalagić squeezed into her laundry room with two children, her husband, and her mother-in-law. It was safer downstairs, anyway.

These "safe" rooms were inevitably dim and smoky, with the sandbags over the windows blocking any light. Candles were expensive—at least $1 apiece, if you could manage to find any. People devised homemade lamps from empty beef cans and humanitarian-aid cooking oil. Suada Čaušević, who had been hospitalized during a problem pregnancy, swiped a length of intravenous tubing, which her husband hooked up to a Bic lighter to make a gas lamp. It was a dangerous contraption, but it beat sitting at home in the dark.

On a listless afternoon, Minka Kaljanac was drinking coffee and smoking a cigarette. Her boys were sprawled on the living room rug, bickering as they played a board game in the vanishing daylight.

Suddenly, there was a faint popping sound. A single lightbulb over the kitchen table flickered on.

The younger boy, Tarik, went into fits of ecstasy. "*Struja, struja, struja*," he chanted repeatedly, using the Bosnian word for electricity as he dashed over to the television. Immediately the board game was abandoned and the children were watching a Superman cartoon on the VCR.

It was like that for much of the war. Life on Logavina Street, as elsewhere in Sarajevo, was measured out in kilowatts.

Some people had electricity some of the time. The same for water, gas, and telephones. When the utilities switched on, the city sprang to life. Often, the electricity came on only after midnight. Those were long nights, filled with the whirring of washing machines and vacuum cleaners. Jela Džino marked the date August 22, 1993, in her calendar. It was one of the few times during the war that she had water and electricity simultaneously.

"I got up at 5 A.M. I made pies, I did laundry. I took a shower. I tried to iron all the clothes. By the time I was done, there was no more electricity, no more water, so I went to sleep," Jela recalled.

As unpredictable as the weather, the utilities were an endlessly fascinating source of conversation and dark humor. Delila told me one of the bleaker and more revealing jokes about wartime Sarajevo: What's the difference between Sarajevo and Auschwitz? Auschwitz had gas.

When Ekrem called home—assuming the telephones were working—the first questions were always about the utilities. Walking down Logavina Street, you could hear the same dialogue replayed again and again between neighbors and family members.

"*Imal' struje?*" "Is there electricity?"

"*Nema.*" "There's none."

"*Imal' plina?*" "Is there gas?"

"*Nema.*" "There's none."

"*Imal' vode?*" "Is there water?"

"*Nema ništa*" would be the exasperated reply, finishing off the conversation. It meant literally "There's no nothing." It was repeated so often it was almost a mantra of Sarajevo life.

Electricity bills were more constant than the supply, and Sarajevo residents received bills throughout the war. Electricity was always the most popular utility and people would do just about anything to get it. Dino Duran, a thirteen-year-old student at the Razija Omanović elementary school, told me his parents made him pedal a stationary bicycle that was attached to a homemade generator. It didn't work.

Sarajevans' technique of "borrowing" electricity was more effective. Throughout most of the war, Sarajevo had a tiny bit of electricity that came into the city through what one UN official called the equivalent of a gigantic extension cord from central Bosnia. It was only about 15 megawatts—down from the 300 megawatts consumed by the city in peacetime—and was rationed sparingly to the police, the army, and high government officials.

If you had friends in the right places, it was simply a matter of running a discreet wire into a priority building. Ekrem Kaljanac was the master of this scam. He tapped into both the police station and the school next door, part of which had been taken over by the Bosnian Army. He ran a wire over to Esad Taljanović's to thank him for some free dental work on Minka's fillings. He also gave some to Jela and Zijo Džino and to an impoverished elderly couple, Serbs, who lived across the courtyard.

By Christmas 1992, Logavina looked like it was covered in garlands. Lengths of red garden hose and assorted wires snaked in and out of the windows along the street.

"Anybody who asks me, I can give them electricity. I never charge," Ekrem declared. "They get only 1.5 kilowatts an hour. It's enough for a little television, the VCR, and one lightbulb, nothing more. If someone tries to use their washing machine, that's it. We cut them off."

The biggest problem was that the rare lightbulb glowing through the curtains into the relentlessly dark Sarajevo night caused resentment from neighbors without electricity. At night, Minka began to hang thick quilts over the windows.

"It is so that the Chetniks can't see our lights and start shooting," Ekrem explained. "And, well, also because of the jealous neighbors."

The system was not terribly reliable. Tarik and his brother learned to switch around the plugs in the Kaljanac apartment. If the school lost electricity, they'd plug in pilfered electricity from the police station. They had to change cords again if the real electricity popped on.

Often enough, there were crackdowns on the electricity bandits. The Kaljanacs were frequently unplugged and left sitting in the dark.

As the war dragged on, they grew bolder in their quest for electricity. In autumn of 1995, Logavina Street pulled off its most audacious electricity heist ever. They ran a wire more than five hundred yards—all the way down Logavina and around a corner, where they plugged into the private home of Haris Silajdžić, the Bosnian prime minister.

"That's what this war has done to us," Jela Džino said, with a touch of sadness. "We've become a nation of thieves."

5

SERBS, CROATS, AND MUSLIMS

DESA STANIĆ DIDN'T HAVE a candle to put on her husband's grave, so she lit a cigarette. She took one puff and placed the cigarette upright in the snow, next to a sprig of plastic flowers.

"Pero loved to smoke, especially Marlboro. If I had a Marlboro, I would have left it," Desa said.

Pero Stanić was a soldier with the Bosnian Army who was killed on May 30, 1993, in an aborted campaign to dislodge the Serbs from Mount Trebević. He was forty-one. He left forty-three-year-old Desa with no money and two scrappy teenagers. The younger one, Vedran, thirteen, had been hit in the head by shrapnel and had a jagged scar running down his forehead.

Desa herself had the saddest face of anybody I'd met in Sarajevo. Her dark hair was pulled back severely and her blue eyes were ringed gray and red from long nights of insomnia and tears. The family lived in a nondescript concrete apartment building at the upper end of Logavina.

Like thousands of other war widows, Desa visited the cemetery whenever she could, talking quietly to her dead husband or just weeping, but what separated Desa from the many other grieving wives of Sarajevo was that she was a Serb. Her husband was a Croat.

"It is all the same. A widow is a widow, especially if she has children," Desa said with a dismissive shrug.

The most misunderstood aspect of the Bosnian war is the role of ethnicity and religion. Television commentators abroad—most of whom had never been to Bosnia—pointed to the blood feud between the Serbs, Croats, and Muslims. The reality was far more subtle and complicated.

According to the Serbian relief agency, Dobrotvor, an estimated 50,000 of the 300,000 people living in Sarajevo in early 1994 were Serbs. (In pre-war Sarajevo, 28 percent of the population was Serb, 49 percent Muslim, and 16 percent Croatian.) The Serbs suffered the same privations, and dodged the same snipers and exploding grenades, as their Muslim neighbors. Many Serbs fought heroically in the Bosnian Army.

"We are all just regular Sarajevo guys defending our homes and our city," said Mladen Marković, the soldier and poet. "In my unit, you have all religions. It is quite normal."

Logavina Street was home to one of the most prominent Serbs in Sarajevo. Jovan Divjak, a four-star general, became the highest-ranking Serb in the Bosnian Army and a wildly popular war hero.

To be sure, there were prejudices and unspoken tensions. Muslims thought the Serbs were not sufficiently fastidious about taking off their shoes before entering a house, as is the Muslim custom. There was lingering jealousy from the Communist years, when Serbs held a disproportionate share of the high government posts. Periodically, rumors would surface that Serb spies in the city were tipping off gunners to choice targets, such as water lines and bread queues.

Still, given the brutality of the war it was stunning how well the Muslims treated the Serbs living in their midst. Their behavior was very different, for example, from the way the United States interned Japanese-American citizens during World War II.

Jela Džino's closest friend on Logavina Street was Desa Stanić. Jela's husband, Zijo, worked on fixing car batteries and radios with Milutin Đurđevac, another Serb. The most surprising relationship was the Džinos' continued friendship with a wizened, elderly neighbor named Mara. She had a son who had left for the other side and was fighting with the Bosnian Serb army. Yet when the telephone lines were working, he would call his mother at the Džinos' house, since Mara had no telephone.

Jela would run next door at all hours to get Mara. After the call was finished, Jela would send her neighbor home with a loaf of bread or vegetables from the garden. "Mara's just an old woman. She hasn't done anything to hurt anybody," Jela said matter-of-factly. "Before the war, nobody really knew who was a Serb, who was a Croat, or who was a Muslim," said Zijo. "It was better that way."

Logavina Street was so cohesive that few of its Serb residents followed Radovan Karadžić to his self-proclaimed Republika Srpska—although many fled simply to get away from the war.

It was far easier for a Serb or a Croat to escape Sarajevo than for a Muslim. A Serb would be automatically granted citizenship or refugee status in Serbia, a Croat likewise in Croatia, but the Bosnian Muslims had no identifiable homeland except Bosnia. Unless they were lucky enough to be granted refugee status in Germany, the United States, or another country, they were stuck in Sarajevo. It took a fair amount of determination and courage for a Serb to remain.

In the library of his Logavina Street apartment, Brigadier General Jovan Divjak kept the casing of a 76-millimeter artillery shell, engraved with the signatures of men who had served under him in the Yugoslav National Army. The general showed off this memento with pride, turning it over in his hands. But, as he examined the names, his mood turned melancholy.

"He is over there. He is over there. He is on the other side," Divjak murmured, reading off the names. All were fighting with the Bosnian Serb Army—all except Divjak.

The general was an engaging man in his late fifties, with a penchant for speaking French and kissing ladies' hands. Everybody in Sarajevo claimed to be his friend. When I met him, in the pitch-dark stairwell of his apartment, he didn't have a flashlight so I gave him mine. He accepted this gift, worth maybe $3, as if it was priceless.

A lifelong soldier, Divjak had been educated at the military academy in Belgrade. He moved to Sarajevo in 1966 with his wife, Vera, to take a position with the Bosnian territorial defense—roughly comparable to the National Guard in the United States. Divjak became disenchanted with the army in 1991, after witnessing its violent intercession on behalf of the breakaway Serbs of Croatia. He was turned off by the Serbian nationalism that was sweeping Belgrade. A 1987 speech by Serbian president Slobodan Milošević was particularly upsetting to him. Milošević called for Serbs to stand up for their rights in areas where they were a minority.

"I had heard what Slobodan Milošević was saying—that all Serbs were supposed to live together in the same country—and that was simply not acceptable to me. In my family, there was never any of that kind of talk. I found it insulting to suggest that we wouldn't want to live with other peoples."

The Divjaks' older son was married to a Croat, the younger son to a Muslim. Everyone in the family voted for an independent, multiethnic Bosnia in the referendum of February 1992. Divjak estimates that 50 percent of Sarajevo's Serbs voted in favor of the referendum, with most of the rest boycotting the election.

Two months later, when Sarajevo came under attack on April 6, Divjak did not hesitate. "I walked from my apartment on Logavina to the new headquarters of the Bosnia-Herzegovina army and volunteered." As one of the few professional officers in the fledgling army, Divjak was named second-in-command. His presence was testament to the fact that it was not a "Muslim army," as it was often described. The original Bosnian Army was made up of about 30 percent Orthodox Serbs and Catholic Croats. That percentage dwindled to about 10 percent later in the war.

As the lone Serb in the high command, Divjak was eyed with suspicion. Despite the four stars on his epaulets, he was excluded from sensitive strategy sessions. Once, at a peace conference in Geneva, a Bosnian Serb negotiator approached President Alija Izetbegović and hinted strongly that Divjak was a spy. Izetbegović called Divjak aside and confronted him.

"What if you really are one of them and you provide them with data?" the president asked Divjak. "But what if I fire you and you're not?" Ultimately, Divjak kept his job, but the doubt remained. In 1994, when Divjak was being interviewed by a history professor, the man told him: "You will become a part of history. Either as a legend or a famous spy."

"It is understandable," Divjak said dismissively. "It has nothing to do with Muslim nationalism or anything like that.

Refugees arrive here from Foča or some other place where they might have been tortured, expelled. They get to Sarajevo and they cannot understand why they should trust me or why Serbs are allowed to live here."

Despite such suspicions, many Serbs, particularly the elderly, refused to leave.

Milutin Đurđevac and his wife, Cvijeta, lived in the dingy kitchen of their third-floor apartment on Logavina Street. It was the only room they could keep warm. They had an aluminum stove the size of a bread box in which they burned all sorts of things. Once, when I visited, they were feeding an outdated Communist-era textbook, *Social Harmony and Management*, into the flames, page by page. The Đurđevacs had been rich before the war. Milutin had retired as an executive of a large trading company in 1990 with $68,000 in savings and a monthly pension of $1,100—a fortune by Yugoslav standards. It was all wiped out in the collapse of the Yugoslav banking system.

When I met them in 1994, they were so poor that Cvijeta made coffee from lentils. Milutin couldn't afford cigarettes so he rolled his own with shaking, bony hands. Aside from UN rations, they subsisted on handouts from the Jewish Community Center, the result of Milutin's military service fighting the Nazis during World War II. At the age of seventy, Milutin looked like a skeleton in a three-piece wool suit that was the last relic of his former stature. He suffered from a variety of ailments, not least of which was a bullet wound in his buttocks. He had been shot on July 23, 1993, while hobbling past an exposed intersection with a bundle of firewood in his arms. He lay on the pavement for thirty minutes before the sniper stopped shooting and somebody pulled him to safety. Had Milutin not used his T-shirt to stanch the bleeding, it's likely that he would have bled to death.

"These are evil people, criminals," Milutin said of the Bosnian Serbs. "In World War II, we had snipers that were used for military purposes only. These people are shooting children and the elderly."

"As far as I'm concerned, Radovan Karadžić can go to hell," piped his birdlike wife, looking surprised at her own use of profanity.

The Đurđevacs were actually acquainted with Karadžić. The leader of the Bosnian Serbs was not from Bosnia at all but from the rural hillside around Mount Durmitor in Montenegro. Milutin was born in the region and knew of Karadžić's father as a Chetnik soldier in World War II with a penchant for looting. Milutin considered Radovan Karadžić a peasant and his nationalist ideology primitive and dangerous.

In the late 1970s, when Karadžić was a young psychiatrist, he came to visit Milutin to talk about how Serbs needed to guard their own interests.

"All the stuff about Greater Serbia, I wasn't interested in. We didn't want our children to hear that kind of crap," Milutin said. "We had lived with Muslims all our lives."

The Đurđevacs had no complaints about their Logavina Street neighbors. In the first month of the war, with fears of terrorism running rampant, Ekrem Kaljanac's duties as a police officer had included confiscating weapons. Milutin's hunting rifle was taken. But the neighbors stayed on good terms. When Ekrem wired his own apartment for electricity, he ran a cable across the courtyard into the Đurđevacs' to give the elderly couple a bit of light.

Then, in February 1994 an ugly incident took place that taught the Đurđevacs how fragile their acceptance in Sarajevo was. Cvijeta, sixty-six, had walked downtown in desperation to find some bread. She went into a restaurant where bread was being distributed, but a young man chased her away. "I know who you are. Get the hell out of here," the man yelled.

Cvijeta said she was so frightened that she slipped down the stairs fleeing. She pulled down her sock to show me an ugly green bruise on her shin. It was the first time anything like that had happened to them, and it touched a deep nerve. Their greatest fear was that if Bosnia was divided into ethnic enclaves, as Karadžić wanted, they'd be forced to move out of the neighborhood and go to the Republika Srpska.

"The Serbs are forcing Muslims to leave their apartments elsewhere. If the same thing happened here, I guess we would have to leave, but I wouldn't want to," Cvijeta said. "It is tough here—no food, no electricity, no heat. But having to leave, that would be the worst thing."

The Serbian Orthodox Church of St. Michael the Archangel has stood since 1589 a few blocks from the foot of Logavina Street, on what is now Maršala Tita. In August 1992, the chief priest announced he was taking a vacation. He never returned.

"I was sent here for three weeks to fill in for him. I was fooled. He's gone, and I'm still here," said the Reverend Avakum Rosić, who became the head priest.

Father Rosić is a wizened man of nearly eighty, but tough. He kept the church operating under the most adverse conditions. There was no heat, no lights—only the flickering illumination of the oil-burning chalices. Most days, less than a dozen worshipers attended the 9 A.M. service. Father Rosić occasionally conducted services in an entirely empty church.

"A lot of our members left Sarajevo. Others were killed. Others don't come because they are scared of the shelling," he said.

Despite animosities created by the war, the church had never been vandalized or threatened by Sarajevo's Muslims—except for an incident in which a few children were caught stealing candles.

There was no comparison to conditions in Serb-controlled Bosnia, where virtually all the mosques had been destroyed. In Banja Luka, Father Rosić's hometown, now part of the Republika Srpska, Serb rebels had dynamited every mosque. They did not even spare the sixteenth-century Ferhad Pasha mosque, one of the finest examples of Islamic art in Yugoslavia and Banja Luka's chief tourist attraction.

Father Rosić had been good friends with the imam of the Ferhad Pasha mosque, who fled Banja Luka in terror. "They were houses of God," Father Rosić said, shaking his head. "It is a disaster that they destroyed the mosques."

Serbs in exile in Pale, ten miles east of Sarajevo, couldn't believe the televised reports that the Sarajevan Orthodox church had not been destroyed by Muslims. Another religious man, Mustafa Orman, who ran the fifteenth-century Muslim prayer house next to the cemetery on upper Logavina, said: "No matter what the Serbs do, we will never destroy a church or any other religious monument. Islam is very forgiving. Islam is very tolerant. We respect all religions." He spoke about this tolerance three days after his wife was killed in the February 5 shelling of the Sarajevo marketplace.

In wartime, spiritual leaders were as important as the defenders on the front lines in protecting Sarajevo from annihilation. At the Christmas Eve mass, leaders from all religions sat in the front row at the Roman Catholic cathedral—thumbing their noses at Karadžić and the others who said the people of Bosnia could not live together.

It was not that Sarajevans possessed superhuman quantities of tolerance and forgiveness. The explicit policy of the Bosnian government was to encourage a spirit of reconciliation as it tried to establish itself as the legitimate, legally elected government of all Bosnians—Serbs and Croats, as well as Muslims.

In Sarajevo news broadcasts from Television and Radio BiH (Bosnia and Herzegovina), the enemy was referred to as "the Karadžić Serbs," "the Serb aggressor," or "the Chetniks"— but never simply as "the Serbs." The message that was repeatedly hammered home was that not all Serbs were culprits.

Alija Izetbegović and Prime Minister Haris Silajdžić maintained that the Serbs on the other side were mostly decent people who had been cleverly manipulated by a handful of war criminals.

The propaganda from the Bosnian Serb capital of Pale was exactly the reverse. With language evoking the Crusades, the announcers spoke of a holy war to eliminate Muslims from Serbian land. Muslims were "the Turks," the "fundamentalists," or "the Mujaheddin," Islamic freedom fighters. Sometimes they used the pejorative *balije,* which writer Tom Gjelten noted was the rough equivalent of a TV news anchor in the United States referring to blacks as "niggers."[1]

Serb television could be so offensive that it upset ten-year-old Haris Kaljanac. Haris, who liked to watch the cartoons on the Belgrade channel when there was electricity, hated it when announcers referred to President Alija Izetbegović as "Ali Baba." "They insult us all the time. They're always making fun of the Muslims," the child complained.

In Serb nationalist folklore, June 28, 1389, is a day to remember. That is when Ottoman Turks conquered the medieval Serbian empire at the Battle of Kosovo Polje. Even though six centuries had elapsed, Serb militants harked back to Kosovo as though the battle were yesterday and referred to it to justify whatever violence was inflicted on twentieth-century Muslims.

In 1995, an Orthodox priest in the Serb-held municipality of Ilidža told me that even the children of Muslims "will grow up to kill Serbs again." In contrast to the gentle clerics of Sarajevo, the priest insisted that Serbs could "live with any other nationality except the Muslims and Croats.

"The one who forgives is worse than the one who did the bad deed in the first place," he intoned.

Yet there were tales of extraordinary kindness and courage on both sides. Fatima Sokolović, a seventy-five-year-old refugee from Grbavica, recounted how her closest Serb friends risked their lives to help her, in defiance of the Serb militants who were terrorizing Muslims.

"The whole time we lived in Grbavica I cannot tell you of a single conflict between neighbors," Sokolović said. "I don't know if even over the next hundred years, people will be able to write the history of this war. The longer you're here, the less you understand."

No wonder, then, that Americans were baffled by the Bosnian war. So, too, were Bosnians.

The conflict was commonly defined as "ethnic warfare," yet everyone comes from the same ethnic stock. The difference among people is primarily in the religions they practice, yet to explain the fighting as a "religious war" would be equally misleading, since most Yugoslavs were not religious people.

The Yugoslav (literally "south Slav") people are mostly descendants of the Slavic tribes that wandered through the region in the third and fourth centuries. Those who settled to the west took the faith of the Roman Catholic Church in what is now Croatia. To the east, the Serbs assumed the Orthodox Christianity of the Byzantine Empire. The Muslims were Slavs who converted during the four centuries that Bosnia was ruled by the Ottoman Turks.

If you watch a Sarajevo street scene for a few minutes, you will see brunettes, blonds, and redheads, blue eyes and brown eyes, tall and short people. They are more diverse in appearance than the residents of many European capitals. You cannot tell a Serb, Croat, or Muslim by appearance. The only way to tell the difference is by traditionally Muslim, Catholic, and Orthodox given names—although even that method is not foolproof. Lana Lačević, so named because her mother liked the actress Lana Turner, once told me with her wicked sense of humor, "I'll decide whether Lana is a Serb or a Muslim name when I see who wins the war."

In the former Yugoslavia, religion and ethnicity are contentious subjects. Even some of the historical scholarship is slanted by underlying political disputes. Serb and Croat militants—who agree on little else—consider the Muslims to be lapsed Christians who betrayed their faith by collaborating with and taking the religion of an occupying power. The Serbs trot out historical treatises that suggest the Muslims were originally Orthodox. In this way, they have tried to bolster their claim that Bosnia is truly part of "Greater Serbia."

In 1993, when fighting between Croats and Muslims broke out in western Bosnia, the Croat nationalists adopted a similar tack—insisting that the Bosnians were really lapsed Catholics and that Bosnia belonged historically to Croatia. Actually, some historians have theorized that the medieval Bosnian Church was neither Catholic nor Muslim. Some evidence suggests that pre-Islamic Bosnians were Bogomils—members of a heretical Christian sect. Under this theory, the Bosnians eagerly embraced Islam and the protection the Ottoman Empire provided them from persecution by the Bosnian Church.

In any case, the prevailing view among modern historians is that it was not the Ottoman Turks' policy to force conversions. Other than the Albanians, the Bosnians were the only Turkish subjects to convert to Islam in large numbers. Nevertheless, under Ottoman rule, Muslims enjoyed certain tax benefits and stood a better chance of retaining large land holdings. As a result, much of the feudal aristocracy converted. This set the stage for a dynamic that would persist into the twentieth century.

Conflicts between Serbs and Muslims were often about economics—a Serb peasant class revolting against a better-educated and wealthier Muslim elite. Not surprisingly, after World War II the Serbs joined the Communist Party in disproportionately high numbers. Muslims lost out when private estates were socialized. The Chetnik militia was inspired by the Hajduk bandits—Robin Hood figures in Serb folklore who robbed Turkish merchants. In 1992, the Serb militiamen who perpetrated the "ethnic cleansing" of Muslims in northern and eastern Bosnia boldly carted off the Muslims' televisions and VCRs, often in stolen Mercedes.[2]

These class distinctions were more or less obliterated in Sarajevo by the 1990s. There were rich Muslims, poor Muslims; rich Serbs, poor Serbs—and Communists of all religions. On Logavina Street, the last vestiges of the old class order were apparent only in where people lived. The Serbs tended to be clustered in the newer apartment houses, built in the 1950s and 1960s, some of which were used as army housing. The descendants of some of the area's oldest Muslim families—people like the Džinos, Telalagićs, and Kasumagićs—occupied the single-family houses.

Logavina Street is in the heart of Sarajevo's old Muslim neighborhood. Nineteenth-century postcards, printed during the Austro-Hungarian period, refer to it as the *Turkische Viertel*—or Turkish Quarter. Along the street, which stretches less than a third of a mile, there are three mosques, their minarets piercing the distinctive Sarajevo skyline.

Under siege, the call for Muslim prayers came not from the minarets, but from behind a brick wall. Fear of sniper attacks kept muezzins from climbing the stairs of the minarets. At one mosque, a microphone and loudspeakers were installed so that prayers could be called safely from inside. The electricity went off soon after the installation, so the muezzin began summoning the faithful from within a walled courtyard. "It was better before, when you could call from the minaret. It was higher up, louder," said Alija Žiga, head of a tiny mosque on Logavina.

Despite the faint call, more and more faithful responded. While the cosmopolitan residents of Sarajevo had always thought of themselves as just like other Europeans, the war had made them acutely conscious of their differences. As Šaćira Lačević commented, "We never knew we were Muslims before. The Serbs forced it on us, so now I try to remind my girls not to forget who they are."

Religion was one of the few refuges for those with little hope. With most businesses closed, no movie theaters or electricity to watch television, praying at the mosque was at least something to do. "People are coming back to Islam, sort of like rediscovering themselves and their roots," said Edin Smajović, an army officer in his late twenties who lives on Logavina. Like others of his generation, he had come of age under Marshal Tito's Communist regime, when religion was discouraged.

"Islam is very appealing to people right now because Islam is a religion that is not afraid of death. Every day here is a game of Russian roulette—you don't know if you will be alive or not—so you have to believe in something," he said. "We used to say 'Thank Tito.' Now we say 'Thank you, dear God.' "

Most of the Muslims on Logavina Street did not follow the religious strictures. Some didn't eat pork, but very few were averse to an occasional beer or brandy. Ekrem and Minka Kaljanac showed me their old photo album filled with pictures of the boys sitting on Santa Claus's lap. "I celebrate all the holidays—Christmas, too," Ekrem said.

Muslims visited their Catholic friends for Christmas dinner, and celebrated Christmas again with their Orthodox friends in early January. For Bajram, the most important Muslim holiday, Muslims hosted their Christian friends and neighbors.

"You invite people who are poorer than you to eat. No matter if all we have are UN rations, there are a lot of grandmothers and old widows in the neighborhood, and we'll have them over," Minka explained.

Ekrem started observing the Muslim fasting period of Ramadan during the war. Since food was in such short supply the difference between fasting and eating was negligible. Delila Lačević also fasted, even in 1993, when she was recuperating from her shrapnel wounds. Delila was always a little embarrassed by her religious grandmother, swathed in black and reading the Koran. She would apologize profusely whenever I visited and her grandmother instructed me to remove my shoes. Delila also fretted that she would get to the United States and people would think she was a fundamentalist. She occasionally saw American television coverage of the war—it was often rebroadcast on Television BiH—and she was appalled by all the footage of Muslim peasant women who kept their heads covered.

"They show these old ladies from Srebrenica with babushkas," Delila complained. "It makes me really angry. We are Muslims, but we are not mujaheddin."

Nor was Delila bent on vengeance against the Serbs. "I went to the cathedral on Christmas Eve with my friends to hear the music for midnight mass. I was taught not to hate Serbs and Croats. . . . Even now, if I ran into a Chetnik, even the one who had fired that shell, the worst thing I could do is spit in his face."

Both Delila and Lana were scornful of the girls their own age who were wearing veils as they strolled through the Old City. The Communists had banned the veil in 1950, but it was enjoying a trendy revival in wartime. At one café in the Baščaršija, you would often see teenagers in veils, smoking and drinking coffee, flirting with boys. Lana said about 3 of the 250 women in her medical school had started covering their heads. She believed they were pandering to the Arab charities that were funding Islamic culture programs in Sarajevo.

"I respect it if they come from traditional Muslim families, and are truly religious. But if it is for a few extra packages of humanitarian aid or a scholarship from some Arab committee, I can't agree with that," Lana said.

The Sarajevo Muslims often seemed deeply conflicted about their religion—fiercely proud of their unique tradition, but also apologetic and embarrassed. Once, at a restaurant owned by Minka Kaljanac's in-laws, a group of Saudi Arabians arrived for lunch in traditional attire. The entirely Muslim restaurant staff eyed the covered women suspiciously. It was the chilliest reception I had ever witnessed in this most hospitable city.

The dentist, Esad Taljanović, told me the Bosnian Muslims felt more in common with the European Jews than with the Muslims of the Arab world. "Our women wear miniskirts and blue jeans. We drink beer and wine. If Bosnia was ever going to be an Islamic state, I would be the first to leave," Esad said. "We want to be like America, with everybody having equal rights."

Much debated was a treatise that Izetbegović had written in 1970, his "Islamic Declaration," which expounded on the relationship of Islamic law to secular government. Although he did not call for an Islamic state in Bosnia, the treatise gave rise to fears among Serbs and Croats, as well as many Muslims, that the president had a secret Islamic agenda planned for Bosnia.

Sead Vranić was the most devout Muslim I met on Logavina. He was one of the few who read Arabic fluently and attended mosque regularly. Yet he, too, expressed distaste for the idea that Bosnia could become a Muslim state. "The Serbs may not want to live with us, but we stubbornly persist in wanting to live with them," Sead said in late 1995, as the international community was drawing up another plan to partition Bosnia. "I like it when people talk about mixed marriages. That is the real Bosnia."

Sead found it endlessly irritating that the Catholics referred to themselves as "Croats" and the Orthodox as "Serbs," even though they might have no family ties whatsoever to Croatia or Serbia. "How can somebody be a Serb when his family's been living for five hundred years in Bosnia? Somebody might be Orthodox or Catholic or Jewish, but if they're from here, they're Bosnians," he challenged.

Sead's position was the prevailing attitude in Sarajevo, but there were many exceptions. Once, when I knocked at the door of Edin Smajović's apartment, he demanded to know whether the translator accompanying me was a Muslim. He would not admit a Serb to his home.

Nermin Džino, who served with the Bosnian Army, also became increasingly militant as the war dragged on. "I would never trust a Serb anymore," Nermin declared one day, as his parents, Jela and Zijo, looked on disapprovingly. I asked him how he felt about his neighbor, General Jovan Divjak. Nermin seemed offended by the question. Of course he trusted Divjak. He considered him a great Bosnian patriot. Then Jela reminded her son that his own sister's husband is Serb.

"Well, he's a great guy," Nermin said.

We started teasing Nermin about the Serb girl he was dating. "That's a different story. I don't care about the religion of a woman I'm involved with, as long as she's pretty."

And so it went. Nermin was forced to concede there wasn't a single Serb he knew that he didn't like, but his attitude underscored how fragile Sarajevo's tolerance had become in the brutality of war. The soul of Sarajevo—its legendary tolerance—was as gravely endangered as the lives of its inhabitants.

6

COMING OF AGE

IT WAS THE FIRST DAY of school on Logavina Street and, not surprisingly, there were more than a few glitches.

For one, there were no chairs. Refugees had stolen most of them to burn for fuel. In classroom 29 of the Razija Omanović school, seventh-graders sat on their desks and giggled hysterically until principal Lejla Hadžiomerović came striding in and ordered them to the basement to hunt for more chairs.

"No chairs," shrugged Hadžiomerović, an unflappable and impeccably dressed woman in her mid-forties. "Well, that's the least of our troubles."

The school had no heat, no electricity, hardly any windows, and no running water—not to mention any of the usual school paraphernalia, like erasers, and globes, computers, and audio-visual aids.

The kids didn't have physical education anymore. The Bosnian Army had taken over part of their gym in the basement and the rest was being used as a bomb shelter. Besides, the gymnasium floorboards had been ripped out and burned for fuel.

The school still offered music classes but had no instruments. "The kids sing a lot," Hadžiomerović said.

The textbooks were laughably obsolete. "The people of Yugoslavia live and work on an equal basis and in togetherness," declared a social studies book, published in 1991, that fourth-graders were still using.

What remained of the Razija Omanović school were the sturdy stone walls and the dedicated teachers, who worked for less than $2 a month. It was an old dilapidated place that had defied the historical odds by its continuing existence. It had survived two world wars, despite being bombed repeatedly by the Allies in 1944 when it was a Nazi headquarters. The broad side of the building faced Mount Trebević and it had taken countless mortar hits in 1992 and 1993.

The place was filthy. The walls were covered with graffiti reading "Bulldogs" and "Tigers," the mascots for Logavina's popular soccer team. Janitors swept up daily, but there was no water or detergent for washing. The lavatories were so unspeakable that "the kids are forbidden from using them unless they absolutely can't stand it anymore."

The public schools in Sarajevo had operated in fits and starts since the beginning of the war. The school day was abbreviated to three hours. They simply couldn't keep the children—ages seven to fourteen—any longer without heat or functioning toilets.

When I visited in March 1994, the school had been closed for nearly four months. An extended winter holiday had been declared the previous November after a school in the Alipašino Polje neighborhood of new Sarajevo was shelled. Three children were killed in the attack and twenty were wounded. Around the same time, a popular second-grader, Dijana Kadrić, eight, was killed by a grenade near her apartment.

"That one was very, very tough on the kids," said Hadžiomerović. "Every day they would bring flowers to leave on the desk where she used to sit."

While American students go through fire drills and bomb scares, the students at Razija Omanović were going through the real thing.

"We were sitting at this table right under where this sniper was shooting," thirteen-year-old Maša Lačević recounted. "The teacher, she was really scared. She grabbed her books and fell under the table. We were all laughing."

"I even found the bullet," interjected Maša's cousin Mirza Kapić. "I wanted to keep it but the principal made me give it to the police."

"It was really funny," added Maša.

Haris Kaljanac, ten, told me excitedly about the time a shell landed right outside his fourth-grade classroom. "All us kids hid under our desk. The girls were crying, but not the boys. We told them, 'Why are you crying, stupid?'"

The students were prohibited from loitering in the courtyard outside school. The basketball hoops were removed to discourage practice. The children were instructed to walk home in pairs, not in large groups, which were tempting targets for Serb gunners.

Other adjustments were made to the curriculum. The school began Saturday classes in English. Foreign languages were enjoying a tremendous boom in wartime, because so many families hoped to emigrate. Arabic was also added, for children interested in exploring their Islamic roots, and those thinking about emigrating to Arabic countries.

"I don't think it is so much a religious thing as it is that children hear about the great wealth in the Arab countries and think, if they go there, they'll be eating bananas and choco-late," Hadžiomerović said.

The school also shortened, but did not eliminate, the time they regularly devoted to teaching the Cyrillic alphabet, used in Serb areas of the former Yugoslavia. (As Hadžiomerović ex-plained, the kids wanted to be able to read the subtitles on Belgrade television, which broadcast the best American mov-ies.)

The school directed students to call their own language Bosnian-Serbo-Croatian, instead of Serbo-Croatian, as it had been known in the past. It was too long, so the kids simply called it Bosnian. The idea behind the change was to resurrect Bosnia's independent history and instill a sense of ethnic pride. According to Hadžiomerović, the Yugoslav school sys-tem had given short shrift to Bosnia in the past. Muslim names were not used in reading material until the mid-1970s. Even then, the schoolbooks had subtly derogatory references to Muslims.

"You'll see all the time, things like 'Dragan's [a Serb name] father is an airline pilot. Sejo's [a Muslim name] father is an auto mechanic,'" Hadžiomerović said.

Recently, a humanitarian organization gave a grant to schools to buy new reading material. But it made a tremen-dous gaffe by including a poem by Radovan Karadžić.

"I'd say that the lack of current books is our biggest single problem. The teachers all try to improvise, with more or less success, but it is hard without the reading material," the prin-cipal said.

The parents on Logavina Street were fretful about the war's toll on their children's education. The Kaljanacs had bought a computer for Haris with math and English-instruction software just before the war started. He could use it only on those rare occasions when there was electricity.

Minka Kaljanac was especially upset that her younger son wouldn't be able to go to school until he was seven—the traditional age for first grade throughout the former Yugoslavia. "Almost all the kindergartens are destroyed, and nobody would take a kid to kindergarten anyway. It's too dangerous," said Minka. "But I worry that Tarik doesn't get a chance to socialize with kids his own age."

"These poor kids," complained Esad Taljanović. "My brother called the other night from Michigan and said his son's school took them on a nature walk. They examine nature. My son, I send him to examine the basement."

Still, there were few complaints about the school itself. If anything, the frequent interruptions caused by shelling made the students more attentive. "A couple of times when school was closed, we'd have parents coming here anyway, saying, 'I couldn't keep my son home. He really wants to go,'" said Hadžiomerović. "You never saw that before the war."

The students were willing to endure the shabby conditions. They wore ski jackets inside the unheated classrooms, bundled up as though they were dressed for an afternoon of sledding. "When we're all breathing at the same time, it is not as cold in the classroom," a chipper thirteen-year-old, Mirza Ustamujić, suggested.

By any standards, the students seemed to be performing well enough on their first day back after the four-month hiatus. They met in a dank, unfinished basement converted into a classroom. Without apparent difficulty, the fourth-graders in Haris Kaljanac's class were able to multiply 3,456 by 324. The seventh-graders were able to fluently recite the chemical symbols, even though their school had no science lab.

In English class, they read enthusiastically from a textbook that was poignant in its obsolescence:

"Have you been to Yugoslavia?"

"Yes. I have just arrived from Belgrade. Belgrade is a beautiful city. . . . I have been on the Adriatic and the Alps in Slovenia."

Perhaps the most traumatic incident of the war for the Razija Omanović school took place October 8, 1994, about seven months after my first visit. It was a crisp, irresistibly sunny afternoon in the middle of what was supposed to be a cease-fire. Thirteen seventh-graders set out to visit their favorite math teacher. She lived a fair distance away in the Čengić Vila neighborhood of new Sarajevo. The trams had resumed running along Sniper Alley. For most of the kids, it was the first time they'd ridden the trams since the war began.

Amir Goro wasn't thinking about danger when he got off the tram to the sound of gunfire. "Oh, forget about it," the thirteen-year-old remembered telling his apprehensive schoolmates. "We've gotten so used to shooting. I didn't even notice it."

Even after everyone started to run, even as Amir's own legs stopped obeying a command from his brain to keep going, he wasn't thinking about death. Not even when a man picked him up off the ground and drove him in a Volkswagen Golf to the hospital, not even a little later when the numbness started giving way to a horrific pain in his stomach. Not until he was lying outside the operating room and heard a surgeon screaming at her colleagues—"You idiots, hurry up. We've got a child dying out here!"—did Amir realize with a start that they were talking about him.

The sniper had fired with a 7.9-millimeter machine gun

just after the tram opened its doors at the last stop, near the Holiday Inn. Returning from their excursion, three of the children from Razija Omanović were hit. Two recovered quickly from leg wounds. Amir Goro did not.

When I visited Amir two months after the shooting, he was in the State Hospital of Sarajevo. It was on a ridge above the Holiday Inn, the façade so demolished you wouldn't believe a hospital was functioning inside. Amir's ward was in the back. The room was long and narrow with plastic sheeting taped over a bank of windows, potbellied stoves in the corners spewing out gusts of warmth. The boy was all cheekbones and ears. His skin was like parchment draped over knobbly bones. A tall boy, maybe five feet ten, who had weighed about 120 pounds before the shooting, Amir now weighed barely 50 pounds. Most of his teeth had fallen out from malnutrition.

But Amir had lively brown eyes and an engaging manner. Without much to do in the hospital other than read a well-thumbed copy of *Denis Napast*—Dennis the Menace—he was well-versed in the causes of his own misery.

"It was only one bullet," Amir explained. But it was quite a bullet. It was not a direct hit, but it ricocheted off the pavement and into his hip. Spinning through his body, the bullet ripped its way through his stomach, intestines, and rectum. His colon was still sitting in a plastic bag. He wasn't strong enough to undergo surgery to put it back in.

Amir had already undergone three operations. With boyish bravado, he explained how he'd almost died in the most recent operation, three weeks before my visit. It had taken the doctors ninety minutes to revive him.

"I am better now," Amir said in carefully articulated English for my benefit. Then turning to reassure his other visitors, he said, "I am happy today because my mother, my sister, and my best friend came to visit."

His best friend, Mirza Ustamujić, was standing by the bedside, looking on skeptically. Every time he came to visit, his friend was noticeably thinner. Once we were in the corridor and out of earshot, tears filled his long-lashed eyes.

"Amir looks like one of those pictures from Bangladesh," Mirza whispered.

Fresh outrage swept through Logavina Street after the attack on the schoolchildren. "This is not a war. A war is where soldiers shoot soldiers. This is just crime," Zijo Džino ranted to the neighbors. Ekrem Kaljanac collected food from the neighborhood for the Goro family. General Divjak arranged to get Vahid Goro, Amir's father, who was a soldier, transferred from central Bosnia to a unit in Sarajevo so he could tend to his injured son.

Amir's shooting was just one of a number of misfortunes that had befallen the Goros. They had been expelled from their five-room apartment in Ilidža and were confined to a squalid one-room flat a few blocks from the foot of Logavina.

Before the war, Vahid Goro had been a well-paid crane operator. Amir's mother worked in a sock factory. Now, they had no income other than the cigarettes Vahid received instead of salary from the army. Vahid would swap the cigarettes for orange juice to bring Amir. The boy's mother and teenage sister pawned their jewelry to buy food for him. The hospital had nothing but powdered mashed potatoes, powdered soup, beans, rice, and bread, so patients were expected to provide their own food.

Vahid Goro began to obsess over the unknown sniper who had shot his son. He was convinced it might be somebody he knew from Ilidža. It was impossible to prove, of course, though not out of the question, given how many of his ex-neighbors and coworkers had enlisted in the Bosnian Serb Army. "These were the same people I used to sit with in restaurants and cafés. I can only imagine that they were promised money or misled by politicians," Vahid said morosely, nursing a cup of muddy Turkish coffee in the Goros' miserable apartment. "The one who fired saw the group of children and wanted to kill them all."

Everybody figured that the sniper had been no more than five hundred yards away—no farther than a deer hunter would shoot. Most probably he had been in the high-rise Metalka building, just across the river in Serb-occupied Grbavica. The area around the Holiday Inn, where the shooting took place, was by far the worst stretch of Sniper Alley. Scores of people were shot there. The exposed intersections were plastered with droll bilingual warnings. OPASNA ZONA—"Danger Zone"—advised one hand-lettered sign, U'RE A TARGET. There was another advisory in a grassy field nearby: RUN OR R.I.P.

The kids on the ill-fated school excursion were angriest not with the sniper, but with the United Nations troops. An anti-sniper UN patrol had been only a few feet away when the sniper opened fire on the crowded tram.

Mirza Ustamujić said the whole gang of kids tried to run behind a UN armored personnel carrier for safety. He and most of the others made it, but Amir Goro and Džana Kazić stumbled and fell after they were shot.

"The UN people did nothing," said Mirza. "They were wearing flak jackets, but still they were hiding behind the car." An old man wearing nothing but a regular jacket went out to drag Džana back behind the van. "Somebody else started yelling at them, 'If you won't shoot back, give us your weapons so we can do it.'"

Amir, too, said, "I gave my hand to the UN guy and he didn't want to help me. He wanted to stay behind the APC."

All three injured children were taken in civilian cars to the hospital. So were another six people who were shot inside the tram, trapped as though in a cage, in clear view of the sniper. They included a young mother shot through the stomach, a teenage athlete whose hand clutching a rail in the tram was shattered by gunfire, and a fifteen-year-old whose penis was sliced off by a bullet.

"We were all covered in blood," said Mirza. "This whole time I was so worried, I just kept screaming that they shouldn't amputate my leg."

Džana had more pedestrian concerns. "At first, I thought I was dreaming and I was going to wake up," she said. "Then, I figured it out and I was thinking, my mother is going to beat me for taking the tram."

Mirza and Džana were hospitalized on the floor below Amir with gunshot wounds in their legs. They filched wheelchairs when the nurses weren't watching to sneak upstairs and visit Amir. They were released after two weeks, leaving Amir alone to read and reread the stack of comic books the kids from school gave him on his fourteenth birthday, November 6.

Occasionally, Amir wrote letters from the hospital to his school friends. "Do you miss me? I've forgotten your faces for the moment," read one letter to Mirza. "Who is dating whom? You better tell me what's going on." There was not a lot to tell. The trams stopped running shortly after the shooting. The schools shut down again—the walk to school was simply too dangerous.

"All there is, is war and more war," Mirza said after reading Amir's letter. "Maybe Amir will go abroad to get medical treatment and when he comes back all his friends will be soldiers."

By late 1995, nine out of almost eight hundred students at Razija Omanović school had been killed; another eleven students had been seriously wounded. Fifty-seven students had lost one or both parents in the war. On Logavina Street, more than a few of the children exhibited signs of post-traumatic stress. Desa Stanić's son, Vedran, spent most of his time in the apartment, often talking to his pet cockatiel. He bit his fingernails compulsively and would curl his toes or clutch his head. He had been wounded in the first summer of the war, when he was twelve. A piece of his skull had been removed and replaced with plastic.

"He acts like a much younger child than he was before he was injured," Desa fretted. "The boy is awfully nervous. He has all these headaches." Vedran's older sister, Marijana, started smoking at fourteen, exactly three weeks after she learned her father had been killed. "I know I shouldn't let her, but what can you do? There's no chocolate, no sugar, nothing for the children," Desa told me.

Even the children who were unscathed by death or injury found life numbingly dull. Sarajevans had been wild about skiing before the war. A couple of families on Logavina Street had owned mountain chalets on Trebević or Jahorina; the mountains were now infested with artillery and soldiers. The most popular swimming lake was in Ilidža. During the war, it was off-limits to Muslims and Croats.

Parents were stricken with guilt as they wrestled with whether or not to let their children outside. In the yard shared by the Kaljanacs and the Telalagićs a compromise was forged: All the kids were confined to the eighty-foot-long driveway that led into both families' homes. Haris Kaljanac and Hamza Telalagić, Kasema's teenage son, strung a blue electric wire across a stoop to make a Ping-Pong table. (Ping-Pong balls were among the few things readily available in Sarajevo. Some shops handed them out to customers instead of small change.)

Only electricity provided relief from the eternal dilemma of how to keep the children entertained and safe. The kids could stay at home when the electricity was on, glued to the television, although usually only the goriest American action films were showing.

"That's what I like best," Haris Kaljanac told me, adding wisely that "reality is much scarier than anything you see in the movies."

His kid brother, Tarik, confused what they watched on television with what was happening in Sarajevo. "Why can't we send that girl to fight the Chetniks?" he demanded of his father, as the family was watching a film heroine annihilate a half-dozen villains with some phantasmic laser gun.

There was now an entire generation of children who had no recollection of normal life. They couldn't remember milk that wasn't made from powder, or water coming out of a tap. Kasema tried to compensate by teaching her younger child, Dženana—born in 1990—about the lions and giraffes in the zoo. There had been a zoo in Sarajevo, up on the front lines above Koševo Hospital, but it was one of the first casualties of the war.

"What happened to the animals?" Dženana asked her mother. Kasema lied. To teach Dženana about the ocean, Kasema filled a plastic bucket with water and tilted it to simulate waves. Her daughter was enchanted. She and Tarik would put straw mats on the driveway and lounge on them, pretending to be sunbathing on the Adriatic coast.

It was much more common, though, for the children to imitate the aberrant lifestyle of war. Dženana used to yell at her doll, mimicking her mother's behavior: "Hurry up. We have to go to the bomb shelter. No, no. You can't play outside today." The children scoured the streets for scraps of trash to burn—empty cigarette packs, plastic soda bottles, cardboard. "They're scared of being cold," said Minka. "They know there is no firewood. They see grown-ups picking up garbage, so they do the same."

The adults on Logavina were constantly looking for new, safe ways to entertain the children. At the Razija Omanović school, they started a children's choir. It was named the Princess Krofne, after a sickeningly sweet Bosnian pastry, and was led by a musician named Zlatko Bostandžić. Before the war, Bostandžić had been playing with a band in Switzerland. In March 1992, he flew back to Sarajevo to pick up a new passport—Yugoslav passports were no longer recognized after Bosnia's declaration of independence—and got stuck in the onset of war.

"The choir keeps me busy. And it keeps the kids off the street," Bostandžić said.

There were no instruments, unless one of the young people could borrow a guitar. The choir sang poignant Bosnian folk ballads. For percussion, they used maracas filled with humanitarian-aid rice.

Seventeen-year-old Mahir Čaber was sitting on the bench at a soccer game I attended in February 1994. Vrbanjuša, Logavina Street's soccer team, played indoors—they'd been under cover since the Serbian shelling began in the spring of 1992—and indoor soccer uses only five players, instead of the normal nine.

"Outdoors, it's more interesting. More guys get to play. There's more action. But in the war, indoors is better. It's safer," said Mahir, a polite and skinny young man.

The Vrbanjuša soccer club was an attempt to provide young people a bit of normalcy. It was named after a hilly neighborhood above Logavina Street and was headquartered, improbably enough, in the orphanage. The players kept in shape by doing calisthenics in the basement. They practiced running and kicking in a dank seventy-five-foot-long hallway.

They played soccer matches at an indoor stadium in Skenderija, a neighborhood across the Miljacka River where UN troops were based. The quarterfinals for the Bosnian Winter Cup were taking place the first week of February 1994.

To get into the sports complex, you had to pass a UN checkpoint, then zigzag through an obstacle course of tanks, sandbagged blockades, and barbed wire. (Getting there was so dangerous that, when I visited, we rode in a bulletproof car. The players had walked to the arena earlier.) Despite the precautions I took, it didn't seem all that safe. The glass-bricked windows above the playing field were riddled with bullet holes. It was dim and chilly inside, and only a handful of fans sat on the wooden benches.

Like Mahir, the boys had an air of genial acceptance. It was remarkable that they were able to play *fudbala* at all. One member was shot in the stomach by a sniper, another grazed by anti-aircraft fire. Four of the best players had fled Sarajevo. One had become a star with a team in Stuttgart, Germany. Two other players were out sick with hepatitis—probably the result of Sarajevo's tainted water system. The team had so little money, the boys had to sweep the stands in the arena to cover the rent for practices.

None of them got enough to eat. "Before the war, the kids had to run a hundred meters. We cut that in half. They don't have the strength," said Sejfudin Tica, their coach. "They have no meat, no milk, no chocolate, no vitamins." Still, the biggest obstacle to wartime soccer was security. In April of the previous year, two teams played an outdoor game to commemorate the anniversary of Sarajevo's liberation from the Nazis. Five people at the game were killed when a shell exploded on the stadium.

Even though the soccer team was wildly popular on Logavina Street, only the most fervent fans made the twenty-minute walk across the sniper-targeted bridge that crossed the Miljacka River to Skenderija.

Coach Tica was always nervous when the boys went to practice. "I have this pit in my stomach. I'm always thinking, my God, what will I tell the parents if something happens to the kids on their way?"

Still, there were some advantages to wartime soccer. Since the boys attended school only occasionally, there was plenty of time to practice. "We haven't had a lot of other things to do but play soccer," Mahir Čaber said. "We might have to get in better shape, have more rigorous practice and all, if we start playing outdoor soccer again. But we are really pretty good."

Coach Tica, in his early thirties, wore a suit and tie for the game. He spoke with such animation that he seemed to be bouncing on the balls of his feet. He explained that he had been orphaned at the age of three and was raised in the Logavina Street orphanage. He still lived there—the only resident who was not a refugee.

There were photographs of the teams from 1991 through

1993 on the walls of his office. The players had always worn the same uniforms. There was no money to replace them, but there was no need—judging by the boys' photos, they were getting smaller, not bigger. Tica displayed one of his proudest possessions on his desk: a soccer ball autographed by members of Belgrade's Red Star (Crvena Zvezda) soccer club, the former world champions. Red Star was now sponsored by Zeljko Ražnjatović, better known by his nom de guerre, Arkan. He was the most vicious perpetrator of anti-Muslim violence in northern and eastern Bosnia.

"I still keep the ball here. I've always felt sports should not be mixed with politics," Tica said. "It's the same way with the kids. They're always trying to imitate the big stars, no matter where they are from." Tica had been a soccer player himself. He decided in 1988 to organize a team to instill the neighborhood children with the discipline and spirit he had gotten out of soccer.

The Vrbanjuša club finished in last place among Bosnia's youth teams its first full year, 1989. The next year, it rose to fourth place. In July 1991, the team had its first great hurrah—and its last.

Vrbanjuša won first place in a Sarajevo tournament. "We had this huge picnic, invited all the family. We got 7,000 čevapčići [a Bosnian kebab], beer, Cokes," recalled Tica. After that great success, the Red Star club invited the Vrbanjuša to Belgrade. Of course, the team never got to go. "We had such great ambitions, but then the war started," said Tica.

The players experienced the first sign of serious trouble at a game on September 14, 1991. They were playing Pale, a nearby city, now the capital of the Bosnian Serbs. There was one young Orthodox player with the Vrbanjuša team, an eleven-year-old. Serb nationalists in the crowd recognized him as a Serb when his name was announced and they started hissing, yelling that he was a traitor for playing with a team whose members were predominantly Muslim.

"We avoided serious trouble because the coach of the other team was a good friend of mine, but we were really scared," Tica recalled. "I was so afraid for the kids that while we were waiting for the bus, I wouldn't let them go to the bathroom."

The Serbian player remained with the team, the smallest player on the field the day of the quarterfinals. The Vrbanjuša team has not returned to Pale since.

The boys played magnificently at the quarterfinals. Trailing their opponents 3–2 in the last three minutes of the game, they managed to score a tying goal. Both teams took penalty shots, and the Vrbanjuša team prevailed.

There was no *čevapčići,* no beer, and no Coca-Cola after the game. The team just had a dangerous walk home, but Tica was ecstatic. He probably would have been even if the team had lost. In Sarajevo, it was not important whether you won or lost. What was important was that you played and that you stayed alive.

February 1994—In this time-lapse photo, stars streak to the right and tracer bullets fired from the Serb-held hillside streak to the left across downtown Sarajevo behind the Bosnian parliament building. The view is from the Holiday Inn, from which Bosnian Serbs fired on pro-unity demonstrators at the beginning of the war.

Shrapnel scars virtually every building, street, and sidewalk in Sarajevo.

A woman sprints toward safety—trying to avoid the bloody path left by a sniper victim, whose body had been dragged away moments before.

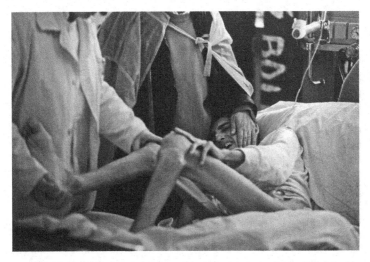

Amir Goro was one of four students from the Razija Omanović school who were machine-gunned in the street. He lost half his body weight in the State Hospital of Sarajevo, which was without heat, medicine, or basic equipment and where families had to bring food for patients.

Boys at play set up a make-believe checkpoint on Logavina Street.

Children play behind a barricade of cars shredded by artillery and bullets. The barricades limit the line of sight for snipers a couple hundred yards away.

Muslim men and boys pray at a six-hundred-year-old mosque. The prayer service took place only days after a Serb shell killed sixty-eight people, including a woman from this congregation.

Haris Kaljanac, nine, is stuck inside along with his cat during one of the most dangerous times in the war.

Ekrem Kaljanac with his three-year-old son, Tarik.

Stolen gas runs through a garden hose past Adnan Čaušević and his daughter, Lejla. His wife, Suada, was to take the children the next day and walk a dangerous route over Mount Igman and then to refuge with her sister on the Adriatic coast.

Desa Stanić (right) and a friend share a meal made from humanitarian rations in the Džinos' downstairs kitchen. Next to them is a wood stove used for cooking and heat.

Sarajevo women prided themselves on looking good, despite the war. They dressed well, put on makeup (often homemade), and did their hair before going out—even if it was just for the daily chore of finding firewood. It was a form of defiance.

The Lačević/Kapić cousins, outside their house at 63 Logavina Street, look warily up the street after hearing a thud. For a moment, they thought it was an incoming mortar shell. Left to right: Delila Lačević; her cousins from northern Bosnia, Selma and Mirza Kapić; and Maša and Lana Lačević, who are sisters.

Sarajevans waited for foggy days to bury their dead. The fog obscured them from Serb snipers in the hills above.

During the third winter of the siege, Zijo and Jela Džino bathe their son, Nermin, a solider in the Bosnian Army suffering hepatitis and so weak he can barely stand.

7

RESISTANCE I: THE ARMY

NERMIN DŽINO WAS STUFFING a cotton sleeping bag and an extra sweater into his blue knapsack. It looked like the sort of thing a schoolboy would bring to summer camp. In fact, Nermin was about to climb Logavina Street in subfreezing weather to one of the front lines above Sarajevo.

Jela wouldn't sit down. She fussed around the kitchen, packing a tin cup, a plate, and two bottles of water. In a brass hand-operated mill, Jela ground up a plastic bag full of coffee and mixed it with some sugar. When Nermin turned his back to look for his cigarettes, Jela slyly slipped a piece of pie into the knapsack.

"I am so nervous every time he leaves," Jela confessed as the inevitable tears filled her eyes. "And the whole time he is up there, I am always trembling from fear."

"Shit, I don't have any cigarettes," he responded, ignoring the outburst.

This same ritual between Jela and her son was reenacted every few days when Nermin trekked off to war. He was a commuter soldier. Hardly any of the Bosnian soldiers lived in military barracks because, as Nermin explained, "it would be too expensive to feed everyone."

The Bosnian Army was the purest embodiment of Sarajevo's favorite saying, *Nema ništa*—"There's no nothing." People often lamented the army's lack of heavy weapons, but the inadequacies were far more fundamental. They had no food for the troops, no water, no coffee. Most soldiers lived at home, where their wives and mothers cooked their rations. There were certainly no armored personnel carriers—just a couple of buses, but they didn't have gasoline. The soldiers walked to the front lines, which were not so far off since the war was right in Sarajevo.

They bought their own uniforms. Nermin paid $60 for a pair of khakis and an army surplus jacket from the Vietnam War, and Jela sewed on the patch of the Bosnian Army—fleurs-de-lis scattered against a blue shield.

Nermin Džino is tall and strikingly handsome, with curly dark hair and an aquiline nose. He was twenty-three years old and working in a café for pocket money, trying to decide what to do with his life, when the war erupted. The decision was made for him. Although he had been wounded in the foot when a grenade crashed into his parents' kitchen, Nermin received a prompt draft notice, on May 16, 1992.

The short commute made for constant culture shock. "I don't really mind. It is my duty. It is just that when I come back, I feel like I'm coming from Mars," he said. "I'm so dirty, so tired that I can hardly stand, and I see girls and boys sitting in cafés, and I have a pain in my heart."

All the young men were similarly plucked from the mellow, café-hopping lifestyle they had enjoyed before the war. Delila Lačević's boyfriend, Haris, eighteen years old and fresh out of high school, was drafted.

The army tapped some of the not-so-young, too. Ekrem Kaljanac continued to do utility installations by day, changing into military fatigues at night to work with the military police. Esad Taljanović, by dint of his profession as a dentist, was assigned to a military medical unit. Notwithstanding that he was a Serb, Mladen Marković found himself in the Bosnian Army, fighting in a pair of wool tweed trousers his wife had sewn before she fled to Germany.

Before long, 70 percent of the men on Logavina Street were in some form of military service. Sarajevo, which had once enjoyed the easy atmosphere of a university town, was transformed into something more like a vast military barracks. In place of MTV, where Sarajevo's youth got their fashion and music taste, they now listened to BiH, the state television network, which broadcast a steady diet of inspirational war footage against a soundtrack of rock and roll and Bosnian folk tunes. The war permeated every inch of the city.

From the very start, the Serb rebels held an enormous advantage. They had inherited the infrastructure and much of the arsenal of the Yugoslav National Army. Before its collapse, Yugoslavia had an improbably large military for a nation of 24 million people. Its army was reputed to be the fourth-largest in Europe, nurtured by Tito after his break with Stalin to repel either an invasion from the West or a Soviet crackdown, as had happened in Czechoslovakia in 1968.

As Yugoslavia disintegrated along ethnic lines, the army's raison d'être was subsumed into the Serb nationalist cause. There was a gradual blurring of the lines between the Yugoslav army regulars with their crewcuts and military discipline and the brutal Chetniks with their ski masks. Months before actual fighting began, the army had begun deploying additional units

in Bosnia. The explanation offered by Serbian president Slobodan Milošević was that the army would serve as a neutral buf-
fer between Serbs and Muslims should ethnic warfare erupt.
Even as the Yugoslav National Army's MiG-29s were buzzing
the skies over Sarajevo, residents looked up with gratitude, be-
lieving that their army had come to protect them.

In their grand pink mansion on Logavina, the Vranić family argued over the army's intentions.

"Don't worry so much," Vetka Vranić would tell her husband when he fretted about the possibility of war in Bosnia.
"The Yugoslavian Army will protect us."

"No, you're wrong. They'll start the whole thing. You wait
and see," retorted Sead, a pessimist by nature.

Tarik Vranić was the most bewildered of the family. Having enlisted in the National Army in December 1990 at the age
of nineteen, Tarik was a loyal soldier, unaccustomed to questioning his superiors. He had been stationed in Karlovac, in
Croatia, with other recruits of Muslim, Serb, Croat, Macedo-
nian, and Slovenian origins.

"Everybody really got along fine. It was not an issue. We
were still attached to the phrase 'Brotherhood and Unity,'"
Tarik recalled, referring to the late Marshal Tito's slogan for
the unified Yugoslavia.

Nobody was more surprised than the young recruits when
the Yugoslav army charged with guns blazing at the Slovenians
and Croats.

"All the soldiers had the same attitude. We couldn't believe
that the JNA [Yugoslav National Army] was committing these
atrocities. This was our army," Tarik said.

Almost all the Croats, about half the Muslims, and even a
few Serbs started deserting. Tarik says his best friend, an Orthodox Serb from Montenegro, slashed his wrists in a fake sui-

cide attempt so he would be transferred to a low-security military hospital. Tarik was not able to get away. He remained with the army, most of the time working radio communications, until his term was up in January 1992.

"That was the happiest day of my life. I thought I was done with the military," he recalled two years later, as he was packing a knapsack for the front lines, this time to fight with the Bosnian Army.

Bosnia had no army of its own, having entered nationhood only a few days before it was plunged into Europe's worst conflagration since World War II. As a Yugoslav republic, Bosnia only had its Territorial Defense—more like a National Guard or state police than a real military.

In September 1991, the Territorial Defense units were ordered to turn over their weapons to the Yugoslav National Army. Jovan Divjak, assigned to Sarajevo's Territorial Defense, balked at the order, suspecting rightly that it was part of the army's secret preparation for war in Bosnia. His courageous act of insurrection turned Divjak, an ethnic Serb and army careerist, into a hero in Sarajevo. Moreover, the few weapons he retained were invaluable to the future Bosnian Army.

When war erupted in April 1992, Bosnia had to cobble together a military from scratch. Serb propaganda had accused the Bosnian Muslims of having long plotted an Islamic revolution, but such claims were belied by Bosnia's woeful lack of preparation. "There was absolutely no armed organized defense in Sarajevo before the war," recalled Divjak. "We had at best one weapon for every third soldier."

When the Serbs opened fire on Sarajevo it was rare to meet a Bosnian soldier with a gun, let alone a full chamber of bullets. The Bosnian Army assembled its pitiful arsenal by confiscating hunting rifles and retooling antiques from World Wars I and II. They captured rocket-propelled grenades and other artillery from an army officers' club in downtown Sarajevo and enlisted the support of the city's more unsavory characters—criminal gangs that knew best where to get their hands on guns.

The UN slapped an arms embargo on all of the former Yugoslavia in 1991, which sealed the disparity of weapons between the warring sides. Although Iran and other Islamic countries began supplying Bosnia with weapons in 1993, its army could never quite catch up. In November 1994, Jane's Sentinel—a military analysis firm in London—estimated that the Bosnian Serbs had 335 tanks in service compared to the Bosnian government's 145. However, the Bosnians made up for their lack of firepower in their manpower and zeal.

"We are defending our lives and our homes, and they are only looking down at us from the hills," Nermin Džino declared.

Sarajevo was ill-situated for defense. Splayed out along the valley of the Miljacka River, the city was an easy target for the Serb artillery entrenched in the mountains. There was hardly a nook or cranny the Serbs couldn't see from their fortified perches above. Choked off by the surrounding mountains, Sarajevo had only a handful of access routes for roads and rail lines. It took relatively few soldiers with their tanks strategically placed to hermetically seal off the city from the outside world.

Not only was Sarajevo surrounded, the enemy lurked within. Some Serbs sympathizing with Karadžić's separatists remained in the city. The bombing of the central post office on May 2, 1992, was carried out by people who were still working in Sarajevo. A sniper who lived around the corner from Logavina Street wasn't caught until August, after a dramatic chase through the Džinos' backyard. Confusion and panic reigned; the very nature of this war between neighbors made it hard to determine who was friend and who was foe.

This late-twentieth-century war adopted medieval tactics. Serbs filled barrels with explosives and rolled them down the mountains. Sarajevans defended themselves by whatever means they could find. In Dobrinja, a town of high-rises built for the Olympics, young professionals threw potfuls of boiling water and furniture out the windows as commandos tried to storm the neighborhood.

"It was more of a means of maintaining morale than a truly effective defense," recalled Divjak, who, as a commander of the fledgling army, could only urge residents not to abandon their homes.

Each neighborhood had its own brigade of defenders. Logavina's men met regularly at the Stari Sat (meaning "Old Clock"), a wood-paneled café across from the police station that looked like a British pub. Young men went to Stari Sat when they wanted to enlist.

Among the first volunteers were Ekrem Kaljanac and Divjak's elder son, Želimir. Džemal Hajrić, twenty, who lived on Logavina, and his younger cousin, Alden, rushed to volunteer. Mahir Čaber, the soccer player, whose brother worked in the Stari Sat, was only fifteen. Too young to be of use on the front line, he carried pots of hot soup to the soldiers.

"Some of these boys were underage. They were schoolchildren. We tried to send them home, but they wanted to fight," recalled Ekrem.

Other residents contributed to the war effort in whatever way they could. Jela Džino distributed sandwiches to the volunteers. Next door, Fuad Kasumagić, a jeweler in his fifties, stood out on the street at 6 A.M. as the shifts changed, serving the troops hot tea.

The volunteers marched off to strategic points around Sarajevo where the Serbs were trying to penetrate the city, but many of their duties were right on Logavina Street. After all, the war was on their doorsteps. When Muniba Kaninić was killed by shrapnel on May 23, 1992, one of the first fatalities on Logavina Street, Ekrem and a young soldier from the neighborhood carried her body, wrapped in a blanket, to the morgue. Later that same day, the young soldier was killed.

"I felt terrible around that time. Until then, I did not know the human brain was yellow. I knew nothing of death. Now it was as though everybody I touched was dead. It was the beginning of the war and we were all very brave. It was crazy, the stuff we did. We didn't think about anti-aircraft guns, tanks, artillery, until so many of our own were killed," Ekrem recalled.

"It changed later. After we saw so many dead, many of us became angrier and wanted to fight for the city at any price. Others just got scared and wanted to escape, no matter what."

For all the patriotism and courage Bosnia could muster, the Bosnian Army could do little but defend the status quo. The Serbs managed to capture close to 70 percent of Bosnia within the first month of war and held that position for more than three years.

It was a long and bloody stalemate. The Serbs tried to carve the city in half by storming the Bridge of Brotherhood and Unity west of the Holiday Inn, which connected Sarajevo with the Serb-held neighborhood of Grbavica. Radovan Karadžić readily told visiting journalists his theory that Sarajevo should be partitioned with a Berlin Wall—the old heart of the city going to the Muslims, the new western suburbs to the Serbs. The Bosnian Army defended the bridge and the twenty-square-mile swath of besieged Sarajevo that the government controlled.

The conventional wisdom in Sarajevo was that the Serbs could pound the city into rubble but they couldn't get in. "They'll shell us until we're all in the basements, but there is no way they will ever take this city," boasted Zijo Džino.

But by the same token, the Bosnians couldn't get out. Sarajevo, the saying went, was like a can that could only be opened from the outside.

Periodically, rumors that the Bosnian Army was about to bust through the siege lines swept through the city. They did manage to score small successes by virtue of their superior numbers with guerrilla-style ambushes that cost many lives. The Bosnian Army boasted 200,000 soldiers, although about half of them were reservists and only about 50,000 had weapons. The Bosnian Serbs, with about 80,000 men, were a smaller force, but better equipped, having inherited much of the weaponry of the Yugoslav National Army. Invariably, the Serbs would redeploy their troops and recoup their losses.

The Bosnian Army's gains were loudly heralded on Television BiH and in the daily newspaper, *Oslobođenje,* giving solace to those waiting impatiently, trapped within the city. As often as not, the truth could be found on the back page—in the columns of obituaries with postage-stamp-size photos of the men who had perished.

When Desa Stanić's husband, Pero, was killed May 30, 1993, on Mount Trebević, the family found out only after Belgrade television broadcast footage from the battle. Desa went to watch the videotape at an army barracks. Her husband's face was battered beyond recognition, but she spotted a purple schoolbag draped around his shoulder that their son had given him for good luck.

The older of the Hajrić cousins, Džemal, was wounded in September 1992 and nearly lost a leg. He was lucky to be evacuated to San Diego for reconstructive surgery. He stayed in the United States, studying English and becoming a real estate broker. His cousin, Alden, was killed in 1994 ambushing enemy troops in central Bosnia. Alden was wearing a camouflage T-shirt that Džemal had sent from California. He was only twenty when he died.

Alden Hajrić's death hit Logavina Street hard. "I cried like a child. I couldn't help it," said Zijo Džino. "I only hope that my son and all the others will come home soon. We don't care so much about ourselves, but all these young people we are losing."

With Alden's death, Tarik was the last member of his old Logavina Street gang. Two of his best friends had been killed; two others had been wounded and evacuated. Another had suffered a nervous breakdown and was in treatment in Vienna. Three simply had fled.

"They call me the last of the Mohicans around here. There used to be nine of us and now there is just me," Tarik told me despairingly as we sat in his parents' freezing living room a few days before Christmas 1994.

His cousin, Emir Đanđanović, twenty-one, recalled how he had given up an engineering scholarship at the University of Texas to volunteer for the Bosnian Army.

"Now it's getting to be like Vietnam. The rich people's sons are no longer in the army. They send their sons out, and the poor people are left fighting the war," Emir said.

A thriving black market developed providing the documents that military-age men needed to leave the city. Everybody knew whom you had to pay in order to get "demobilized." Soldiers were often sent home because of psychiatric problems—a condition that Sarajevans refer to simply as "losing one's nerves." When Nermin Džino was hospitalized with a severe case of hepatitis, the other soldiers in his unit kissed him good-bye with the hope that they, too, might be sent off on sick leave.

Divjak's two sons fled Sarajevo with their wives and children in 1993. One went to Munich, the other to London. "I would have preferred, truthfully, if they stayed," Divjak said. "The kids tell me this is not our war. I feel this is not my war, either. We didn't start the war, but we still have to defend ourselves."

The war became an endurance test. Unable to advance and unwilling to retreat, the soldiers spent their time in the trenches trading curses with the enemy. Often enough, those on the other side were former colleagues or schoolmates.

"We speak to the Chetniks very often," Nermin said after one forty-eight-hour stint at Špicasta Stijena, a rocky outcropping two miles uphill from Logavina. "Sometimes they call us to have coffee with them. Or else, they want to sell us something. They have meat, whiskey, everything over there. Somebody wanted to sell us a whole veal. We'd rather starve to death than do that."

The Bosnian Army never had enough money to pay salaries; the best the soldiers could hope for was a ration of cigarettes. In summer, many picked wild irises from the front lines to sell in the city for spare change. In winter, they chopped wood to bring back to their families.

"I used to be a pacifist. I didn't particularly want to fight. Even now, I'm full of fear," Mladen Marković told me one evening, newly back from the trenches, as he sat in his dark and empty apartment. Like other soldiers, he increasingly lived from cease-fire to cease-fire, waiting for whatever chance came to recover his nerves and energy.

"The other night was very nice and quiet. There was no shooting. We had time to chop wood," Marković said. "We sat around and talked about how good we had life in Sarajevo before the war."

8

RESISTANCE II: CIVILIANS

WHENEVER LALA MEMETI HEARD the thud of an exploding shell, she would reach for her lipstick. Then, with trembling hands, she would fasten her earrings.

Then she'd dash for the bomb shelter.

"Even if there is shelling, I am running to the bomb shelter and putting on my makeup at the same time. I've been doing it since I'm seventeen years old, so I'm pretty good at it," she said, laughing.

Lala was only half kidding as we sat around one afternoon sipping coffee in her sister's Logavina Street apartment. A thirty-six-year-old hairdresser, Lala was a hearty bleached blonde who had her own beauty shop in the Baščaršija, although the place was closed most of the time because of the incessant shelling.

War or no war, Sarajevans were dead serious about the way they looked. Many women saw maintaining their appearance as an act of defiance against the Bosnian Serbs.

"We don't want to give up," Lala declared emphatically, all

trace of humor now gone from her voice. "We don't want them to say that they defeated us."

It might seem trivial to equate a brush of blue powder across the eyelids with the soldiers hunkered in the trenches, but keeping up appearances was, in its way, an integral part of the resistance. As it became clearer that the Bosnian Serbs' grip on the city was not loosening, Sarajevans seemed to have decided that living well was their best revenge.

If a woman gave birth to a healthy baby, or if the soccer team played a match, it was not taken merely as a cause for celebration; it was a sign that the war was not yet lost. By 1993, as the first anniversary of the siege passed, Logavina residents started venturing from their basements more frequently, trying to put their lives back together. Every day it seemed that somebody was hosting a party. "You don't need a reason to celebrate around here. When somebody loses a 100-German-mark bill, we celebrate, then cry later," Ekrem Kaljanac joked.

Yet, of all the forms of resistance, the attention Sarajevans lavished on hair, makeup, clothing, and hygiene was the most startling to outsiders. The foreign journalists who came to Sarajevo stood out like sore thumbs in their combat gear, muddy boots, and unkempt hair. The Sarajevans were immaculately coiffed, with crisply pressed clothing. After a while, we journalists were no longer surprised by the elegant women in mink coats hauling wood or waiting in a queue for humanitarian aid.

Lala Memeti claimed that war conditions brought about a boom in hair coloring. She made emergency house calls—touching up Minka's red hair every month or so—and had transformed herself from a brunette into a striking platinum blonde.

"My husband never wanted me to color my hair. But his

attitude was changed by war. He wanted me to fulfill my wishes, since you never know when you are going to get another chance," Lala explained.

The war also boosted Lala's business by giving women more gray to cover. "I don't care how long this war lasts, I'll figure out a way to do my hair. Lejla, too," Suada Čaušević said, talking about her five-year-old daughter. "She likes to put on makeup, play with perfume. She wants to look good."

I hardly ever met anyone in Sarajevo who smelled bad or who wore dirty clothes—despite the lack of running water and basic products like toothpaste and deodorant. During a sultry stretch of summer, Minka demonstrated the system she had developed for keeping things clean. If one of her boys didn't finish a glass of water, she would pour the remains onto a sponge to wipe off the kitchen table or a counter. She washed the dishes over a bucket, instead of the sink, so that the rinse water wasn't wasted. She saved the dirty water in the bucket to flush the toilet.

Bathing was challenging. Jela Džino would warm water in a big spaghetti pot over the wood-burning stove. She and her husband took turns pouring the water over one another for an improvised shower. The laundry, too, was boiled in the same big pot on the stove, the only way to be sure of getting it clean. Jela also ironed, despite the lack of electricity: she simply heated her electric iron on top of the wood stove.

No household was quite so inventive as the Lačevićs'. They had four teenage girls, all aching for cosmetics. They still had some old makeup left from before the war, and "we keep it stashed away like gold," Delila said. If the UN had airlifted in shampoo and lipstick instead of canned beef, the girls probably would have been happier—but they soon learned to make their own cosmetics.

Delila made facial cleanser out of yeast and water. For moisturizer, she would use humanitarian-aid rations of cooking oil, although she had to sneak it out of the kitchen while her grandmother was napping.

Her cousin, Lana, kept herself looking like a California blonde with a homemade potion of hydrogen peroxide and crude lye soap, also supplied by the United Nations. Lana's thirteen-year-old sister, Maša, was designated the hairdresser for the entire family to save money. Like most of the girls, Maša kept her hair short "because when there aren't enough vitamins in the diet, your hair breaks and falls out a lot."

Still, the Lačevićs looked elegant in photographs taken in 1994 in the basement of the orphanage. The photos show Šaćira and the girls, all immaculately coiffed and made up, grinning for the camera as though they were at a wedding instead of cowering in the bomb shelter.

The girls had developed an active fantasy life, since they had no place to go. Delila was obsessed with all things American. "We like to get dressed up and pretend that maybe we're going to Geneva for the peace talks or having dinner with Bill Clinton," she explained with a laugh.

Before the war, Sarajevo was a singularly fashion-conscious city. There were nearly as many *frizerski salon*—hairdressers— as there were cafés. Chic Sarajevans made routine shopping trips to Italy, particularly during sale months. Asked what they missed most under the siege, more than a few people answered, without hesitation: "New clothes."

The Lačević girls swapped sweaters to give the illusion of an extended wardrobe. Nothing was discarded. Delila was grazed by a bullet as she ran up Logavina Street and she meticulously patched the hole in the jacket she'd been wearing.

Many Sarajevans had lost so much weight they could no

longer wear their own clothes. Šaćira Lačević, at forty-nine, borrowed jeans and sweatshirts from her teenage daughters. She, too, would always bring a bag of makeup to the bomb shelter.

"First thing in war, you have to take care of yourself and maintain your self-respect," Šaćira instructed her daughters, nieces, and nephew.

Nearly two years into the war, demographers started charting another phenomenon that defied conventional wisdom: a baby boom. In January 1994, Sarajevo recorded 170 births, about 20 percent more than in pre-war Januaries. It was also the first month since early in the war that the number of live births exceeded the number of abortions.

The phenomenon could be ascribed, in part, to a shortage of birth-control pills and long, boring nights without electricity. But many saw the baby boom as a conscious effort by parents to replace children they feared might be lost in the war, or as an act of defiance against Serbian extremists who were trying to eradicate Sarajevo's Muslims.

"If we didn't go ahead and have our kids, if babies weren't being born, the city would die," Edin Smajović said. Edin and his wife, Lejla, lived in a second-floor apartment on Logavina. Their living room windows looked out over the Vrbanjuša cemetery, where Delila Lačević's parents were buried.

When I visited, Lejla was smiling as she sat nursing her eight-day-old son. Lejla, a twenty-year-old dark beauty, seemed blissfully oblivious to the scene outside the window behind her, where workers were digging fresh graves for victims of the latest shelling. Edin, twenty-eight, was already profoundly embittered by the war. He pointed toward the field of graves and remarked that he had been featured in a famous war photograph, weeping at the graveside of an army buddy. For the city's survival, they must create new life, he said.

Edin and Lejla plowed on with their lives, despite everything. Theirs had been a wartime romance; Lejla had met Edin, a Bosnian Army officer, at a party during the summer of 1992. "It was like two souls meeting," she recalled. They were married six months later in a huge wedding, "just like in peacetime." Their son was born January 30, 1994. They named him Džan (pronounced like "John"), which is an Arabic word for "soul." "We cannot just sit around and wait for the war to end," Edin declared. "We have to live our lives."

Kira Prgovski was far less starry-eyed about wartime pregnancies. Kira, a tough and pragmatic woman with an unruly mane of black hair, lived in an apartment directly below the Kaljanacs and was Minka's best friend. She was horrified when she discovered she was pregnant in 1993, during a singularly miserable stretch of war. For one thing, she was not yet married. She and her boyfriend, Mirsad, had been living together for several years in the overcrowded apartment on Logavina with far too many of his relatives. Both were exhausted from overwork. He was doing double shifts with the civilian defense unit on Logavina Street, and she was working as a pediatric nurse at Koševo Hospital.

Kira knew how difficult the war was for children. "There was one day that they brought in thirty wounded children. Can you imagine what it is like to be in a room with thirty wounded children? It's too horrible for the eyes," Kira said.

Mirsad was also skeptical about starting their family in war. "Let's think about it," he told Kira. "Is it such a good idea to have a baby right now during the war? So many children have been killed." The couple discussed long and hard whether to have an abortion. Finally, they opted to go ahead with the pregnancy. "I told Mirsad, 'If it's this baby's destiny to stay alive, he will stay alive.'"

Once they made their decision, they needed to find enough food to keep Kira healthy during her pregnancy. "I looked around to try and find whatever I could. Sometimes I could get an apple, but never an orange. That was impossible," Kira said. "I was lucky. My baby weighed three kilos [6.6 pounds], but many of the babies born these days are really small."

The average weight of newborns in Sarajevo dropped from more than eight pounds to six pounds between 1991 and 1993, according to city hospital records. Premature births rose from 5.3 percent to nearly 13 percent, and more than one out of ten babies was stillborn.

It was hard to believe that Suada Čaušević was in her sixth month of pregnancy. Suada, a fine-featured woman, twenty-eight years old, weighed barely a hundred pounds and smoked compulsively, stamping out her cigarettes only after the plastic filters were burning. "Nobody's told me to stop smoking, and if they did I wouldn't do it. I'm nervous all the time and I have nothing to eat."

With obvious disdain, Suada displayed a tin of biscuits she had received from the United Nations as a dietary supplement because of her pregnancy. The date stamped on the bottom was 1967, more leftovers from the Vietnam War. "Who would eat that stuff?" she demanded. "I'm afraid of it."

Suada's pregancy was proving nightmarish. In her fourth month, the doctors had hospitalized her because of heavy bleeding. She checked herself out after a few days because she was frightened by the shelling around Koševo Hospital. Once home, she refused to go out of the apartment, even for medical checkups.

"The nurses say she might lose the baby," said her husband, Adnan, a pale man with thinning hair. "She's so exhausted all the time. She can't sleep at night. They've tried to give her intravenous feeding. She is so thin, you would think she isn't pregnant."

Suada and Adnan had made a conscious decision to have another child, despite a set of circumstances that might seem imprudent. Adnan, twenty-seven, a year younger than his wife, had been recently released from the Bosnian Army with a bad case of shell shock and frostbite. The family had no income whatsoever. They already had difficulty coaxing their five-year-old daughter, Lejla, to eat the UN beans and rice. Lejla was adorable, but stubborn.

Nevertheless, Suada firmly defended their decision to have a baby. "If a shell is going to hit you, it is going to hit you if you're pregnant or not," she reasoned with irrefutable logic. "When we see how many children are being killed, we feel we have to have more."

Despite all attempts at defiance, Sarajevo looked like a dead city. Only a handful of shops were operating and they had little to sell. By night, the city was a void of darkness. There was little incentive to violate the 9 P.M. curfew, since there was no place to go.

Almost all the cafés were shuttered. The only animation in nighttime Sarajevo came from the stars. The few UN vehicles that were on the roads at night were driven with the headlights off, to avoid attracting snipers.

As if the relentless shelling and power blackouts weren't enough, Sarajevo faced another monumental problem: Its economy barely had a heartbeat. There was no currency. The Yugoslav dinar had collapsed even before war erupted in Bosnia; the only money of any use was the German mark. The Bosnian Labor Ministry estimated that as of the end of 1993, 75 percent of the workforce was unemployed. Those who worked were not paid.

In Sarajevo, the only factories that operated throughout the war were the brewery and the cigarette factory. There was no malt, so the Sarajevsko Pivara produced an anemic brew from rice and served as a water-collection point. It was the Drina cigarette factory that, more than anything else, was a mainstay of the tottering economy.

Drina cigarettes—named for the river along Bosnia's eastern border—quickly became the basic unit of currency. In wartime, Drinas used a harsh blend of tobacco from Herzegovina. The shortage of paper was so critical that cigarette packages were wrapped in the pages of discarded books, often printed in the disfavored Cyrillic alphabet. (One television journalist in Sarajevo kept as a collector's item a pack of Drinas wrapped in a page from a Serbo-Croatian edition of Marcel Proust's *Remembrance of Things Past*.)

With no money to pay salaries, the Bosnian government distributed cigarettes instead. Ekrem Kaljanac received five packs per month for his work with the police department. He didn't smoke, so he'd give two to his wife and sell the rest. A pack of Drinas traded for one German mark, roughly 60 cents. Thanks to her more prestigious occupation as a doctor, Kasema Telalagić received a larger distribution of cigarettes.

"Neither of us smokes, so we'll usually try to swap it for meat or cabbage," Kasema said. "My daughter doesn't remember what money is. She said to me the other day, 'Let's take your cigarettes and buy me a new dress.'"

In this bleak business climate, there were a couple of bold strokes of entrepreneurship. Working at his kitchen table, Zijo

Džino made pipes and other wooden objects intricately inlaid with silver, a craft he had learned as a boy from his uncle. Cigarette holders were his best seller, since the Drina factory often ran out of filters.

Zijo's cousin and next-door neighbor, Fuad Kasumagić, was perhaps the wealthiest resident of Logavina Street. He had donated the gold for the 1984 Olympic medals. In May 1993, he opened a small store downtown selling Sarajevan jewelry and crafts. Although the store wasn't making any money, Fuad said, "I really did it out of spite. I wanted people to see beautiful things in the window, the kinds of things we had in normal times."

Fuad also kept his jewelry workshop operating, around the corner from Logavina on Remzije Omanović Street. When the electricity went off, Fuad found an antique gas stove in the storage room that he pedaled with his foot to smelt gold.

"Look what the war has done. I'm making gold just like they did a hundred years ago," Fuad exclaimed as he labored over a 14-karat nugget. He also showed off his now-useless computer where he'd kept inventory and payroll before the war. It had been replaced by a manual typewriter.

Nevertheless, Fuad Kasumagić's workshop was a bustling enterprise by wartime standards. He employed a staff of fifteen, who were compensated with an odd assortment of cigarettes, bread, jam, and cheese and occasionally German marks out of Fuad's savings. Revenues had sunk to about 5 percent of pre-war levels, but the workshop kept busy producing the gold lilies that the Bosnian Army awarded soldiers for heroism. They also did a brisk trade in inexpensive lily earrings and tie pins that were a popular expression of patriotism. Every now and then, the shop would make a wedding ring. "People still get married," Fuad explained.

Logavina Street had a couple of storefront businesses interspersed with apartments and private homes. Kasema Telalagić's husband, Dino, ran an auto repair shop out of a garage in front of their home. When he wasn't on the front lines, Dino would tinker about in the shop. But with gasoline running $100 a gallon, there was little demand for auto repairs.

A business that customers would have actually used, the shoe repair shop at 58 Logavina, was shuttered due to lack of supplies.

Before the war, the Stari Sat on Logavina Street had been one of the most popular cafés in Sarajevo. Customers used to spill out onto the sidewalk on warm summer nights. It reopened in December 1993 when the police station across the street began sharing its supply of priority electricity so they could have a place to sit and drink coffee. But the Stari Sat was a pale shadow of its former self. A foreboding stack of sandbags nearly blocked the entrance. Empty bottles of Glenfiddich scotch and Grand Marnier were kept behind the bar to remind the few customers of what used to be.

A tiny mom-and-pop grocery store on Logavina reopened the same month as the Stari Sat. It had been a gourmet store before the war, with "ten different kinds of cheese and pineapples," said the manager, Kadira Hadžibegović. Its wartime merchandise was outlandishly eclectic. There were single cans of Italian tomatoes and imported *champignons de Paris*—gifts that Sarajevans had received from relatives abroad and traded for more basic foodstuffs. The store offered bargain prices on automatic dishwasher detergent and a Dustbuster—useless items in a city without electricity.

Before the war, Hadžibegović had worked as a kindergarten teacher, but the place had been destroyed. She said she reopened the store because "sitting at home after twenty-two years of working was driving me crazy."

If Logavina residents truly needed to buy something, they had to make the trip downtown to one of the public markets. There were two across from one another on Maršala Tita Street: an outdoor produce market and a covered hall called the Markale—the site of a thriving black market. Both places were as crowded as a New York subway car at rush hour and just as unpleasant. Going to the market was like foraging for food in a barren forest.

The black market was a clear symbol of an economy in collapse. The market functioned on a crude barter system. People from all over the city came to swap their children's outgrown sneakers for sugar or odd plumbing and electrical parts, or they traded tiny tins of fish they'd received from relief organizations for something more desirable. They usually wanted coffee or cigarettes—the staples of the Bosnian diet.

Kira Prgovski had those staples in mind the day she took me along to the covered market. She left her seven-week-old baby at home with his father, and threw two plastic Baggies of powdered milk into her tote bag. We shoved our way through an unhappy crowd, everybody bundled in threadbare winter coats. Kira quickly became irritable. It was clear that coffee was well beyond her budget. The only vendor who had coffee was charging 160 German marks per kilo—roughly $50 a pound. Kira's powdered milk was worth maybe $9.

"So how about some cigarettes?" Kira demanded.

The three packs of cigarettes that Kira wanted were worth less than the milk, and the vendor had no change. Kira walked on, discouraged. She tried several other vendors who either had nothing to swap or no change. She gave up on cigarettes and coffee and decided to look for some cheese. Behind the cheese counter, the man had no cheese but passed on a rumor that you could find some at another market—located about five miles away at the far end of Sniper Alley.

After nearly an hour of haggling and pushing, Kira had swapped her powdered milk for six small potatoes. "This is the kind of lunch we're going to have, potatoes," Kira said with a grimace, as we trekked back up the snowy hill to Logavina Street.

Prices fluctuated wildly, depending on the grip of the siege. Prices began to drop toward the end of 1992 as the UN relief operation became fully functional, but the fighting that erupted in early 1993 with militant Croat nationalists in Herzegovina made getting anything at all into Sarajevo twice as difficult.

By the second winter of the war, one egg cost the equivalent of $3. Luxury items—a can of Coca-Cola or a pack of Marlboros—went for $7.50. Esad Taljanović, the dentist, complained, "Even the Japanese couldn't afford this stuff."

"I get nauseated just being here. When I realize I can't afford a tube of toothpaste, I actually get sick," Jela Džino said as she roamed the market one day.

Almost all the food products for sale were humanitarian aid flown in on the UN airlift. They were easy enough to spot—a can of herring in tomato sauce was labeled "Gift of the Federal Republic of Germany." Other items had obviously been smuggled from UN bases in Sarajevo. The best loot came from the French base in Skendarija; you could occasionally find a can of pâté de foie gras or a bottle of Beaujolais.

The PX-type store that the United Nations ran for its own staff was a source of smuggled goods. It was a discouraging experience to see Sarajevans stare with sad, aching eyes at a box of chocolate chip cookies offered for $11 at the market when the same cookies were sold for just $2 at the UN store.

The trade conducted at the public markets was technically illegal. Police swept through several times a day, and vendors would simply tuck their wares under their winter coats. Sarajevans said they despised the "black market," although that in part reflected the lingering distaste for free enterprise left from the Communist era. Actually, the salespeople in the market were pretty much the same as anybody else, struggling to survive.

Visiting the market was an especially intense experience for Jela Džino. Many of her former coworkers from the shuttered textile plant were now peddling goods there. During one visit, Jela embraced an elderly man who was standing out in the snow, selling a fistful of cigarettes that were clutched in his red-mittened hand. Jela found another friend trying to sell her single can of margarine for $35.

"I hate working here. I hate it every time somebody asks me what something costs," Mirsada Pobrić said as the shoppers scowled at her margarine. "Rarely do you see anybody smiling here. They all look sad, but they buy anyway because there is nothing else." Detested though it was, the market had become the lifeblood of Sarajevo's economic life under siege.

9

AWAKENING

THE MORTAR SHELL that ripped through the market on February 5, 1994, struck at the soul of Sarajevo. Everybody knew somebody who worked at the market or someone who shopped at the market.

It had been a sunny Saturday, the kind of rare winter day that practically begged the unwary to leave the relative safety of their homes. War or not, it was impossible to stay inside all the time. The shell struck at 12:37 P.M., when the market was jam-packed. Suddenly, there was a crash. A whirlpool of metal shards. The bustling street scene was reduced to the rawest elements of human life: flesh and blood.

From the foot of Logavina Street, it is roughly four hundred yards down Maršala Tita to the market square. On Logavina, they heard only a distant, dull thud. It was an anomaly that a mortar shell makes less noise exploding in the middle of a crowd than if it lands harmlessly on empty pavement. But news of the calamity traveled up the street quickly.

Jela and Zijo Džino were in their downstairs kitchen—the safest room of the house. The electricity was off, so Zijo hooked up the television to the car battery and tuned in to the scene on the market square. It was all there—indistinguishable body parts amid the potatoes and onions, the severed head, the puddles of bright crimson, the wails of the wounded. BiH Television showed the sort of explicit footage routinely expurgated from American television.

Jela put on her reading glasses and peered closely at the television to seek out familiar faces in the on-screen carnage. The authorities did not release the identities of the victims until nightfall. Jela and Zijo listened quietly, their hearts pounding as the television announcer read each of the names.

"That was the worst part," Jela said the next day. "My heart still can't stop pounding. I feel so sorry for everybody."

None of their close friends or relatives were among the dead and wounded. However, the mortar shell had claimed two victims from the neighborhood. One was a merchant who owned a glove shop downtown. The other was the wife of the popular leader of the Islamic prayer house at the top of Logavina. The woman had told her husband she was going to buy groceries and would be gone for thirty minutes.

The day after the shelling, the city was in a collective state of shock. Sarajevans telephoned one another, asking if everybody in their families was okay and if they knew anybody killed.

They swapped anecdotes of their own brushes with near death. Almost everyone on the street had a tale to tell. Delila Lačević had wanted to buy cigarettes at the market but was delayed—as it happened, showing me around the neighborhood. Nermin Džino was supposed to meet his girlfriend at the market square at 12:30. He was hurrying down Logavina Street at the moment of the blast, thinking that his girlfriend would be angry he was late. Luckily, she was late, too.

"She's okay," he said, shaken, the next day. "But I know one of the ladies who was killed. She worked there selling food."

Kira Prgovski had scheduled a small party for Sunday to celebrate the fortieth day since her son's birth—a Muslim tradition. The get-together seemed inappropriate in the wake of the shelling, but she had already used her last sugar to make a cake—her famous war recipe using ground Vietnam-era biscuits—and her ground-floor apartment was safe enough, facing north. Still, only Ekrem and Minka Kaljanac, who lived just upstairs, were willing to leave their homes.

The party turned out to be a grim affair. The adults traded stories about people who were hurt and killed. The baby fretted. Minka's children misbehaved, upset that they weren't allowed to go outside and play. Television BiH was broadcasting classical music for the dead and reruns of the gruesome market scene. Four-year-old Tarik Kaljanac grabbed the tube of a vacuum cleaner and brandished it menacingly at the TV set.

"Chetniks," he growled. Minka took the vacuum cleaner away from him and went to deal with her ten-year-old, Haris, who was trying to climb out the window into the courtyard. "Get back in here. There could be shells," she snapped.

"I feel like I was just run over by a tram," Minka whined as she finally settled down on the sofa to light a cigarette.

"The trams don't run anymore," Kira retorted.

Ekrem made lame jokes, trying to lighten the mood. He told how he had begged Minka to go to the market in search of coffee. "If she had been there when the shell exploded, I would have killed myself," he declared, and then paused for theatrical effect. "That or fallen into the arms of another woman."

Minka looked fondly at her husband and they both laughed aloud. For a moment, everybody smiled. But then Kira abruptly burst into a flood of tears.

"If it continues like this, they're going to kill us all. There's a shell with everybody's name on it. It is only a matter of time," she wailed.

The market shelling came at the end of a lethal couple of weeks for Sarajevo, in which its citizens were perishing at an alarming rate, and the world was paying attention. Just the day before, ten people had been killed as they waited in line for humanitarian aid in the Dobrinja neighborhood. Two weeks earlier, six children had been killed while they were playing in the snow. This was the standard fare in Sarajevo, barely worth a mention on the evening news. But the 68 deaths and 200 injured by this deadly 120-millimeter mortar shell were of a magnitude impossible to ignore. From a public relations standpoint, it didn't hurt that the massacre occurred a week before the tenth anniversary of Sarajevo's Winter Olympics, and the upcoming opening of the 1994 games in Lillehammer, Norway. As sports fans around the world tuned in to watch the Olympic coverage, they were met with footage of Sarajevo's marketplace.

World leaders decried the outrage. They called it genocide. President Clinton, who four months before had dismissed the Bosnian debacle "as ultimately a matter for the parties to resolve," now declared that the United States and its allies would not stand by idly and watch the "slaughter of innocents."

Since May 1993, Sarajevo had been one of six Bosnian cities designated by the United Nations as "safe havens," despite the fact that Sarajevo was clearly one of the least safe places in the world. More than twenty thousand UN soldiers were stationed in Bosnia, but their primary task was to safeguard the delivery of humanitarian aid—not to stop the killing. Now, world leaders were calling loudly for the United Nations and NATO to take a more interventionist stand.

Radovan Karadžić sputtered and equivocated. He denied that Bosnian Serbs were responsible for the market shelling and threatened to cut off humanitarian routes into Sarajevo unless this "outrageous" accusation was retracted. He then claimed the Bosnian Muslims had bombed themselves to elicit international sympathy. The Bosnian Serb media in Pale advanced the even more ludicrous theory that the entire massacre had been staged—that Sarajevans had dragged out corpses from the morgue and artfully arranged them for the benefit of the television cameras.

UN investigators examined the crater left by the shell at the marketplace but were unable to say with any certainty who had launched it. Given that the Bosnian Serbs had lobbed more than two million rounds of tank and mortar shells into this densely populated downtown, NATO didn't buy Karadžić's denials. Two months earlier, Karadžić had promised to intensify the assault on Sarajevo, telling his deputies in Pale, "Sarajevans will not be counting the dead. They will be counting the living."[1]

Enough was enough. The shelling of Sarajevo had to stop. Led by the United States and France, NATO issued an ultimatum: The Serbs were to withdraw their heavy-caliber weapons twelve miles away from Sarajevo or place them under the control of United Nations forces. Any weapons left within striking distance of Sarajevo would be subject to air strikes. The Serbs were given ten days to comply. The deadline was set for one o'clock on the morning of February 21—D-day as the Sarajevans were calling it, giddy with anticipation.

The planes were invisible, obscured by the persistent cloud cover of a Bosnian winter, but they made an impressive roar, drowning out normal conversation and rippling the plastic sheeting taped across the broken windowpanes. Sarajevo shuddered, but nobody complained about the noise. They looked up to the fog-shrouded skies with anticipation that the roar was a message from above and redemption was on its way.

"I'm so happy. I'm trembling when I hear the airplanes," said Delila, her eyes glittering with excitement.

NATO forces had been patrolling the skies over Bosnia since 1992 as part of a limited mandate to enforce the no-fly zone, and to provide air cover for the UN troops on the ground. The United States had the largest number of planes in the NATO fleet, and Sarajevans had cherished the belief that these Americans would eventually come to their rescue. It was a hope nurtured by a steady diet of American films, television, and recollections of World War II.

Alija Žiga, the seventy-two-year-old head of the mosque behind the courtyard, had just finished leading services for the start of Ramadan when he came out to talk to some neighbors. He had fought with Tito's partisans. "I was behind the front lines. The Germans had us surrounded and they were trying to starve us to death. Then, all of a sudden, these American planes flew overhead and they dropped—you are not going to believe this—hot goulash."

Some had darker recollections. In 1943, when the Allies tried to bomb a Nazi headquarters housed in the Razija Omanović school, they mistakenly hit the Hajrić house two doors down. Suad Hajrić's father was killed in the accident.

Almost all anybody could talk about was how the Americans were about to liberate Sarajevo. They imagined it would be a cross between the Normandy invasion and the Desert Storm bombing of Iraq in 1991. Nermin Džino declared, "The Americans missed a few targets in Iraq. I want the air strikes, even if they end up bombing my backyard by mistake."

Delila agreed. "If I get killed by an American bomb, I won't mind so much as if it's a Chetnik bomb."

As the deadline grew closer, and the Serbs continued to balk, the NATO planes flew lower and more frequently, buzzing the Serb artillery positions in warning. Everybody was convinced the Serbs would be bombed into submission. Delila was out of control. Four nights before the deadline, she ran out of the bomb shelter in the orphanage at midnight to cheer at the NATO planes flying low through the clouds.

"Come on! Come on! Do it!" she yelled, until a policeman walked by and urged her to go back inside.

Tarik Kaljanac woke up one morning, stumbled into the kitchen as his parents were watching the television news, and asked Minka, "Mom, is this the end of the war? Are the Americans really going to help us?"

The weekend before Monday, February 21—D-day—police knocked on doors up and down Logavina Street, advising people to take precautions in case the air strikes missed their targets, or, more likely, the Serbs sought retribution. A rumor swept Sarajevo that the Serbs had a new weapon, a poison gas they planned to unleash on the city. The police showed residents how to fashion a gas mask out of dishwashing liquid and a cotton rag.

After one police visit, Minka confessed she was more afraid than ever. "I worry that the Chetniks will be so angry they have to withdraw that they'll shell us with all they've got. They are sore losers."

As darkness descended on Sunday evening, Minka hung a heavy blue wool blanket over her living room window, which faced Mount Trebević. You never wanted any light glinting out to make a target for the gunners in the hills. She packed sleeping bags for the family, bread, and a canister of water in case they needed to take cover in the basement of the school. The dishwashing liquid was on the kitchen table, just in case.

The anticlimax should have been predictable. First, the Serbs balked at the conditions set by NATO and Sarajevo filled up with television crews from around the world who were expecting a rerun of the Persian Gulf War. Then Russian president Boris Yeltsin offered to send Russian troops to secure areas from which the Serbs had withdrawn. The Serbs viewed Russia as their political ally and accepted a deal under which most of their heavy weapons were delivered to UN-monitored collection sites.

Ekrem and Minka had stayed up until 1 A.M., playing cards and listening to the radio. "You always expect something to happen, and then the next morning, it is just the same old crap," Ekrem complained the following day as he wolfed down a lunch of rice and canned meat.

Kira was also annoyed, having stayed up all night not to await the NATO bombardment, but because the baby was fussing. "Let me tell you about the world," she said wearily. "I've heard all of it before. They always make promises they don't keep. They said they would attack—they didn't do it—and now, whatever they do or say really doesn't interest me."

Yet it couldn't be denied: The shelling had stopped. Sarajevo was quiet again. You could even hear the birds. Sure, there was an occasional burst of gunfire around the Holiday Inn, or an odd boom from the direction of the front lines, but Sarajevo was, for the most part, safe.

The kids were the first to rush outside. The boys from the soccer team started kicking balls around behind the orphanage. "They are feeling relaxed," said their coach, Sejfudin Tica, peering nervously from the window of his office. "I don't really approve, but it's something they need to do for their souls."

It was an early spring, the air balmy and shrouded with a soft mist. Jela put a green plastic table out in the yard. For the first time in almost two years, her family could sit and sip coffee outside. They started working in their garden. Zijo ripped out some of the rosebushes to plant lettuce. He also removed the cobblestoned driveway that led to the garage out back. It seemed unlikely that they would be able to afford gasoline to take out their Volkswagen Jetta anytime soon, so they figured the precious space could be used to grow carrots, squash, cabbage, beans, and spinach. "There is no other way we'll ever get to eat a green vegetable," Zijo explained.

Ekrem converted a small backyard shed into a chicken coop. By Sarajevo standards, it was a gold mine, since a single egg cost $3. He and Mirsad, his neighbor Kira's boyfriend, cleared away the debris left from a cluster of garages that had been blown up in the summer of 1993, and made a collective vegetable garden for their apartment building. In the heart of the city, Logavina Street was transformed into a small agricultural village.

Delila slept in her own bed for the first time in six months. This was a big step for the shell-shocked teenager, who was still leery of this unaccustomed peace. Since 1992, the extended Lačević family had been traveling up to the orphanage nightly. There were so many of them—Delila and her cousins Lana and Maša; their mother, Šaćira; Selma and Mirza, the refugee cousins from Derventa—that the family had been assigned its own room, with mattresses lining the floor. The neighbors, most of whom had long since abandoned the dank, smelly shelters, thought they were a tad eccentric.

"I'm embarrassed. I would never tell my colleagues where I

sleep," confessed Šaćira, a gynecologist at Koševo Hospital. The family had held frequent meetings about sleeping at home. ("Like NATO, we've actually passed a couple of resolutions to go back, but we never do anything," Lana explained to me.) They had tried it a few times, but Delila had such terrible insomnia that they all went back to the shelter.

"My cousins laugh at me, but I'm as afraid of shells as the devil is of the crucifix. Whenever I hear shells, I have the sensation that shrapnel is hitting me in the same place all over again," Delila told me. "I'm feeling pretty safe now. I'm an optimist. I simply cannot believe that things are not going to change. If they don't, I'll lose my mind. My hair will turn gray and I'll go crazy."

Delila made slow steps to normalcy. She ventured warily into the city. Walking down Logavina Street for the first time in months to visit the Baščaršija, she asked a friend to accompany her. "I was so scared at first I was standing behind him every time I caught a glimpse of Mount Trebević," she said.

The first weekend of March, Delila and Lana decided to make a more ambitious excursion. They went to BB, the only discotheque still operating in Sarajevo, safely tucked underground below the shuttered Hotel Belgrade. Nobody bought the drinks—a beer cost 5 German marks and a Coca-Cola cost 10—but Delila and her friends danced wildly until fifteen minutes before curfew.

The next day they went to play billiards at the pool hall at the Skenderija sports arena, another underground facility that had stayed open. It was a mile-long walk, which included crossing a bridge over the Miljacka River. A pedestrian walkway dotted with cafés ran along the south bank of the river. It had been one of the prettier places to stroll before the war, and Delila was stunned by the devastation there. The Austro-

Hungarian buildings with their ornamental trim were bashed and blackened by mortar shells.

"Look, that was our biology lab!" exclaimed Delila as she grabbed Lana's hand to point out a building across the river. It now had a crater large enough to drive an eighteen-wheel truck through.

During the first few weeks after the cease-fire, Sarajevo was caught up in a mix of euphoria and despair. Without the numbing fear of mortar shells, Sarajevans tallied their losses. People grew morbid with reflection, yet they were excited by the slightest glimpse of normalcy: sanitation workers hosing down a street, shopkeepers sweeping up broken glass, and crews repairing the electric lines for trams.

On Vase Miskina, the pedestrian mall where the first big shelling had taken place in 1992, killing twenty people, a pineapple was displayed in a store window. Passersby stopped to gawk, as though a UFO had suddenly descended on the city. Suada Čaušević saw the pineapple as she was strolling by with her five-year-old daughter, Lejla, and had to stop to explain what a pineapple was.

"The worst is over, surely," declared a radiant Sead Vranić, ecstatic after seeing the offices of a travel agency preparing to reopen. Within a few months, Sead was convinced, he could return to his job with a Croatian trading company. His neighbor Kasema Telalagić kept cautioning him and the others. "If this really meant the end of the war, people would celebrate. It would be like the wedding day of Princess Diana."

Spring 1994 brought another breakthrough. On March 1, 1994, President Clinton held a news conference in Washington to announce a peace pact between the Bosnians and the Croats. The pact would end a nasty chapter of the war, in which Croat nationalists had turned against their former Muslim allies. The Croats had claimed a swath of Bosnia as their own state. They wanted to carve out a slice of Bosnia before the Serbs took everything. The vicious fighting between the Muslims and the Croats had been concentrated in Herzegovina, an austere, mountainous region to the west of Sarajevo, and had redoubled the difficulty of getting goods into the city since most commercial trade bound for Sarajevo originated in Croatia and had to pass through Herzegovina to make it through Serb siege lines.

The deal with the Croats was as welcome as the NATO ultimatum. The United Nations opened roads into Sarajevo. Prices crashed. Suddenly you could buy coffee, apples, and oranges at prices that at least vaguely resembled those in the rest of Europe. You still couldn't make a telephone call from Sarajevo, but with persistence, international callers could sometimes call in. The siege seemed to be crumbling.

On Logavina Street, the most remarkable herald of peace was the arrival of Selma and Mirza's parents in Sarajevo. More than anything else, the reunion of the family made it seem like the ordeal of war was over.

The first reports that Selma and Mirza had heard after they fled Derventa in 1992 was that their parents were dead, murdered when their hometown fell to the Serbs. It was not until 1993 that they received a sketchy message hand-carried into Sarajevo by a Catholic archbishop that the couple had escaped to Croatia. "They are alive and well" was all the message conveyed about their circumstances. After that, there were a couple of indirect contacts through a ham radio operator. Finally, in March, they were able to make a telephone call. Mirza was so overwhelmed he couldn't speak a word.

On June 18, Selma and Mirza went to the Sarajevo bus station to pick up their parents with their aunt, Šaćira. As they scanned the passengers disembarking, the kids were nervous.

Selma rushed to embrace her mother, but got a rude rebuff. Mejasa Kapić didn't recognize her daughter, who had been a plump adolescent when Mejasa had last seen her.

"Get away from me. You're not my child," she cried, distraught at the attentions of the slim, pretty sixteen-year-old.

Fadil Kapić, Selma and Mirza's father, tried to comfort his wife as she continued to push Selma away. In desperation, Selma pulled back her freshly permed hair to show her ears, ever so slightly pointed since birth.

"Mother. Look at my ears. It's me, Selma," she implored.

It had been over two years since Selma and Mirza said their hasty farewells to their parents in Derventa. The transition back to normal family life was slow and painful. Selma and Mirza were not only taller, they were more mature, and the rigors of war had toughened them. They couldn't quite bring themselves to say "Mommy," and would catch themselves addressing their parents as "Aunt" and "Uncle." But then, there were the evenings when the two teenagers, now sixteen and fourteen, would cuddle into bed on either side of their mother.

"I still couldn't believe that these were my children in my arms and that I was hugging and kissing them again," recalled Mejasa, whose round and gentle face crumpled into tears.

Fadil and Mejasa had not had an easy time during the separation from their children. They had stayed in Derventa to protect their house and land, but finally gave up in July. Mejasa washed the dishes and closed the shutters of her house before they left, hoping they could return in a few days. It was impossible. They still had a functioning car, so the couple drove through northern Bosnia, skipping from town to town ahead of the Serb advance.

At last, they found shelter across the border, in the Croatian town of Slovonska Požega. A couple named Slavko and Nada took pity on them and gave them housing, food, and clothing. "We didn't know anybody in this town when we arrived and we were treated like family. We made real friends," Fadil said.

It was too good to last. In the summer of 1993, after the fighting erupted between Croats and Muslims, Slavko received anonymous letters in his mailbox. One warned that his house would be firebombed if he didn't expel Muslim refugees. Slavko filed a complaint with the police and begged Fadil and Mejasa to stay, but they were too frightened. In November 1993 they moved to Zagreb.

Šaćira tried to find somebody willing to evacuate Selma and Mirza to their parents in Zagreb. It proved impossible and so, in June, Fadil and Mejasa moved to Sarajevo.

"Compared to Zagreb, Sarajevo is nothing but a concentration camp, but we wanted to live with our children," Fadil said.

The trip took four days and required permission from Serb authorities. Mejasa was terrified, especially when their bus was stopped at a checkpoint under the sign welcoming them to the Republika Srpska.

As they entered Sarajevo, Mejasa couldn't believe her eyes. The apartments were all blasted away, and battered trams and buses had been piled high as sniper barricades on the side of the street.

Fadil tried to reassure her. The NATO ultimatum was still in place. The Serbs had withdrawn their heavy guns from the hills above the city. There was no more shelling, no more shooting. In Sarajevo, the family would be safe.

10

BETRAYAL

December 1994

ALL ALONG LOGAVINA STREET makeshift aluminum stoves were devouring people's possessions. Desa Stanić burned her summer sandals, the slipcover of an armchair, the clothing her teenage children had outgrown, and their old schoolbooks.

Sead Vranić had chopped down a cherry tree from his garden and was resisting pleas from his son and wife to tear up the parquet floors.

Zijo and Jela Džino were among the few families on Logavina who had real firewood to burn. Their son, Nermin, had carried it home from the front lines. But he had contracted hepatitis and couldn't provide more wood, so Zijo was eyeing the toolshed in the backyard.

The third winter of the siege had descended on Sarajevo with a vicious bite. The household items that were easiest to burn—the bookcases and cupboards—had gone up in smoke long ago. Sarajevans had ravaged the hillsides. The temperature in the average Sarajevo home was 40 degrees—about the same as a refrigerator—and people worried that they would die of hypothermia.

"The slipcovers smell terrible. They're made of some kind of synthetic fabric," Desa said apologetically as we visited her chilly apartment. "The shoes burn so hot that the stove turns red and you get the feeling it is about to take off, but what else are we supposed to do?"

It had been eight months since John Costello and I visited Sarajevo. When we left in March, the mood was optimistic. The trams were running again. Café proprietors had set out tables on the sidewalk. If people didn't necessarily believe the war was over, they believed they had survived the worst of it.

"It was just an illusion. No gas. No electricity. We will not be able to survive the winter if it is like this. This is a new beginning of the war for us," Zijo told us.

All of Logavina Street was in hibernation. The soccer team had stopped playing. There was hardly any life on the street. It was dark by 4 P.M. and with no electricity, most people went to bed by 7:30 P.M.

"I slept late today, too. Until 8:30 in the morning. You have to stay in bed as long as possible to conserve firewood and to eat less," Jela Džino explained.

The Razija Omanović elementary school was closed for a winter recess. Even in the one classroom with a wood-burning stove, it was cold enough to see your breath. "As you can see, we are still besieged," principal Lejla Hadžiomerović said as she watched the children filing out on the last day before the break.

In the Kaljanac apartment, Minka was feeding empty egg cartons into the stove. There was nothing else to burn. The boys complained incessantly about the cold and the lack of electricity. They wanted to watch television. To pass the time, they were stacking packs of cigarettes into a tower, which Tarik kept knocking over with a frustrated kick.

"In the summer, the roads were open. We ate well. We put on a little weight. People thought it was all over. I told Minka this is only going to last until September. She laughed at me, but look, I was right," Ekrem Kaljanac said.

At the top of Logavina Street, across from the cemetery, Selma and Mirza's parents were not doing well. Fadil Kapić, who had once been one of Derventa's wealthiest men, was rising at 5 A.M. to scour the dumps for burnable garbage. He had to go early because the competition for the best pickings was fierce. The day we met with him, he had scored big: a broken plastic garbage pail.

"See how it burns. So fast, like gasoline," boasted Fadil, a large, ruddy-faced man.

Selma and Mirza looked on, wrinkling their nose at the stink of the blazing plastic. "It's so cold I have to sleep with a hat on," Selma told me in a whisper, not wanting to offend her father.

People were more obsessed than ever about the utilities. During the summer, when temperatures had climbed into the nineties, there had been no running water. Now, when it was too cold to bathe, there was plenty of water but no gas or electricity for heat. They scanned *Oslobođenje* for reports about why the gas and electricity kept going on and off and when it might happen.

One evening, after ten straight days without utilities, the gas came back on with a sudden hiss. Most households on Logavina had gas stoves, and through the darkened windows of the street you could hear the occupants exclaiming, *"Došao plin!"*—"There's gas!"

"Karadžić turned back our gas again," exclaimed Mejasa Kapić. "I'm as happy as if we got to go back to Derventa again."

Of course, like so much else in the war, it proved a cruel

tease. By morning, the gas had dwindled to practically nothing.

The cease-fire didn't collapse with a big bang. It eroded steadily. Each day there was another burst of sniper fire, or a couple of mortar shells, and the sinking realization that the respite from war was over. Then, on October 8, gunmen, who were hidden in a Grbavica high-rise, opened fire on the tram in front of the Holiday Inn. This was the incident in which Amir, thirteen, and two other students from the Razija Omanović school were injured.

By November, people were terrified to set foot inside the trams. They stopped running on November 28. The United Nations grounded its flights of humanitarian aid into Sarajevo because the Serbs had positioned SAM anti-aircraft missiles around the airport. The food supply rapidly dwindled to a selection of dried beans, rice, and macaroni, all of which were nearly impossible to make edible without gas, electricity, or firewood.

The first week in December, Jela and Zijo were in their downstairs utility room—the safest part of the house—when they thought they heard knocking. Zijo opened the door and no one was there. The next morning they found a bullet embedded in the door. "You are safe absolutely nowhere," Jela told me later that afternoon.

The next weekend the Džinos' next-door neighbor Fuad Kasumagić found out that two jewelers from his workshop had been shot by a sniper while walking by the Holiday Inn. Rifat Ibrović, forty-five, was killed instantly. The other jeweler, Nihad Hadžikalfagić, who was twenty-eight years old and had been married just two months earlier, was left paralyzed from the waist down.

NATO had executed maneuvers during 1994 to try to dissuade the Serbs from their attack. In April, U.S. F-16s and FA-18s bombed Serb troops when they attempted to overrun the UN safe haven, Goražde, in eastern Bosnia, and NATO warplanes struck again in November to protect the enclave of Bihac.

The air strikes were timid measures—pinpricks, denounced the critics. They only enraged the Bosnian Serbs, who retaliated by seizing UN soldiers as hostages and cutting off humanitarian access to Sarajevo.

The NATO ultimatum was a bluff and the Serbs had seen through it. By mid-December, the Bosnian Public Health Institute reported 109 Sarajevans killed and more than 500 wounded since February 9, when the ultimatum was issued. Former U.S. president Jimmy Carter flew into Bosnia the weekend before Christmas to patch together a new cease-fire. He was in Pale with Radovan Karadžić the afternoon of December 20, when two 120-millimeter mortar shells hit Marije Bursać Street, around the corner from Logavina. They mangled a bicycle, sent laundry flying, and annihilated the kitchen of a house whose elderly occupants were out collecting humanitarian aid.

Logavina residents were enraged, none more so than Esad Taljanović. The dentist's six-year-old son, Emir, was playing outside when the shells detonated about a hundred yards away. Emir came back home, frightened and tearful.

"You see, I should not let my son out for thirty seconds," raged Taljanović. He was furious with the Serbs, the United Nations, and Jimmy Carter. "It is the same thing as if Truman stood next to Hitler and negotiated with him."

Ekrem Kaljanac picked up the telephone, the only working appliance in his apartment, since the electricity was off again.

"Yes, hello," he said. Then, cupping his hand over the mouthpiece, "It's Hillary Clinton. She's worried about us and was wondering how we're doing."

Ekrem's mischievous performance was intended to point out the absurdity of the idea that anybody in the United States, least of all in the White House, cared about Sarajevo.

Sarajevans were fed up with politicians, diplomats, bureaucrats, relief agencies, and everybody who had promised to help, then failed to deliver.

People were especially frustrated with the United States and the vacillating policies emanating from the White House. Sarajevans had believed Clinton when he promised, during his presidential campaign, to be more proactive in Bosnia than George Bush. "If the horrors of the Holocaust taught us anything, it is the high cost of remaining silent and paralyzed in the face of genocide," Clinton had said in August 1992, while Sarajevans were huddled helplessly in their bomb shelters.[1]

Ekrem mercilessly teased his wife. Minka, like many of the women on Logavina, had been charmed by Clinton, who they thought resembled John F. Kennedy.

"I saw Clinton a lot on television. He was so good-looking. He was promising a lot and I believed him," Minka confessed sheepishly. "I was convinced that the Americans were going to bomb the Serbs and end the war."

"Clinton lies. He behaves like an actor," interjected Ekrem bitterly. His brother, Safet, joined in. "I watch the news. Americans are more interested in a cat in New York than they are in Bosnians."

It was not only Clinton's political rhetoric that persuaded Sarajevans the United States would rescue them; they saw America as the embodiment of the multiethnic state they hoped to create in Bosnia.

A popular poster hanging in cafés around Sarajevo de-
picted an American flag with a Bosnian lily next to the stars,
suggesting that Bosnia become the fifty-first state. Moreover,
Bosnians were so utterly convinced of the righteousness of
their cause, they simply couldn't believe that the United States
would not do something—anything—to intervene.

The invective was also directed against journalists. An
emotionally unbalanced woman in her thirties who lived in
the Kaljanacs' apartment building cursed and spit on the
ground whenever she saw us coming. Although most Logavina residents remained unfailingly polite and hospitable,
they, too, vented their frustration.

"Aren't you ashamed that your country has done nothing
but stand by and watch us die?" Esad demanded of us as his
wife served us coffee in their dining room.

Sead Vranić best encapsulated the mood of Sarajevo during that increasingly dangerous month of December 1994. "All
days are the same now. You get up and see if you have electricity, or water. You listen to what Clinton says in the morning,
and hear that he's changed his mind by afternoon, then discover in the evening he has forgotten what he said in the
morning," Sead said wearily.

It was not as though Bosnia was being ignored. The peace-
keeping mission in the former Yugoslavia was the largest and
costliest in the United Nations' history, consuming some $1.6
billion a year. That didn't take into account the extra $700 mil-
lion spent by the Office of the UN High Commissioner for
Refugees.

The UN Security Council had passed more than one hundred resolutions dealing with the Yugoslav conflict. Most of
them were laughably ineffectual. For example, Resolution 752

stated: "The Council demands that all parties concerned in Bosnia and Herzegovina stop the fighting immediately."

Between the diplomats and bureaucrats, the soldiers, aid workers, and journalists, there were more foreigners in Sarajevo than there had been since the 1984 Olympics. By a conservative count, there were at least 150 nongovernmental agencies working in the area, ranging from Médecins sans Frontières (Doctors without Borders) to the comic spin-off Clowns sans Frontières, which brought jugglers to entertain Bosnian children.

Yet all the money and good intentions didn't alleviate the cold, dark nights with nothing to eat. It didn't stop the shellings and it didn't stop the sniper fire. Sarajevans resented the foreigners, witnesses to their indignity. They scorned the UN anti-sniper teams who did too little to stop the snipers. They hissed at the TV crews that staked out the dangerous intersections, waiting to film the next sniper victim.

Sarajevans had turned against the United Nations since Secretary-General Boutros Boutros-Ghali's visit to the city on New Year's Eve 1992, after which he commented: "I understand your frustration, but you have a situation that is better than ten other places in the world. . . . I can give you a list."[2]

Their anger had turned to outright paranoia. "It is like they are experimenting on us to see how much we can take," remarked the normally sensible Jela, echoing an increasingly common sentiment.

Suada Čaušević recalled how she had gone out with her five-year-old daughter, Lejla, one day when she heard that the UN Egyptian battalion was distributing kiwi fruit. Pregnant, Suada stood in line for an hour with Lejla.

Lejla was given a shriveled and brown apple. They got back in line and waited again, hopeful that they would get kiwis, but when it was their turn, a UN soldier spotted the uneaten apple in Lejla's hand and shooed them away. "No, you got yours. Get out of here," he told Suada and Lejla.

"I can't tell you how humiliated I felt," Suada said. "You know, sometimes they even throw potatoes at us from the armored personnel carriers. It's useful, we need the potatoes, but it makes for a very ugly scene."

Sarajevans were angry—at everyone. Their free-floating rage hung over the city. The summer of 1994 had been like a furlough from prison, a chance to relax. Having let down their guard once, they couldn't psychologically gird themselves for the relapse of war. They were starting to lose it.

The spirit of cooperation that had sustained Sarajevo through 1992 and 1993 was under enormous strain. Hardliners in Izetbegović's ruling Party of Democratic Action proposed banning Serbian songs from the radio. Sarajevans cherished the maudlin Serbian love songs and the proposition failed, but the militants persisted and in October, BiH Television censored a comedy skit poking fun at Islamic fundamentalists. *Ljiljan*, an Islamic magazine, set off another debate by questioning the propriety of mixed marriage.

"To be honest, I hate Serbs a little more now. The Croats, too," Ekrem Kaljanac declared in a pique of resentment. Sarajevans were quicker to speak deprecatingly not only of Serbs and Croats but also of the Muslim refugees who were pouring in from the villages of eastern Bosnia. They called the refugees *papaks,* or peasants.

The neighbors on Logavina Street quarreled more frequently. Jealousy was rife, especially when it came to utilities. One evening when I was visiting the Kaljanacs, the family was using enough stolen electricity to illuminate a twenty-five-watt lamp. Each time they heard steps in the hallway, they guiltily unscrewed the pathetic little lightbulb, lest anyone discover their secret.

"A lot has changed. People have changed. They've withdrawn into themselves. They are not as social as they were. They are just surviving," Ekrem explained.

They were less inclined to invite neighbors for coffee. It took twenty minutes' worth of precious firewood to boil the water. People were stressed out, nervous. They complained of upset stomachs, ulcers, insomnia, heart palpitations. Some admitted to me that they were taking tranquilizers.

Eccentric characters were spotted on the street. A middle-aged man wore nothing but shorts and running shoes in the middle of winter. A wrinkled woman in widow's black would sit for hours, bawling, on the window ledge of Fuad Kasumagić's house. A strikingly pretty young, black-haired woman paced, babbling to herself.

"I think there are a lot of people here who went insane out of fear. You can tell, they'll burst out laughing at strange times, or else start crying," Ekrem said. "I can't entirely blame them. I think if I didn't have to hold it together for the kids, I might be that way, too."

The shelling that resumed in late 1994 wasn't as relentless as before, but people were more traumatized than ever. It was one of the ironies of Sarajevo that more people were killed when the fire was sporadic and unpredictable than in the stretches when fire was heavy and residents remained underground.

"At the beginning of the war, we didn't know what a mortar shell could do to you. Now even a fool is afraid," explained Minka. "If I hear an explosion, even a car backfiring, my legs get weak. My heart starts pounding. I think it is the chemistry in my body that has gotten like this."

Esad Taljanović was walking past the Sarajevo Music Academy, a block away from Logavina, when he heard a whistle. He crashed to the pavement, thinking he was hearing an incoming mortar shell. It was only a student whistling a tune.

At the other extreme, some Sarajevans became inured to war. After his two employees were shot on December 10, Fuad Kasumagić wondered why they had risked their lives walking in front of the Holiday Inn, rather than taking a safer back road.

"A normal person would avoid going that way, but we don't act like normal people anymore. A normal person would run away if they heard shooting, like you would put up your umbrella if it started to rain. But it's this syndrome we have. We are not even aware of it," Fuad said.

The randomness of the violence made people obsessed with fate and destiny. Superstition raged out of control. Sarajevans would spit three times on the sidewalk when they saw a black cat. The old women—the *babe gatare*—read fortunes in the muddy grounds at the bottom of coffee cups. A popular telephone psychic rendered predictions about which days were better to stay inside and when the electricity might pop on.

"It is a lot of crap," Selma Kapić said, admitting that she called on occasion. "At least it's free."

Everybody had an amulet against danger. Ekrem and Minka put up a horseshoe in the frame of their front door. Minka, like the Lačević girls, Delila, Lana, and Maša, always wore a dangling gold die for luck. Nermin Džino would never go to the front lines without a silver-inlaid wooden ball that his father had carved for him. When the Serbs opened fire, he would put the charm in his mouth. Foreigners in Sarajevo urged one another to "be careful," but the Sarajevans were more likely to say, "Be lucky."

Minka wouldn't let her children go out to play if she had a bad dream. Fuad, sober and sensible, recounted how, in 1993, he had gotten a sudden impulse to move his teenage daughter's piano out of a room. Within an hour, a mortar shell crashed through the window. The piano was spared.

Mladen Marković was convinced he would have been killed in the February 5 market massacre had he not gotten a rare telephone call from his wife in Germany. "We spoke from 7:30 A.M. to 10:15 and all my plans for the day were delayed. The call cost her 500 German marks. That's what a great love is."

"We are all a little weird here," Mladen admitted. "We believe in destiny. In superstition. A phone rings and we jump. When people come back here who didn't live through this, or if we go somewhere else, everybody is going to think we're nuts."

Christmas Eve 1994 brought another cease-fire. Jimmy Carter's tête-à-tête with Radovan Karadžić had been productive. The Bosnian Serb leader agreed to stay his guns. People did not believe the truce would last, but they were determined to make the most of it.

Tarik Vranić, Sead's son, explained while he was getting ready for midnight mass, "We expect this will last at least until New Year's, maybe through the Orthodox Christmas [January 7], so why not enjoy it?"

Desa Stanić was hell-bent on celebrating the holidays. In 1993, after her husband's death on the front lines, she had been morbidly depressed. Now she ventured down to the basement storage bin to retrieve her Christmas lights and a small artificial tree. Even though Desa and her late husband had been Communists—she still hung a portrait of Tito in the hallway—

she loved Christmas. The tree was about the only flammable item left in the basement that hadn't been burned for fuel. She set up the tree in the living room and painstakingly decorated it with the string of red, yellow, and blue plastic pinecone lights. When dark came, hope got the better of Desa and she tried plugging the lights into a socket.

"*Nema struje*," Desa apologized to her teenagers, who snickered at the unlit tree. "No electricity."

Desa bought a chicken with money her children had received from Merhamet—the Muslim charity. She baked it in her makeshift aluminum stove fueled by crumpled paper and schoolbooks and invited her upstairs neighbor, Seid Ganić, a Muslim, to dinner, along with friends of the children. As midnight approached, Desa put on a pair of borrowed boots that were two sizes too big to trek down icy Logavina Street. She and Ganić stopped to pick up Jela Džino on their way to mass. Desa, a Serb, celebrated Christmas with a Muslim and a Catholic.

"All nations, all confessions. It is the way Sarajevo always used to be," Ganić boasted cheerfully. "I'm a Muslim, and I've never missed a Christmas Eve mass yet."

Christmas Eve mass was a huge event in Sarajevo's social calendar, more so this year than ever because the archbishop of Sarajevo, Vinko Puljić, had been newly elevated to cardinal. The city suspended its 10 P.M. wartime curfew. The previous two years, attendance had been down because of the unremitting shelling.

The cathedral itself had taken a couple of direct hits. In the crucifixion scene behind the altar, the entire torso of Christ was missing.

Cardinal Puljić delivered the sermon wearing a cross around his neck made of molten shrapnel. "All those who have power, let them get enlightened to do something to stop this war," he told a standing-room-only crowd. More than two thousand people were jammed into the cathedral, which was designed to seat two hundred. Together, they prayed that this latest truce might stand a better chance than its predecessors.

Christmas Day at 9 A.M. Mirza Kapić gave the cease-fire its first road test. He wanted to surprise his parents and bring home some firewood. His mother was sick and Selma was whining constantly that the house was so cold "penguins couldn't stand it." They were tired of burning garbage.

Mirza, fourteen, borrowed two sleds and took a saw from the garage. He was joined by his friend Hasan Husić, seventeen, a refugee who lived with his mother in the orphanage. Proceeding straight uphill from Logavina, where the landscape was mountainous and rustic, the boys hiked about two miles until they reached Špicasta Stijena. It was the front line—the very place where Nermin Džino reported to duty—but there weren't any trees left. The boys disregarded the Bosnian soldiers, who were yelling at them to watch out for land mines.

They ran to the biggest tree they thought they could handle. It was almost down when the bullets started dancing through the trees, showering the boys with pine needles.

"I was so scared, I left the sleds and the saw. I rolled all the way down the mountain," Mirza admitted later with embarrassment.

"It was a foggy day so I thought it would be okay," Hasan said. "But too many people had the same idea. We were making too much noise. The Chetniks could hear us. Some of them got up to five trees. We didn't get a single one. Maybe if we had picked a smaller tree."

By 1994, so many truces had come and gone that graffiti scrawled on a wall at the Sarajevo airport read "the last cease-fire held for . . ."—with the answers ranging from five minutes to twenty seconds. The very term *Bosnian cease-fire* had become an oxymoron.

11

ESCAPE

SUADA ČAUŠEVIĆ FLED Sarajevo on a chilly December morning. She walked out of her apartment carrying her infant daughter, while her six-year-old, Lejla, skipped behind. They made their way toward her husband, who was behind the wheel of a waiting car with the engine running.

Suada's tearful sister-in-law, Aida, watched them from the front stoop, murmuring an Islamic prayer as she spilled water from a glass onto the pavement. It was a traditional Bosnian ritual to bring a traveler good luck.

Suada was going to need all the luck she could get. She was escaping with the children and a few hundred German marks hidden in her clothing. At twenty-nine, she had never been out of Yugoslavia, had never traveled alone, and spoke no foreign languages. The route out of Sarajevo was dangerous and she only had vague plans for once she got out of the city. But she believed that she and her daughters could only survive the winter if they left Sarajevo.

"This has become hell, really," she declared on the eve of her departure.

On her last night at home, Suada sat smoking and talking with her husband, Adnan, at the kitchen table, next to their stove, which was devouring a cushion from their sofa. Shadows flickered from the flame of a lamp made out of an empty tuna-fish can that burned vegetable oil. In the corner, Suada's knapsack and a small, shabby suitcase were neatly packed and ready to go.

When I had last seen Suada in March, she was in precarious condition. Her doctors thought it was unlikely that she could carry her baby to full term, but the cease-fire had arrived in the nick of time for her.

Adnan had cleared away the trash behind their apartment and had planted a small vegetable garden. He sold his produce at the market and earned a little money. "There was no shelling. I ate well. I got fat," Suada told me. Their second daughter, Adna Čaušević, was born July 11, 1994, eight pounds and five ounces, robust and healthy.

All was well until winter set in. Adnan, an electrical engineer, couldn't find work. They tried to raise money by selling off their VCR and stereo, but they got less than 100 German marks. With no money to buy firewood, they burned their chairs, then their couch. The furniture didn't provide enough heat and the baby contracted a chronic cold and had to stay with Adnan's parents.

Lejla, a talkative girl, now sat quietly sucking her thumb, cuddled next to her father. Adnan was glum. He would not be able to leave with the family. Even though he was on medical leave from the army, as a draft-age male he could not obtain a Bosnian passport to leave the country.

"I never thought of sending my family out. We've stayed the whole time," Adnan explained. "No one is leaving Sarajevo gladly. We love this city."

"It's the same old story, just like the beginning of the war. They've started shelling all over again," Suada said.

"We have hardened with regard to the shelling," Adnan interjected. "We are not afraid of the hunger. We are afraid of the winter. We have no money to buy firewood."

Suddenly their discussion was interrupted by knocking on the door. A breathless child from an apartment upstairs had come to tell them the gas was back on. Cautiously, Adnan twisted open a gas valve. It hissed. He extinguished the chunk of his sofa that had been burning in the oven, and immediately lit the gas.

Suada wavered. If the heat was working again, she wouldn't have to leave her home after all.

Suada and Adnan stayed up most of the night, talking, smoking cigarettes, and watching the fire. As the first morning light broke, the gas flame flickered lower and lower until it went out.

"No. I'm leaving. If Bill Clinton himself called and promised me the gas would stay on, I'd still go," Suada declared in the morning.

Suada's plan was to escape to Split, the Croatian port city. She had a sister living on Ostrvo Cvijeca—Island of Flowers— a tourist spot off the Adriatic coast now filled with Bosnian women and their children. She hoped her sister could help her find a room and work.

Getting out was difficult. The route that she chose—the only way out for most people—was through a half-mile-long tunnel that ran under the airport. The Bosnian Army had excavated the tunnel in 1993 to sneak soldiers in and out of the city. It was classified top secret—neither the Bosnian government nor United Nations personnel acknowledged its existence—but Sarajevo was not the kind of town that guarded secrets.

By March 1994, civilians with proper documentation were allowed to use the tunnel. Although it was mired in ankle-deep mud and so low that you needed to stoop to get through, it was the only escape route for the people left in the besieged city.

The tunnel emerged in the suburb of Hrasnica. From there, refugees faced another monumental challenge: Mount Igman, which rose 5,476 feet to the southwest of Sarajevo. Although Mount Igman was nominally controlled by the Bosnian Army, it was under fire twenty-four hours a day from Serbs in Ilidža, just below. A dirt road, barely wide enough for passenger cars, wended along the side of the mountain, but few dared to drive it without an armored vehicle. The preferred route was a steep footpath that was hidden from view by trees. Suada figured that she would hike the path and once she got to the other side of the mountain, she could hitchhike or pay somebody to drive her the rest of the way.

The entire journey to Split was less than a hundred miles. Before the war, Suada and Adnan would simply pile into their Volkswagen Golf on a Saturday morning and be there in plenty of time for lunch.

"I'm so excited, so nervous. I have no idea how things will turn out," Suada said, as she sucked a last drag of her cigarette before setting off.

Eighteen hours later, at two the next morning, Suada arrived on the Adriatic coast, a quick journey given the logistics of traveling through Bosnia in late 1994. The fog had remained in place, protecting the travelers from sniper fire.

Adnan accompanied his wife through the tunnel and up the footpath, carrying five-month-old Adna against his stomach in a yellow baby carrier. They hiked up Mount Igman in only ninety minutes. Lejla walked the entire way on her own. When they reached the safe side of the mountain and Adnan had to turn back, Lejla realized that he wasn't coming with them. "She started screaming that she didn't want to go," Adnan said. He was so flustered that he forgot to hand over the baby carrier.

Suada telephoned three days later to report that she had found a room on the island in a former resort hotel. There was a cafeteria with plenty of food and the weather was warm, but Suada was lonely. Lejla, too, was worried about her family in Sarajevo.

"Grandma, do you have enough to eat?" the child asked Adnan's mother, Kimeta Čaušević, over the phone. "Are you cold? Are you wrapping yourself in blankets?"

They were unsure whether to reveal that the gas and electricity had reappeared right after Suada's departure. Adnan didn't want his wife worrying about him, but he also didn't want her to second-guess her decision to leave. Besides, his own resolve to remain in Sarajevo was faltering.

"I don't want to leave. But there is no purpose to anything without Suada. What are they going to do without me? What am I going to do without them?" Adnan said as he watched a soccer game during his first weekend of bachelorhood.

It would be a stretch to call Delila Lačević lucky, given all she had been through after her parents' death. But in the end she was able to escape Sarajevo and find her way to Kansas.

Delila had been angling to get to Kansas ever since her brother left in December 1993. She had few qualms about leaving Sarajevo. "I don't even want to be in Europe. Who knows when World War III will start? Everybody here is crazy," she said. "My brother, when he left, he said he couldn't even sleep in Frankfurt. He couldn't wait until he got to America. I'll forget everything that has happened the minute I can walk into a bathroom and turn on the faucet."

The retired couple in Salina who sponsored Berin had offered to pay for Delila's trip and had arranged for her to stay with another family, who lived on a five-acre estate with a Jacuzzi and a spring-fed pond in Overland Park, Kansas. A California foundation called Resolve offered to get Delila's paperwork in order.

In March 1994, Delila was told she would be leaving within days. "This is the happiest day of my life," Delila declared. "I'm going to America!"

The Resolve foundation had promised Delila that she could leave Sarajevo on the UN airlift, but it turned out that the only available transportation was by bus through Serb territory. Delila conferred with her aunt, Šaćira. They agreed it would be too dangerous.

It was a prudent decision. Resolve did manage to get a busload of Sarajevans out as far as Split but had no money to take them any farther. The foundation's president, Lynne Robustelli, was arrested for fraud shortly afterward in California, having left an international trail of bad debts.

In November, the U.S. Embassy in Sarajevo called Delila to say she would be flying out in two days. She thought somebody was playing a practical joke. She asked her uncle, Mustafa, to call the embassy. He was told, "Believe, believe."

Mejasa Kapić immediately began baking burek—stuffed meat pies—for a party. They used their last money to buy a bottle of brandy. Delila's natural exuberance exploded into near mania.

"Karadžić, okay. You can shoot all you want now. I'm leaving tomorrow!" she yelled out through the front gate. As though on command, explosions ripped through the air. Delila scampered back into the house and hid behind the couch, crying.

"It's all your fault," Fadil Kapić teased.

Delila left on the morning of November 15. She took just a knapsack of clothes and her golden stud earrings shaped like fleur-de-lis—her only souvenir of Bosnia. Her grandmother reminded Delila to say a prayer at her parents' graves outside the front gate before she left. There was no time. The UN armored personnel carrier arrived earlier than expected, and she was whisked away to the Sarajevo airport. She got on one of the last flights out before the airlift was grounded.

Delila's dramatic exit had made a powerful impression on the neighbors. Airlifts and sponsors were only available for the most unfortunate—the amputees, the orphans. The Lačević family's tragedy had attracted widespread media coverage. ABC Television did several shows featuring the orphaned children. Kansas senator Bob Dole had pulled strings to get Berin evacuated, and Senator Byron Dorgan of North Dakota actually flew to Sarajevo to bring Delila out. The people who had suffered the ordinary privations of cold, hunger, and fear were left to fend for themselves, and the logistics of getting out were truly daunting.

The opening of the tunnel in 1994 transformed the dynamics of the siege. The Serbs were permitting Sarajevans to escape; they certainly knew about the secret tunnel and could have closed it whenever they chose. But it was in their interest that Sarajevo have fewer people to defend it. At the same time, the

Bosnian government was making it increasingly difficult to get out. Applicants for Bosnian passports—essential, since the Yugoslav passport was no longer recognized—were told they would have to wait more than six months because of a shortage of paper. Males over the age of fifteen, physicians, and anybody else of possible military use needn't bother applying.

Finding someplace to go was even harder than getting out. Croatia, Germany, and Italy were already flooded with Bosnian refugees. The United States had set a generous quota for Bosnians, but refugees needed to apply at the U.S. Embassy in Zagreb since there were no consular services in Sarajevo. But no one could get to Zagreb without a Croatian visa. Croatia granted visas sparingly and set up roadblocks with attack dogs at the borders. The United States never filled its quota for Bosnian refugees.

Desa Stanić planned to seek refuge in Hamburg, Germany, where her late husband's parents had gone. Desa was in closer contact with her in-laws a thousand miles away than with her own mother and siblings living in a Serb village, just across the front lines. She repeatedly asked the UN High Commissioner for Refugees for help evacuating herself and her injured son, who needed surgery to repair the damage from the shrapnel in his forehead.

"They told me there were children who were more seriously wounded who had to get out ahead of him," Desa said.

Those with connections and money could bypass the bureaucratic rigmarole. There was a thriving black market in forged documents. Everybody on Logavina Street knew exactly who you had to pay to obtain papers and how much they cost—even if they couldn't afford it themselves. By late 1994, it was estimated that more than a hundred thousand Sarajevans had skipped town, among them the best educated. Many translators and UN staff used their credentials to fly out on the airlift, never to return.

Delila was one of the few on Logavina Street who had a going-away party. The departures usually occurred in secrecy. People didn't want to say good-bye to their neighbors. They didn't want to flaunt their luck or risk being reported to the police. "After a while you notice that somebody is not in the neighborhood anymore, and then you find out they've gone to Italy or Germany," Ekrem Kaljanac told me with bitterness.

Mladen Marković vanished. One day in June 1994, he went off to the front lines, and he never came back. The neighbors believed he had been killed or that he had defected to the Serb side. Another theory was that he'd fled to Australia, since he'd often talked wistfully of emigrating there. "Why Australia? Because it is so far from this place," Mladen had explained to me a few months before. "It seems that we are all cursed in Bosnia. Every generation here has to live in war. I'm afraid my son will have another life like mine."

Desa Stanić was convinced that he had tried to join Veronika and his son in Germany. "He loved his wife so much, he would cry and cry when he looked at her picture," she said. "Whether he made it to Germany or not, nobody knows. We haven't heard from him." A few days after Mladen's disappearance, two Bosnian soldiers moved into his vacated apartment.

Desa asked them about Mladen, but the soldiers just shrugged. If they knew Mladen's secret, they were not telling.

Many Sarajevans thought it was shameful to leave, an admission of defeat. Ekrem made no secret of his disapproval when Kira and Mirsad and their infant son fled through the tunnel with hopes of sneaking illegally into Italy. "I'd like to bring back all those who escaped and let us who stayed go out for a while. We'll switch places and see how they like it," Ekrem said.

Minka was more forgiving, timidly admitting that she, too, would like to leave. Picking up a toy plane that her sons had left on the floor, she said, "Wouldn't I love to get in and fly away from here. Kira is not shy. I'm shy. If I were the kind of person who could knock on doors and ask for things, I would leave, too."

Deep into the third winter of war, almost everybody on Logavina Street was seriously considering leaving. The deliberations were anguished, and tearful. Many of the people I knew asked for help getting to the United States, but they all insisted that they would go abroad only if they could find work and support themselves with dignity.

The letters and phone calls that came from Sarajevans in exile were not encouraging. They couldn't find work; they didn't know the languages. Even Croatia had become a foreign country after the collapse of Yugoslavia.

Adnan Čaušević told me a story about a ten-year-old Bosnian refugee in Split whose mother sent him to buy bread. The boy asked for *hljeb*, the most common word for bread in Bosnia and Serbia, rather than *kruh*, the word favored by Croatians. The child was kicked out of the store, empty-handed.

"You talk about leaving. But as soon as you get to Croatia, you are homesick. We are not welcome there. You can see it in their faces," said Adnan.

Jela Džino left Sarajevo in October and returned after only three weeks. Her trip was extremely difficult. She left in the middle of the night because there was shelling at the entrance of the tunnel. Jela, fifty-five, with a huge gash in her leg, hiked alone in the dark and got lost during a driving rainstorm. She arrived muddy and bruised on the sun-baked Dalmatian coast, only to be stricken by an acute case of culture shock.

"Now if somebody would offer me a bag of gold, I wouldn't do it again," Jela said after returning to Sarajevo. She hated that her relatives would not let her smoke in the house. "I had to go to the park to smoke a cigarette. There was no way they could understand what we've been going through," Jela said. "They told me I was crazy to go back to Sarajevo. But I felt like there was no state that could take the place of my husband, my son, my home. I couldn't wait to get back."

Although bruised and battered, Sarajevans had fierce loyalty to their city. People feared that if they left, they might never come home again. It was a realistic concern. Men who escaped could be prosecuted for deserting the army. If you vacated your apartment in Sarajevo, it would be assigned within days to a refugee family on the waiting list. Bosnia, like other former Communist countries, had an acute housing shortage. And notwithstanding all the Sarajevans who had fled, the victims of ethnic cleansing continued to pour in.

To stay or to go was not merely a practical question but also a matter of ethics. Fuad Kasumagić felt a responsibility to his city and to the fifteen employees left working at his jewelry business. The first summer of the war he had sent his two teenage daughters out of the country. He could hardly bear to walk into their empty bedroom, where the posters of their idols, Johnny Depp and Patrick Swayze, were still tacked to the wall.

"I think about whether I should have tried to leave, too. The Jews during World War II had to decide, should they stay and try to protect their estates, or should they leave and save their heads. Of course, the ones who stayed lost both their heads and their estates. But for me, I don't think I could ever leave Sarajevo."

Kasema Telalagić felt that, as a mother, it would be better to take her son, Hamza, thirteen, and daughter, Dženana, five, out of the country. On the other hand, there was her husband, Dino, who didn't want to desert the army. She had serious contempt for all the doctors she worked with who had fled Sarajevo at the time their services were needed most.

"I know a doctor in Florida. He is cleaning swimming pools. Maybe he is satisfied with that. . . . I have a friend, a pediatrician. She went to Germany and the only job she was offered was washing old people's asses in a nursing home," Kasema said, rattling off their names with rancor. "I think it is too late to start from scratch. My son doesn't want to go, anyway. We will burn the last piece of furniture and clothing. We will live or die. There is no third option."

At the end of the third winter of war, the fog lifted and the snow melted from the mountains. Apart from the weather, conditions deteriorated. On April 9, 1995, the UN airlift was grounded again because of Serb anti-aircraft missiles pointed at the airport. Flights would not resume for more than five months. On May 7, eleven people waiting to cross through the tunnel were killed by a 120-millimeter mortar shell. Some were only going to get groceries in Hrasnica, the village on the other side of the tunnel.

Whatever semblance of order the United Nations had brought to Sarajevo disintegrated in the last week of May. Serb soldiers marched into a UN-guarded compound and rode off with confiscated tanks and heavy artillery that were off-limits under the latest cease-fire. In protest, NATO warplanes bombed a Serb ammunition depot near Pale.

The Serb retaliation was pitiless and highly effective. They shelled a strip of outdoor cafés in the northern Bosnian city of

Tuzla, killing seventy-one people, mostly teenagers. (Unlike the February 5, 1994, market bombing in Sarajevo, nobody bothered to deny it. Serb commander Ratko Mladić boasted that the shelling was punishment for the NATO air strikes.)[1]

Across Bosnia, the Serbs captured hundreds of UN peacekeepers as a deterrent to further air strikes. Pale television flaunted the Serbs' captives, broadcasting footage of the peacekeepers shackled to poles and bridges. On June 2, a U.S. F-16 flying above the Bosnian Serb stronghold of Banja Luka was shot down and disappeared.

"They are the UN Protection Forces, but they cannot even protect themselves," said Bosnian prime minister Haris Silajdžić.

It was almost unbelievable. The Republika Srpska, with a population of 800,000—about the size of Greater Pittsburgh—had brought the combined powers of the United Nations and NATO to their knees.

Sarajevo shuddered as it awaited its fate. Returning in the first week in June, I found the city bunkered down. On Logavina Street, freshly painted signs had reappeared on the intersections warning *Pazi Snajper*—"Danger Sniper." The Razija Omanović school was closed again because it was too dangerous for the students to walk to school. The few shops that had opened during the 1994 cease-fire were now closed.

The roads northwest of Sarajevo that the United Nations had been using for land convoys were now shut down. The Serbs stepped up their attacks on the Mount Igman Road, opening fire with anti-aircraft guns on the armored cars of journalists and aid workers. With the siege tightening, there was no flour or sugar for sale anywhere in Sarajevo.

I ran into Suada's sister-in-law, Aida, who was desperately looking for powdered milk. She had had a baby in May and her breast milk had dried up from poor nutrition. The monthly distribution of humanitarian aid had dwindled to one cup of oil and half a pound of dried peas, beans, and rice per person.

"Believe me. The person who is eating only that humanitarian aid is dead already," declared Jela.

The sense of abandonment was acute. "The whole world is protesting three hundred UN peacekeepers in chains while we, an entire nation, have been in chains for three years," complained Esad Taljanović.

The skies were temptingly sunny, the air balmy, but no one was out on Logavina Street. People only stirred when a slow yellow water truck drove up Logavina Street every few days. The tanker's arrival was eagerly awaited. Sometimes it came at 2 A.M., but everybody scrambled to meet it.

There had been no running water for a month, and the water-collection sites in town were being shelled regularly. The truck didn't dare stop on Logavina. The driver would park on a side street out of view from the hills and set up the hoses and spigots inside a concrete entryway. It took less than ten minutes for the truck to dispense its quota for the neighborhood, so only the quickest and pushiest people would get any water. The latecomers were inevitably left brandishing their empty jugs in fury.

"You've got to hurry if you want to get some," yelled Selma Kapić, rousing her brother, Mirza, from a nap on the sofa one afternoon as the truck stopped in front of the orphanage.

Their father, Fadil, explained that the kids were permitted outside only for the water truck. After what happened to Delila's parents, nobody wanted to risk his life fetching water in town. Besides, a boy about Mirza's age had been shot by a sniper walking by their front gate. Fadil didn't even let Selma and Mirza visit their mother, who was in Koševo Hospital after a heart attack—Fadil believed that the stress of the shelling had aggravated an early heart condition. Nobody in the family ever saw their favorite cousins, Lana and Maša Lačević, who had moved from the Logavina Street house to their own apartment fifteen minutes away.

"We love our cousins to death, but this family has seen enough tragedy," Fadil decreed.

People could seldom tell you the date or even what day of the week it was. "My brain has shrunk," Ekrem apologized in a husky voice of defeat. "It's like we are all dead. In 1993, maybe it was worse, but I can't compare the mood. Everybody is half-crazy now."

The Kaljanacs never went outside anymore. Minka had taken a job the year before at a snackbar in the Baščaršija owned by her sister's husband, Lala. Minka was now too scared to make the six-block walk to work. It didn't matter. Although the place was famous for Sarajevo's spicy meat dish, *čevapčići,* most customers were scared to leave their homes, too.

They no longer bad-mouthed the people who had skipped town. With the benefit of hindsight, Minka and Ekrem would have left as well. More and more Sarajevans were going. Desa Stanić, having failed to arrange a medical evacuation for her wounded son, also set off on foot through the tunnel with her children, hoping to somehow make it into Germany. Nermin Džino, barely recuperated from his hepatitis and already back on the front lines, defected from the army and escaped through the tunnel. It was a difficult decision for the Džinos, though as Jela explained, "The decision to save his life prevailed over patriotism."

These were desperate times, and they inspired foolish actions. On June 15, the Bosnian Army launched its biggest offensive to try to punch through the siege lines. More than twenty thousand soldiers were deployed to open the roads into Sarajevo. "There is nothing left in the city, no electricity, no water, no gas, no food, no medicines," explained President Alija Izetbegović in a statement read over BiH Television. "The world hasn't done anything to prevent it. . . . In a situation like this, our army has been given orders to prevent the further strangulation of the city."

Sarajevo heaved with explosions. Air raid sirens wailed incessantly. Quite literally, the entire city was smack in the middle of warring armies—cowering underneath a furious volley of mortar shells and rocket-propelled grenades. For three days, the noise was appalling. Then it stopped suddenly without explanation, but nobody needed to be told: The offensive had failed.

The revenge was pitiless. The Bosnian Serbs immediately attacked the water lines and the hospitals. In Koševo, a hepatitis patient was decapitated in his hospital bed by a mortar shell. The man's headless corpse lay undisturbed for hours because the doctors were too busy with the injured to move him. In the last two weeks of June, sixty-six civilians were killed in Sarajevo and more than three hundred were wounded.

If the world wasn't paying attention to Sarajevo, it was in part because the focus had shifted elsewhere—to Srebrenica. Once known for its rolling farmland and silver mines, it had been one of the six UN safe havens, populated mosly by Muslims from surrounding villages who had fled the earlier waves of ethnic cleansing in 1992. Srebrenica was unfortunately situated in the swatch of eastern Bosnia near the Drina River, bordering Serbia, directly in the path of the juggernaut for a "Greater Serbia."

After three years of siege, the town fell to the Serbs on July

11, 1995. The 42,000 inhabitants went running for their lives and most of them ran to a nearby UN base. There, the 400 Dutch soldiers of the 13th Air Mobile Infantry Battalion were quickly cowed by the Serbs. The women and children were rounded up and efficiently expelled by bus from the newly cleansed Serb lands. Thousands of men and boys are believed to have been summarily executed.[2]

Fatima Valjevac, sixty-five, eventually made her way to the orphanage at the top of Logavina Street. She arrived with nothing more than the clothes she was wearing. All her worldly possessions—a coffee grinder, a mixing bowl, a blood-pressure gauge, and five pairs of socks—were in a backpack that her husband, Salih, was carrying when he was taken away.

"We were all trying to get into the buses. Everybody was pushing and screaming. Salih was almost into the bus when they yelled at him to go with the other men."

"Don't take him. He's all I've got," pleaded Fatima. Her husband was sixty-eight years old, with a heart condition, and could never pass for a soldier. It was no use. Another man of nearly ninety, on crutches, fell to the ground in front of the Serb soldiers, begging to get on the bus. He, too, was dragged away.

Zarif Kaljević, sixty-one, lived in the orphanage room next to Fatima. He was from Žepa, another doomed UN safe haven that was overrun by the Serbs a few days after Srebrenica. He survived two weeks in a dugout next to his farmhouse as Žepa was being bombed, not daring to flee because his wife had suffered a stroke and could not move.

"There were so many mortar shells you couldn't blink your eyes between explosions," Kaljević said.

The men of Žepa were luckier than those of Srebrenica. When the shelling subsided, Zarif was able to carry his wife onto a bus bound for Sarajevo. She died six days after they arrived. Most estimates put the eventual death toll from Srebrenica at about 8,000.

The storming of Srebrenica and Žepa was stunning not just because of the brutality but because it occurred under the eyes of the United Nations. Refugees remember Serbs wearing stolen UN uniforms and blue helmets as they conducted their deadly business.

From around the world, there were calls for the United Nations to withdraw completely from Bosnia. In Sarajevo, people started enunciating the very name "Srebrenica" with the same hushed gravity as "Auschwitz."

The fate of Srebrenica made Bosnians wonder what might happen to Sarajevo if a UN enclave could be overrun with such impunity. Even the most resolute optimists had to admit that the situation had never looked grimmer.

12

INTERVENTION

ESAD TALJANOVIĆ WENT to bed early on Tuesday, August 29, 1995. There was no electricity. The days were getting shorter as the fourth winter of war approached. Esad was depressed.

There had been another grisly bloodbath the day before. Thirty-seven people had been killed by a shower of mortar shells in the middle of Maršala Tita Street, near the entrance to the indoor market hall. More dead Bosnians, more amputees, more recriminations and sputtering indignation from the United States and its allies. The United Nations and NATO were in discussons about the need to punish the guilty parties. Radovan Karadžić was suddenly talking about reopening peace talks, as he did whenever the heat was on. Esad was struck with a weary sense of déjà vu. He had heard it and seen it all before. Sleep was the only escape.

Esad slept soundly until just before 3 A.M., when his wife shook him awake. Šaćira had been on her way to use the bathroom when she saw a crimson glow in the night sky. Through the dining room window, they could see it silhouetting the rooftops on Logavina Street. They would have thought the sun was rising but the light was coming from the northwest. There were a couple of booms and a strange rumble, like an earthquake. The house seemed to shudder and the plastic sheeting over the windows rustled. What was it? Perhaps a new weapon of terror devised by the Bosnian Serb army? After so many years of dithering indecision, Esad and Šaćira could barely imagine that NATO had finally struck back.

"They had been crying wolf for three and a half years. I just didn't think they would ever really do it," Esad said later.

It was not until they heard the morning news that most Sarajevans realized that the mysterious nocturnal disturbances were the beginning of the largest military intervention in NATO's history.

From bases in Italy and from the aircraft carrier USS *Theodore Roosevelt* in the Adriatic, more than sixty planes were blitzing Serb military targets around Bosnia. They bombed an ammunition factory in Serb-held Vogošća—a Sarajevo suburb to the north, where Esad had worked in a dental clinic before the war. That produced the red glow Šaćira had seen. On a hillside south of the city, the planes targeted Lukavica, where the Serbs had their main military barracks. Shortly after 4 A.M., British and French UN troops stationed on Mount Igman opened fire with 105-millimeter howitzers on the military positions that the Serbs had used to terrorize travelers on the mountain road. It was eight miles away from Logavina Street, but the residents heard the firing clearly—a dull, repetitive thud.

"That was the most beautiful sound I heard in the entire war," Sead Vranić said later.

Sead and his wife, Vetka, stayed in bed when they realized

what was going on. Their eyes shut, they listened to the sound of the guns in the distance. It mingled with the sound of the muezzin calling the faithful to morning prayer.

Zijo and Jela Džino slept soundly throughout. The next day they turned on the television to watch the news. BiH Television was showing grainy aerial shots released by NATO of the bombs hitting their targets. They flipped the channels to Pale television, which was only broadcasting still pictures—their main transmitter had been knocked out by the air strikes. They sat and watched the disabled station, giggling like small children.

Kasema Telalagić also slept straight through the bombing. When she turned on the radio at 6 A.M., and heard the news, she suspected a hoax. As she walked downtown to work, she wondered why the general alert sirens were wailing and why the streets were so empty. Another window had been shattered overnight in the clinic. It seemed like just another day of shelling in Sarajevo.

"I don't believe it," she stubbornly insisted to her colleagues at the clinic. Another doctor, who had a view from his high-rise apartment in new Sarajevo, assured her it was true. NATO was pounding away at the Serbs. Kasema suggested somebody run out in search of a bottle of champagne. Everybody laughed. It was impossible to buy champagne in Sarajevo, but the doctors poured themselves shot glasses of whiskey and enjoyed a quick toast before getting down to work.

Ekrem Kaljanac was working the graveyard shift with the military police, and he knew what was happening immediately: The military had been notified a few minutes before the strikes. He had the satisfaction of standing out on the street and watching as the smoke curled up above the hills near Lukavica.

Minka was one of the few people on Logavina who had gone into the bomb shelter for the night. From the insulated basement of the Razija Omanović school, she could hear only muffled detonations. Drinking coffee and smoking through the night, Minka watched her boys sleeping peacefully on army cots and wondered what the bombing meant. Something momentous was happening. But Minka was unsure if it augured a new beginning of the war or, she dared to hope, the beginning of the end.

It was an indescribable delight to see the Serb bully get his punishment after three and a half years of torment, but the celebrating was subdued and private. As far as Logavina Street was concerned, August 28, 1995—forty-eight hours before the NATO air strike—had been the worst single day of the war. Five people in the immediate neighborhood were killed.

Merima Žiga, forty-two, a legal secretary at the trading company Svjetlost, was feeling ill and left work to see a doctor. Heading down Maršala Tita at midday, she walked directly into the trajectory of an incoming 120-millimeter mortar shell and was killed instantly. Unmarried, Merima lived at 31 Logavina with her father, Alija Žiga, who ran the mosque.

Adnan Ibrahimagić, seventeen, was supposed to have left town the Friday before to join his mother in Vienna. He had balked at the last minute, declaring, "I can't live without Sarajevo." And so on Monday, he went downtown with a friend to pick up a takeout lunch of Sarajevo's *ćevapčići* at a shop across from the market hall. Adnan ended up in the most widely published photograph of the massacre, a poster boy for genocide.

The gruesome picture showed his skinny teenage body,

dead, slumped over a railing outside the *čevapčići* shop. Surgeons amputated both the legs of his friend, sixteen-year-old Dario Glouhi, in an attempt to save his life. He died anyway. Both the boys lived around the corner from the Džinos on Hriste Boteva Street; they had been popular students at the Razija Omanović school.

"We all went and donated blood, but it didn't help," said Jela. "Everybody was out on the street, just crying and crying."

The death toll from August 28, 1995—which eventually rose to forty—was not the highest of the war. The market massacre the previous February and the shelling of the cafés in Tuzla were worse. Yet this one brought the timely punishment by the NATO air strikes, as much because of the political climate in Europe and the United States as the blood spilled on Maršala Tita Street. After the hostage crisis in the spring, the downing of the U.S. F-16, and the fall of Srebrenica, the international community needed to rescue its own credibility even more than Bosnia. Logavina residents, by now well-schooled cynics about American politics, also suspected that the Clinton administration wanted to resolve the Bosnia mess before the upcoming reelection campaign.

"Maybe if the United States had presidential elections every year, we wouldn't have had to wait so long," Jela ventured. "But they should have done it earlier and not waited for so many people to be killed and crippled."

The first round of air strikes lasted fifty hours and resumed after a four-day breather for another nine days. NATO pilots flew more than 3,200 sorties over Bosnia and destroyed ammunition depots, command and control bunkers, and communications facilities. U.S. Tomahawk cruise missiles launched from the Adriatic took out anti-aircraft missile sites near Banja Luka.

. . .

Anti-interventionists had warned that air strikes could ignite a wider war, perhaps a rerun of World War I that would draw in Russia, the last ally of the Bosnian Serbs. The doomsday scenarios did not materialize. The Russians protested but made no move to get involved. The Bosnian Serbs shot down a French plane near Pale but did not take any more hostages.

If NATO didn't cripple the Serbs' military, it at least convinced them that the price of continued war would be high. The shelling of Sarajevo stopped, and the Bosnian Army took advantage of the chaos in the Bosnian Serb Army. Backed this time by Croatian forces, government troops swept through central and northwestern Bosnia, reclaiming 1,500 square miles of territory. The map of Bosnia, which had been frozen in place for three and a half years, was radically redrawn in less than thirty days.

There was no defining moment that marked the end of the war. There was no happiness that was not tempered by grief over past losses or by trepidation about the uncertain future.

Sarajevans carried a practiced air of negativity about them, protecting themselves against disappointment. They viewed the events that transpired in the last months of 1995 with skepticism. Things unfolded in a blur of change too fast to grasp.

On September 15, the humanitarian airlift resumed after a five-month absence. The attacks on Mount Igman stopped and the mountain road filled bumper to bumper with trucks hauling commercial goods bound for the city. The United Nations opened a road by the Sarajevo airport; all traffic did not have to squeeze through the funnel of the muddy tunnel anymore.

On Maršala Tita, a Benetton store opened, with sandbags

protecting its plate-glass windows. Sarajevo's markets filled with Western European consumer goods—Spanish melons, Toblerone chocolate bars, German beers. People surveyed these offerings appreciatively—like seeing old friends after a long absence—but they parceled out their last German marks to buy potatoes and firewood.

Minka splurged and bought a liter of fresh milk for Tarik, who, at five, had no recollection of drinking anything but powdered milk. "It cost us 2 German marks [$1.40] and he drank it all up in a minute as though it were water," said Minka. "But who knows when he'll have another chance?"

Ekrem agreed. "The roads are open now, sure. But believe me, once the profiteers fill up their shelves, they will jack up the prices again and it will be over," he said. As he tended his chicken coop behind the apartment house, Ekrem waved his left hand, the one with the missing fingertips, at Mount Trebević and pronounced ominously: "By springtime, you won't be able to stand here without wearing your bulletproof vest."

It was as difficult to adapt to peace as it had been to war. Nobody trusted the unaccustomed calm. The situation bore an uncanny resemblance to the ephemeral cease-fire in the summer of 1994. People didn't want to be lured into a false sense of security or to be caught unprepared again for a winter of war. The Bosnian Serb militia was still entrenched in its bunkers on Trebević. It was a bit like having a paroled murderer living within firing range of your bedroom window. They might be disarmed at present, but how could Sarajevans sleep soundly?

"Our enemies are still around us. They are quiet now. I think NATO frightened them. They will behave until the world forgets," Kasema told me in mid-September. "I have to think it will be better or else I can't go on. At the same time, I try not to think too much about the future. So many times I was disappointed."

On October 10, the lights came back on in a flash, as though somebody had flipped a switch. The Bosnian government had demanded the restoration of utilities as a condition for signing a cease-fire agreement. With its army plunging ahead in northwestern Bosnia, the government was finally in a position to make demands.

The power returned around dusk—the windows of the apartment buildings sparkling with rectangles of light. On Vase Miskina, a popcorn kiosk gave off an unnaturally bright fluorescence. The streetlights cast an asymmetrical glow—none of the bulbs matched. It wasn't exactly Paris, but Sarajevans strolled along the pavements as proudly as if it were the Champs-Elysées.

Logavina Street had no working streetlights—they had all been shot out and they dangled from wires over the middle of the street. But Kasema Telalagić's husband, Dino, switched on the huge pink-and-blue neon sign for his auto-body shop in front of the house. It was like a garish lighthouse, basking the street in a mystical violet light.

The pool hall at the foot of Logavina blasted the street with the Rolling Stones. You could hear a cacophony of stereos, televisions, vacuum cleaners, and washing machines. They were back in the twentieth century.

With the electricity, running water was restored, since the pumps in the municipal reservoir were electrically powered. Distrustful of how long the utilities would last, most people seized the chance to catch up on their household chores.

Sarajevans weren't sitting home and worrying in the dark anymore, but they worried just the same. In November, their concerns shifted to *"Dejton,"* where the future of Bosnia was to be decided. The presidents of Bosnia, Croatia, and Serbia were sequestered inside the Wright-Patterson Air Force Base in Dayton, Ohio, for twenty days.

The peace plan pushed by the United States followed the outlines of a proposal worked out the previous year that gave 49 percent of Bosnia to the Serbs and 51 percent to the Muslims and Croats. ("I suppose it's okay. If it were a corporation, you'd say we were the majority stockholder," Esad Taljanović quipped at the time.) In 1994, the partition was grudgingly accepted by Izetbegović but rejected by the Serbs, who would have had to return territory.

In 1995, the reality on the ground was dramatically different. The Bosnian Army's autumn offensive had squeezed the Serbs' territories from 70 percent of the country to just under 50 percent. The Serbs were eager to accept, fearing more losses. A powerful sweetener had been added: They would get recognition of their Republika Srpska—albeit within the larger framework of something called the Bosnian Federation.

Bosnia-Herzegovina, as drafted in Dayton, would be a most unconventional country. The mapmakers drew squiggly lines running this way and that, carving the country into two entities. The Serb holdings were scattered through western and eastern Bosnia, so a corridor was carved out through the north to connect them. The occupied suburbs of Sarajevo, including Ilidža, were to be handed back to the government, to open unimpeded roads out of the capital. There would be no more trips over Mount Igman, no more tunnels.

From a moral standpoint, it was hard to stomach the deal. The Serbs would hold on to Srebrenica and Žepa, lands that had been more than 70 percent Muslim before the war and that had suffered the worst genocide in Europe since the Nazis.

Perhaps for the first time, Sarajevans grasped what should have been obvious long before: They were not going to win the war. For all the NATO bombs and Tomahawk missiles invested in Bosnia, the West was not going to hand them the victory they thought they deserved.

The streets of Sarajevo were deserted as a powdery snow fell over the city the night of November 21, when the peace plan was being initialed thousands of miles away in Dayton. If there was rejoicing, it was done in the privacy of people's homes. The city reeled with powerful and contradictory emotions. A large mortar shell exploded and there was a barrage of gunfire just as President Clinton began a televised speech to proclaim peace in Bosnia. It was unclear whether the firing had been done in anger or in joy.

Jela and Zijo watched the Dayton ceremonies on television and took their cues from Izetbegović's funereal demeanor. Jela couldn't help but notice that Serbian president Slobodan Milošević and Croatian president Franjo Tuđman gave hearty handshakes to the U.S. diplomats, while Izetbegović averted his eyes throughout.

Jela shook her head disapprovingly as the deal was explained and muttered to her husband, "This may be peace, but it isn't justice."

Step by step, Sarajevo came back to life. Still mostly based there, I witnessed its slow emergence into normal life over the first months of 1996. On the street that Sarajevans were still calling Sniper Alley the police were armed with radar guns and started handing out speeding tickets. The traffic lights were switched back on.

A travel agency opened across from the market hall. A

poster tacked to the glass door advertised the sunny beaches near Dubrovnik. A newsstand on Maršala Tita started selling English-language reading material, although the *International Herald Tribune* was a month old and the computer magazines dated back as far as 1991.

At lunchtime, U.S. marines strolled down the Vase Miskina pedestrian mall. They were a small part of the contingent of 20,000 American soldiers—most of them in the northern Bosnian city of Tuzla—who had been dispatched under the NATO flag to implement the peace agreement. People stopped and nodded approvingly. America was back in vogue. There was even a Dayton Café.

After the war, Sarajevo became an extravaganza of coffee bars—new ones opened daily out of the shells of burnt storefronts. Each announced itself with a neon sign gaudier than the café next door—as though the brazen lights might erase three and a half years of darkness. There must have been more cafés per capita in Sarajevo than pubs in Milwaukee, but they were all crowded with young people. The young men wore Levi's 501s; their girlfriends favored Euro-style black leggings and brown lipsticks. President Izetbegović disapproved and spoke with increasing vehemence about Islamic values. In his New Year's address, he scolded BiH for broadcasting shots of rowdy New Year's Eve parties. Bosnia should not be open to Western vices like "alcohol, pornography, drugs, and debauchery of all kinds," Izetbegović declared. The kids paid no heed.

At the foot of Logavina Street, the Caffe Elvis now opened until a few minutes before curfew, which had been pushed back to 11 P.M. With its new plate-glass window and photographs of the King, immortally young, lining the walls, the place seemed untouched by war. Even the big Bozadžijina mosque at the corner of Logavina and Markovića plastered over the pockmarks, and its minaret was illuminated with bands of bright white lights, clearly visible from Mount Trebević. It didn't matter. There had not been a mortar shell on the street since late August.

Logavina Street was noisy, drivers honking when the traffic got bad at the intersection with Maršala Tita. They were renovating the wing of Razija Omanović elementary school, which was vacated by the Bosnian Army at the end of November. The school desperately needed more classrooms, the student population having been swollen by refugees and Sarajevans in exile slowly returning to their homes.

The shoemaker was working, and the pharmacy was open. The supermarket on Logavina set aside half of its space for shoppers with enough money to buy imported German orange juice, Slovenian chickens, and pretty much all other basic consumer products. In the other half, they still distributed bread and humanitarian aid.

Garbage was piled high on the sidewalk in front of the mosque—there were no regular collections yet. You could see half-eaten tangerines and crusts of bread in the mound, the discards of the affluent.

The average monthly income for a family of four was 45 German marks, about $30. The most popular features on the radio were the public service messages announcing which charities would be giving out aid. Few Logavina residents had gotten around to replacing the plastic sheeting on their windows. Reports were that an Italian charity would be distributing panes of glass for free.

At the top of Logavina Street, the old Muslim cemetery

held 561 graves for people who had perished since the beginning of the war.

The neighbors still referred to the old place at 63 Logavina as the Lačević house, though no Lačevićs lived there. The pre-war occupants were all dead or departed. It was a sad house, made even gloomier by the frequent crying from Mejasa Kapić across the street.

Ever since the night the Dayton pact was announced, Mejasa had been in mourning. Her hometown was given to the Serbs at the last minute in order to seal the deal. Derventa—as a stroke of bad luck would have it—lay smack in the middle of the corridor that Serbs demanded to link up their territory. Mejasa's sister-in-law, Šaćira, a doctor, had been giving her tranquilizers, but it didn't help. Mejasa was so upset, everybody feared she would suffer another heart attack.

"This is a nice house, but it is not ours. We have no way of making a living here. We are hardworking people. We're not used to sitting around collecting humanitarian aid," Mejasa said.

Her husband, Fadil, was in a state that hovered between shock and denial. For three and a half years in exile, living in humiliating poverty and homelessness, the Kapićs believed that they would return to their home, the land their ancestors had farmed since the 1700s. The Bosnian Army was less than twenty miles from Derventa before the cease-fire.

"I don't really care about peace for all of Bosnia. Derventa is everything that matters to me," declared Fadil, his ruddy face reddening in anger. "My personal opinion is we will get Derventa back, with bullets if we need to. . . . This deal isn't fair. The 51 percent of Bosnia that we get will be for Muslims,

Croats, and Serbs. The 49 percent that goes to them will be only for Serbs."

The Dayton pact required the Serbs to permit expelled Muslims and Croats to return. The NATO troops that replaced the United Nations forces were supposed to withdraw at the end of 1996. Who would protect the returning refugees after NATO left? The Kapićs had no intention of setting foot in Derventa while the Serbs were in control.

Fadil still got up at 5 A.M. to scour the trash heaps near the orphanage. He collected pieces of broken metal appliances and used them to build a huge stove that could be fueled by gas, firewood, or garbage, depending on what was available.

Selma would turn eighteen the following month; Mirza was going on sixteen. They were not children anymore. They found their parents' constant talk of Derventa tiresome. They spent as little time in the house as possible. If by chance Fadil and Mejasa were able to return home, their children wanted to stay in Sarajevo to complete their education.

Sead and Vetka Vranić were bundled in thick sweaters on a Sunday afternoon. The gas was off today. Because Bosnia was in debt to the Russian company that owned the gas pipeline, their supply was rationed to every other day. The Vranićs dared not switch on their electric heater. It used three kilowatts per hour and the electricity was rationed, too—only six kilowatts a day per household were allowed.

The Vranićs did not have enough money to buy firewood. Sead started a neighborhood grocery in 1994, around the corner on Remzije Omanović, but it didn't prosper. Sead had some hat-making machines in storage. His grandfather used to have a factory that produced fezzes—the tasseled felt hats popular among Muslim men before World War II. He thought about trying to start a hat factory, but men don't wear many hats these days—let alone fezzes.

Everybody was more or less equally badly off during the siege, but now the Vranićs were realizing how poor they were, compared to people in Sarajevo with money—translators, drivers, the UN and NATO local employees, and the black marketeers.

"It makes me happy to see a Benetton. But let's be honest, not many of us have the money to go shopping. Psychologically, it is better. You can go out on the street without getting killed, but you can't go out and earn your living," Sead said. "We've got everything in Sarajevo now, everything but money."

Every now and then, somebody would knock on the imposing wooden gates to inquire about the pink house with the embossed golden peacocks. Usually it was an embassy looking for headquarters in Sarajevo. The Vranićs wouldn't budge. Their big house might be impossible to heat, but they had survived this war without selling off their antiques or even burning Sead's sports magazines—and they weren't going to vacate their house either.

Kasema Telalagić was radiant. She had a new job in the ophthalmology wing of Koševo Hospital, and a chic new haircut. No matter she had gone entirely gray over the years of war. At thirty-nine, she looked younger and livelier than I'd ever seen her.

"You maybe cannot understand what a great thing it is to turn on your faucet to wash the dishes, to put the laundry in the washing machine, to look out the window at the hills and see all the lights. . . . At the beginning when it was quiet, I woke up at night and couldn't believe that you couldn't hear even gunfire. Now I sleep all through the night without once waking up."

Kasema stayed up late after her children had gone to sleep, with the bedside light switched on beside her. She had unpacked the wedding crystal and paintings that she had stored away at the beginning of the war. She hoped to take a summer vacation. Her husband had been demobilized from the Bosnian Army, along with thousands of other men over the age of thirty. He worked late into the night at the auto-body shop, mostly replacing bullet-shattered windshields. It was a booming business.

Jovan Divjak hated it when diplomats, NATO military, and other foreigners shook his hand with congratulations on the peace plan—or even worse, raised glasses toward him in restaurants in a toast. The portly general was normally one of the most popular figures in Sarajevo, but lately he had been too much of a pessimist to be charming.

"This peace plan is a reward for ethnic cleansing. It's a farce. It was in Clinton's interest to shove Bosnia under the rug until after the elections and not to solve the situation at all," he ranted.

As proof of the American government's hypocrisy, he cited U.S. intelligence reports estimating that up to eight thousand Muslims from Srebrenica and Žepa had been murdered, their remains scattered in mass graves.

"How can they let Srebrenica and Žepa remain in the hands of the aggressor when the fate of these people is still unknown?" Divjak demanded of any American who chanced to cross his path. "How can you expect us to be celebrating?"

.   .   .

Ekrem and Minka Kaljanac had always vowed they would never swallow a partition of Bosnia. But when it came down to it, they realized they would take peace at any price.

During the last days of peace negotiations, Minka was watching the news out of Dayton, practically screaming at Izetbegović: "Sign it! Sign that damn thing now!" They still hadn't quite come to grips with peace. At the stroke of midnight New Year's Eve, when the skies over Sarajevo opened up with a fusillade of gunfire and rocket-propelled grenades, Ekrem had to pinch himself to remember it was only celebration—not war.

Ekrem was demobilized from military duty on December 22, along with thousands of other soldiers. He now lounged around the apartment in a T-shirt and sweatpants, luxuriating in the novelty of peacetime.

"It's a great feeling, not to have to shave every day, not to have to touch a gun," he said. "After two and a half years going to the police at the one A.M. shift, kissing my kids good-bye after midnight, I'm ready for a rest."

Ekrem didn't have much choice. Shortly after his demobilization, he took his discharge papers to the state-owned company where he'd worked before the war. There was a new general manager—a woman he'd never met before—and a roomful of other unfamiliar employees, some of them refugees.

"You'll have to wait. We have nothing for you now," said the general manager, brushing him off.

During the war years, most state companies didn't operate at full staffing, if they operated at all. But the savvier former employees made payments to management to hold places for them on the employment rolls, Ekrem said. "It's not legal, but that's the way things work here." He also suspected that refugees would get first dibs at new jobs opening up, making the market tough for guys like him. He wanted to learn English or German, and he had enrolled his older son in a computer course to make sure his son's prospects would be brighter.

"It's weird now. We've solved one problem and now we have a whole new bunch of problems. The war might be over, but the economic and political war is just beginning."

No matter. Ekrem was profoundly exhausted. What he really wanted was to take a vacation at the seashore, "to pull a beach chair into the shade and read the newspaper, knowing that there isn't a sniper watching me, that nobody is out there trying to kill me.

"When I'm fully rested, I'll figure out something to do."

In the orphanage on Logavina Street, the refugees from Žepa and Srebrenica inhabited a warren of tiny rooms looking out onto a squalid airshaft. Their rooms were on the damp lowest floor, as though to signify their place in the hierarchy of refugees. The people of eastern Bosnia were scorned in Sarajevo as *seljaci*—villagers—and their attire made them unmistakable on the streets. Most of the women wore shawls over their heads and baggy floral pantaloons known as *dimije*.

The women sewed to pass the time; the men played chess in an adjoining room, where a cloud of cigarette smoke hung heavy as a depression. They seldom left the orphanage.

"If it were up to me, I'd go back to Žepa in a minute," declared Zarif Kaljević. "I don't have a wife there anymore. I don't have a house. The Serbs burned everything when we fled, but I have land, and with land I can build something again."

None of the refugees had a job, and none stood much chance of finding a permanent home in Sarajevo. In 1996, the city was in the midst of a tremendous real estate crunch, between the hundred thousand refugees it harbored and the Sarajevans who were moving back. Foreigners were renting one-bedroom apartments at $700 a month.

The refugees would rather have returned home, but since they had to stay here, they had a plan to find housing. "If a Serb is living on my property, a Serb here should give me his property," said Bego Heljić, sixty-nine, the oldest and most outspoken of the group. "The Serbs can live here and nobody does them any harm. It's not fair. If we can't live in Žepa, why should they be allowed to live here?"

The other men nodded furiously in agreement. The logic sounded impeccable.

Milutin Đurđevac wore a frayed hunting jacket, its elbows so ragged it looked as though the sleeves might fall off. His kitchen was coated with smoke from the objects he and his wife had burned to stay warm during the siege. He didn't mind; it was his home and he was here to stay until his last days.

"I bought this apartment. I don't want to leave," said Milutin. His hands were shaking worse than ever, but his mind and convictions were clear.

The only people who would chase him out were the *seljaci* who had brought their village culture and deep reservoirs of anger into the city. Milutin also blamed Izetbegović's ruling Party of Democratic Action (Stranka Demokratske Akcije, or SDA), which, despite its ambiguous name, was an exclusively Muslim party. Although he still held Karadžić responsible for this war, Đurđevac feared the next war would be started by Muslim extremists. "It will be like a dormant volcano that erupts after five to ten years," the old man predicted.

Sarajevo was not so hospitable to non-Muslims. The Serb population had dwindled to about twenty-five thousand, less than 10 percent. Milutin introduced me to his neighbor across the hall. Vesna Miletić was a young widow. Her late husband, Živojin, a Serb who was loyal to the Bosnian government, was killed on the front lines in May 1995, leaving Vesna with a six-month-old baby to raise alone.

Vesna told how she took her young son and went with some friends in similar situations to visit a Kuwaiti charity that was giving out 50 German marks each to children of killed soldiers. At the front of the line, a young man questioned Vesna about her religion. She told him she was born a Catholic and that her husband was raised Orthodox, though neither was religious. She was turned away because her infant son had no Muslim roots.

"I started crying. I was so embarrassed. I wouldn't have gone if I knew. My husband was in the Bosnian Army, like everyone else. I didn't think we were any different," Vesna said.

Zijo and Jela couldn't decide what they should do with the car. It was trapped in their garage in the backyard. They had had to tear up the driveway—they needed the vegetable garden—but now they were on the horns of a dilemma.

The Džinos hadn't used the car since the first weekend of April 1992, when they had last visited their weekend house in Dobroševići—a village northwest of Sarajevo. Under the peace plan, the village was to revert to Bosnian government control. They had no idea if their house had been torched or if there were so many land mines in the area that they couldn't safely get near it.

They had talked about taking a drive to the Adriatic coast to visit Jela's relatives, but so far they hadn't plucked up the courage. Some braver souls were already driving out of Sarajevo through Ilidža, but there had been problems. Nineteen

Sarajevans were arrested the first week of January; some of them were beaten. Jela thought it was better to wait.

They were considering selling the car—it was a 1982 Volkswagen Jetta that could fetch a few thousand German marks if they patched up the shrapnel holes. But they had always planned on giving it to their son, Nermin. Now he was living in Johannesburg with his sister, Alma. After serving nearly three years on the front lines, Nermin was officially classified as a deserter. His parents expected that an amnesty would be passed, but even so, it would be hard for him to find work.

"He's not a member of the SDA. None of us are in this house, and that's the only way to get a job," Jela said in a nervous whisper.

Alma, who was working as a laboratory assistant since the South Africans didn't recognize her physician's license, was reluctant to return because she was married to a Serb, Siniša, who the family feared would not be accepted back now.

"My children will never live in Sarajevo again," Jela predicted with bitterness. "Who knows if they'll ever make enough money to even visit?"

Zijo and Jela missed their family more than anything. Zijo spent a couple of days trying to figure out the VCR—Nermin knew how to work it—and they popped in a videotape from Johannesburg. Their granddaughter, Mateja, now eight, spoke English on the tape. They couldn't understand a word she was saying.

Desa Stanić returned. Her cheeks flushed with excitement, Desa flipped on the overhead lamp and surveyed each of the rooms of her Logavina apartment. She could hardly believe it when she looked out the living room window at the lights twinkling from the hillsides. She was happy to be home.

"The people here look more beautiful than ever," she exclaimed.

Seven months in exile, Desa had always felt like an alien. Even Zagreb was like a foreign country. "I couldn't get used to the language. The minute I opened my mouth, the Croatians could tell I was from Bosnia. And if I told anybody my first name, they knew I was Serb."

Her kids, Marijana and Vedran, had been able to get Croatian passports immediately because their father was a Bosnian Croat Catholic. Desa's application had been rejected. The children had had to go to their grandparents in Hamburg alone— German authorities didn't require Croatian citizens to get visas. Desa eventually got into Germany, but only after paying somebody 2,500 marks to smuggle her over the border.

Desa would live alone in Sarajevo until her children returned. They stayed in Hamburg because her husband's family was still trying to raise money for the surgery to repair Vedran's forehead.

Her own mother and siblings lived in Rajlovac, a Serb-held suburb eight miles to the northwest. Desa hadn't spoken to them since 1992. The barricades were removed in January, but Desa was scared to try to visit.

"I'm not really sure if my mother is alive. I heard that she had a stroke," Desa said hesitatingly. "And I don't know. Will we still understand each other? There has been so much propaganda."

Even coming back to Sarajevo on a bus that crossed through Ilidža, Desa was terrified as she peeked out the window at the Bosnian Serb military police that lined the side of the road. She only felt truly at home in downtown Sarajevo.

. . .

Alija Žiga returned to an empty apartment and blinked in confusion as he looked around for coffee to serve visitors. He was a stranger in his own kitchen.

"My daughter cooked and washed and did everything," he apologized. "She didn't want to get married. She wanted to stay with me," Žiga said as he searched for the coffee.

It was perhaps more tragic to be one of the last victims in war than one of the first. There is something especially sense-less about having survived three and a half years of siege and then perishing in the last big massacre, as Žiga's daughter Mer-ima did.

Alija Žiga had always believed the United States would ul-timately rescue Bosnia—just as he was saved from starvation as a partisan soldier trapped behind German lines in World War II.

"It came too late. My daughter didn't need to die," Žiga said.

He pined not only for his daughter but also the Bosnia that was lost in the war. With an old man's nostalgia, he reminisced about the days when he would donate money to the Orthodox church, and when his Orthodox friends gave him painted eggs for Easter. There were traces of that Bosnia left. His elderly upstairs neighbor, Mara, whose sons fought on the other side, was the first to knock on his door with coffee and a bag of sugar—a traditional Bosnian gift of condolence—after Meri-ma's death.

"I'm seventy-three years old now, not twenty-three, and I can't hope much for things to be better," he said. "We would all like to go back to the way it was when nobody asked your reli-gion, or cared. But now? I don't know. After so many people are killed, how can we trust the Serbs again?"

. · .

It was a Sunday afternoon, but Esad Taljanović had just finished with a patient. His private practice was booming—the wartime diet had been unkind to teeth, and the first thing people did with a little money was visit the dentist.

"It makes me feel better to work. I want to work and nothing else." Esad shrugged as he sank wearily into a chair at the dining room table.

"There are cinemas open now, concerts, restaurants. I never go out. I am exhausted after four years of war. I am realizing now that I am one of those whose psyche is very distressed. I watched the last massacre at the market on television, like it was a movie. A normal person would be shocked, scandalized. I just sat there.

"What can we do with ourselves now?" he asked. "What I'd really like to do is talk to my old friends, Serbs who left, and ask why? Why did you do it? But we can't have everybody knocking on doors, pointing fingers at who's guilty. All I want is for my children to grow up. I lost my father during this war. I could go out and kill a hundred Serbs and it wouldn't bring my father back. There is no way that anybody can take the position that we can't live together again. We lived together for decades, shared the same food, shared the same beds. Four years should not be enough to separate us. I'm against the Muslim extremists, just like I am against all the extremists.

"I'm so tired of this war," Esad said again, slumping lower in his chair. His wife, Šaćira, brought coffee and the conversation turned to economics. "Maybe Bosnia has to be partitioned for now. But you remember what happened in Berlin," he said. "They had bread in the West, none in the East, and the people on the other side practically beat down the wall to get at it. It will be up to the side that has a good economy to bring about reconciliation. We need democratic elections and a free market economy. Maybe the Germans will open a Volkswagen factory here. All this humanitarian aid is the kiss of death. The cans, the packets of flour and rice, they'll make us idiots.

"When you work, you don't have time to do anything stupid. When you work ten hours a day, you forget everything. We have to forget. There is no looking back, only forward."

In front of the market hall, on the exact location where a mortar exploded August 28, 1995, in the last massacre of the war, mourners put together a small memorial, with wildflowers and roses. Police removed it in mid-January, after it kept getting knocked over by cars and buses streaming down Maršala Tita Street.

All that identified the spot were four paper notices, printed simply in black and white and plastered to the outside of the market wall, like theater advertisements. The message read:

Sarajlije nikada neće zaboraviti
"Sarajevans will never forget."

The corners of the notices were curled and starting to peel away from the wall.

13

RETURN TO LOGAVINA STREET

July 2011

JULY IS THE HIGH SEASON in Sarajevo. In the evenings until around 2 A.M., the streets—from the old Turkish market to the cathedral—stream with lovers, giggling teenagers, and families with children who should have been in bed hours ago. Many of them are Bosnian, and they are flocking home from the diaspora to visit their families and spend their money hard earned in Australia, South Africa, Canada, or the United States. If they're not strolling with a cigarette, they probably have an ice cream cone—the most popular flavor the secret-formula vanilla from the Egipat sweet shop, so sugary it gives you a buzz. The Sarajevo Film Festival, started in 1995 to boost the city's wartime morale, is under way, so there's also a gaggle of celebrities. Angelina Jolie is in town to receive an honorary award, having directed her first film in Bosnia the year before, and the city basks in the gratification of her presence. The narrow streets near the National Theater are blocked off by police, and the sidewalk, around what is now called Susan Sontag Square, is covered with red carpet. Behind a roped-off VIP section, young women with bare shoulders and teased hair strut on precarious heels, their cheeks slashed purple with blusher. There's no such thing as too much makeup in Sarajevo. No such thing as too much noise either. The cafés have set out their loudspeakers alongside wicker chairs. They compete for customers decibel by decibel, so as you walk down the street you transition from one noise cluster to the next. People might complain that Sarajevo has become an Islamic city, but the disco music drowns out the call to prayer. The muezzins don't stand a chance against "Funkytown."

People struggle to find the words to describe Sarajevo's spirit—its magic, its joie de vivre, that special *schmeckt* (the German word for flavor). Whatever it is, Sarajevo still has it. It's in the people, in their attitude, but also in the look and feel of the place. Three architectural styles dominate, the most pleasing being the sixteenth-century stone structures of the old Turkish market, or Baščaršija, which were built like citadels and have survived more or less as they did in wars past. Then there are the balustraded façades of the Austro-Hungarian buildings, their look of faded grandeur exaggerated by the largely unrepaired pockmarks of the mortar shells. The least durable buildings were the modernist concrete and glass contraptions of the Communist years in the *novi grad,* or new city; in fact, their demolition might have improved the scenery. Instead, they were rebuilt after the war in all their glaring ugliness, even the stained concrete television building on the road to the airport. The Holiday Inn has been repaired with the same mustard-yellow glass panels that were blown out by the mortar shells from Grbavica. There's a new mini-mall next door and another a little down the road. Otherwise there's not much new: The big excitement is that Bosnia's first McDonald's opened last week on Maršala Tita Street. People are still queuing outside.

. . .

Since the 1990s, I've been back to Sarajevo twice, once in 2007 and more recently in 2011. Each time, I was struck by how much it looked and felt the same. Now that I'm living in Asia, I'm accustomed to dynamic cities constantly reinventing themselves. When I leave Beijing for a holiday, I come back to find the building next door demolished and a new skyscraper rising in my backyard. Not Sarajevo. The city is timeless, almost immutable. Along the stone alleys of the Baščaršija, the jewelers are tapping away behind storefronts with the same names: Kasumagić, Čengić. Even the music is the same 1980s technopop.

So little has changed on Logavina Street I can almost navigate my way with my eyes closed. At the foot of the street, there's the Caffe Elvis. Overhead a messy cat's cradle of electric wires. The metal handrail we used to grab on icy days is still on the left side of the steepest, narrowest first block; the Restaurant Libertas is advertised by a red neon sign. When I peer through the arched windows, there are no customers.

In front of the mosque on the first corner is a pack of half a dozen of the same dun-colored stray dogs, or perhaps their descendants, glaring at me through half-closed eyes. From the outside, the grocery doesn't look much different from the days when it distributed humanitarian aid. Underneath a car parked on the sidewalk, I can see where the pavement was gouged out by a mortar shell, the shrapnel splashing out in a circular pattern from the point of impact. A civic group that started up in the mid-1990s poured red resin into the indentations to make them into a memorial—they call them "Sarajevo roses," though I think the old name we used during the war, "pawprints," is truer to their appearance.

Only the Razija Omanović school across the street has been renovated, thanks to a grant from the Norwegian government. It looks more or less the same except for the plaques giving the names of forty-one soldiers from the neighborhood killed during the war. Many of the names are familiar: Pero Stanić (1951–1993), Desa's late husband. Alden Hajrić (1974–1994), the nephew of Suad Hajrić.

The Džino house is my first stop on Logavina Street. I rented a room from Jela and Zijo while writing my book, and they are the family in Sarajevo I have stayed most closely in touch with. Their house is far from the grandest on the street, though it is painted in a confident fin de siècle pink. A wooden gate with a No Parking sign leads in from the street. I push it open without knocking. The wooden gate opens to the cobblestoned driveway and passes under an arbor of green grapes. Despite their advancing years, they have kept up the garden that sustained them through the war. Onions, chard, beans, and squash are planted in tidy rows, although the flowers are wild, a profusion of blue hydrangeas and yellow rhododendron. It is just past dinnertime, at least for people in their seventies.

Jela and Zijo are watching TV in the small kitchen downstairs next to the garden. The same bronze clock I remember, from the Sarajevo Olympics, hangs on the wall. They spent most of their time in that room during the war because it was safer; now it is more convenient because it saves Jela the trouble of climbing the stairs. She has pain where her left leg was gouged by the mortar shell, and she is broader in the hips than before. But she looks well, her hair dyed a flattering shade of terracotta and her toothy smile still girlish despite years of chain-smoking. Zijo is sprightly, but while he keeps his weight low and doesn't smoke, he has had a heart attack and his overall health isn't as good as his wife's.

Jela gives me the news from the street. Who has gotten divorced and remarried. Who has emigrated to the United States or Canada or Australia or Germany. Who got rich and who is unemployed—more of the latter than the former. Although I've forgotten most of what little Serbo-Croatian I knew, it is easy to understand because the refrain is the same as during the war: *Nema ništa*, "There's no nothing." Jela takes a drag of her cigarette, now a fancy-looking new brand called Aura instead of her old Drinas. "The economy collapsed during the war and it continues to go down."

The Džinos live on modest pensions from the state-owned factories where they worked before retiring. Jela's textile factory and Zijo's housewares company both closed down after the war. To the extent that new businesses have come in, they're small—cafés, boutiques. That's why there was so much excitement about the McDonald's. The timeless quality about Sarajevo that I selfishly find so appealing, Jela points out, is the mark of a failed economy. There's nothing new.

Only because they were sent money by their daughter, Alma, a psychiatrist living in South Africa, were they able to patch over the hole where the mortar shell slammed into their kitchen. Many of their neighbors' houses still have war damage for lack of money for repairs.

The statistics bear out what Jela is saying. Salaries in Bosnia are among the lowest in Europe, between 350 and 400 euros monthly, and unemployment about the highest, 46 percent. The World Bank in its annual Ease of Doing Business Index ranked Bosnia and Herzegovina 110th out of 187 countries in 2010, the lowest of the six former republics of Yugoslavia. One reason is the Rube Goldberg political system set up by the Dayton peace accord in order to keep the Bosnian-Croat Federation and ten separate cantons (they were apparently thinking of Switzerland when they picked the term) and a separate government for the small city of Brčko, because nobody could agree which side should get it. "It is the most complicated political system I've ever seen," a U.S. official told me. "You need to have something like fifty documents to open any kind of business." By the count of the European Forum for Democracy and Solidarity, there are 700 elected officials in the country and 140 ministers.

It's no great surprise that the government is the largest single employer in Bosnia, accounting for 56 percent of jobs. The Džinos' son, Nermin, although he speaks fluent English as a result of a stint living with his sister, when he returned could only get a job as a driver for the state court. It pays so poorly he can barely support his partner (he's been with the same woman for ten years, but they're not married) and their infant son.

"I make in a month what my sister makes in a week," Nermin complains.

The following weekend, I finally get to meet Alma, who is visiting with her husband and two daughters. I've heard about her for years from her parents and neighbors and have been told that she was the prettiest, smartest girl on Logavina Street. Although she is no longer young, she doesn't disappoint. She is a gust of color and energy, fresh from the Dalmatian coast, bare-shouldered and bronzed from the beach, hair frosted blond, pink lipstick, in a low-cut white blouse with flower-patterned crocheted sweater. Her husband, Siniša, Saša for short, is a larger-than-life character—a well-built man of six feet six who even over coffee is the life of the party. Their teen-age daughters are subdued by comparison.

It has been raining all day, but now there is a peek of setting sun. Zijo uses a cloth to dry off the chairs and the red-and-white checked cover on the outdoor table, and Alma opens a bottle of wine. Though it is near dusk, Siniša says he has just gotten out of bed because he and Alma were drinking with friends until 6:30 A.M. They are both in a rapture about Sarajevo, the friends, the café, the pizza, that famous joie de vivre.

"It is driving me crazy: parties, drinking wine, barbecues, drinking, every night," groans Siniša, with a thick Slavic drawl, the only one in the family who hasn't lost the accent.

Alma interrupts with her crisp South African English. "There are other places you can enjoy life, but not like Sara-jevo. The soul is so unique. I miss it so much. I talk to my mother almost every day. Once we had a conversation which was ninety-two minutes long," she says. "You know, we Bos-nians can't just live everywhere. We tried Australia, but it was too reserved, too quiet. We're loud, especially my husband. We only fit in here."

But to move back to Sarajevo? They discuss it between themselves frequently. "Maybe in four or five years," says Alma. "Maybe ten," says Siniša—but as they talk, the more you get the sense they won't do it. Their older daughter, Mateja, spent four months in Sarajevo this spring and told her parents she wouldn't mind moving back, but her parents have coun-seled her against it.

"My daughter loves it here, but this is a fake type of good life," Alma says. "She spends our money. If she had to start working and earn her own money, it would be another story."

If anything, Alma seems more traumatized by the war than her battle-scarred parents or veteran brother. This is some-

thing I notice in many people I meet. The people who stayed
in Sarajevo throughout had a chance to process their grief and
their rage and come out the other end. For those who drop in
every year or so, everything reminds them of the war that they
missed, and the experience feels fresher and more vivid.

Alma left Sarajevo for Belgrade on Saturday, April 4, 1992,
two days before a meeting of European Community ministers
who were expected to recognize Bosnia and Herzegovina as an
independent nation. Siniša, who was worried the road to the
airport would be closed by the checkpoints that Serbs were
erecting around the city, drove Alma and Mateja, then aged
two, to the airport, to make sure they would be out of harm's
way. He gave her all their cash as well, 72,000 German marks.

"Just in case," Siniša told her at the time. Alma wasn't as
worried as he was. In fact, she was so confident the trouble
would be short-lived that she didn't take her diploma or passport with her. She was on one of the last regularly scheduled
departures from the airport, which was besieged the next day.

Two weeks later, Alma was in Belgrade watching Serbian
TV when she saw a report from Sarajevo. "There was this
house with a hole in it. And I thought, Oh my God, that's my
parents' house. I called my mother-in-law and she said, No,
I'm sure you're wrong. Then I saw shots from the hospital.
There was my father, naked, with a sheet over his genitals."
Alma's husband fled Sarajevo in mid-May to join her. The fam-
ily never came back except for vacations.

We've gotten far enough into the conversation without
talking about ethnicity, which hangs like a foul miasma low
over Sarajevo. You might not notice it immediately, and once

you're in Sarajevo awhile, you may forget at times, but questions about who is Serb, Croat, or Muslim lurk in the background. People avoid talking about ethnicity. They steer the conversation away. Or else they speak with excruciating political correctness, using so much euphemism it is hard to grasp their intent. You don't say "Bosnian Muslim" anymore; you say "Bosniak," a cumbersome word we journalists ridiculed during the war. You say "Bosnian of Serbian nationality" for a Serb who still lives in Sarajevo, or "Serb aggressor" for somebody who fought on the other side.

Alma is a direct person, so she plunges into the subject. Siniša is a Serb—at least he identifies himself as such, although his mother is Catholic. Although he wasn't one of the Serbs who went over to the other side, he didn't stay and help either. Six weeks after Alma left, he managed to sneak out of the city by slipping into a convoy of departing Yugoslav National Army vehicles.

"He never did anything bad. His name is still clean. Everybody likes him," said Alma. "We had friends who left because they went over to the Serb side of Sarajevo. As long as they didn't do any harm, it is okay."

Yet the ethnic question isn't dismissed so easily. Everybody knows who is who. Perhaps clowning for my benefit, Siniša jokingly addresses his father-in-law with *Merhaba,* the Turkish word for hello, which is only used by Muslims. Both Alma and Siniša worry about the influence of Wahhabism, the strain of Sunni fundamentalism from Saudi Arabia.

"Everything is different now. Before, nobody knew who anybody was. We didn't care about religion. We had more important things to think about, what you were going to eat, what you were going to buy, where to go for the weekend. Now everybody is so preoccupied with religion. They are supposed to invest in industry. Instead they are building mosques," Siniša says.

Alma wonders where her family would fit into Sarajevo society today. Would her husband really be accepted? Herself? Her given name, Alma, is a traditional Muslim name, but she has a Croatian passport through her mother and a Serb last name from marriage. Her daughters are a perfect Bosnian stew of Serb, Croat, and Muslim.

Just how many Serbs still live in Sarajevo? Bosnia hasn't done a census since 1991, so nobody quite knows or is even willing to hazard a guess, although it is assumed the number is a fraction of the pre-war figure of 157,000. Logavina Street's Serb population has been reduced as much by old age as by ethnic tension. Many of the Sarajevo Serbs have moved out of the center of the city to Pale, the skiing village that was Karadžić's headquarters during the war, and to other Sarajevo neighborhoods that have been assigned to Republika Srpska. The whole area is now called "Eastern Sarajevo." Many of the Serbs who work in government jobs in central Sarajevo feel more comfortable living in Republika Srpska and so they commute back and forth. The license plates are the same on both sides; in a brilliant bit of Balkan diplomacy, they use the letters T, K, J, O, and A—which happen to be the same in the Cyrillic and Latin alphabets—so that nobody knows who's who from their car.

Jela told me she had visited Pale not long ago to see a former colleague, Milica, who had been her best friend at the factory.

She brought her bread and *kajmak,* a traditional clotted cream, and they had lunch along with Milica's daughter-in-law.

"Are there still Serbs living in Sarajevo?" the daughter-in-law asked Jela.

"*Kako da ne,*" Jela replied, with an expression (literally "How that no") that is an emphatic way of saying "Of course." "Maybe there are not as many Serbs as before, of course, but they are still in Sarajevo, even in my neighborhood. How can you ask me such a question?"

The women started quarreling. Milica cut off Jela in disbelief.

"Come on. Let Jela talk," the daughter-in-law persisted.

But Milica wholeheartedly believed the Serb nationalist propaganda that the Muslims wouldn't permit Serbs in Sarajevo.

"I wasn't angry, but insulted. We've known each other for years. How could she not believe me?"

Jela's best friend on Logavina is Desa Stanić, the Serb widow who returned to Sarajevo after getting medical treatment for her injured son, Vedran, in Germany. Nobody expected her to come back to the city where she had lost her husband in the war, certainly not to the very apartment where a mortar shell in the garden had nearly killed her son. Not only did she want to return, so did her children, Marijana, who is now married, and Vedran.

Desa lives in an undistinguished mid-rise apartment building uphill and across the street from the Džinos. When I visited, she was repainting with the help of her son. The living room was empty except for a cluster of plastic chairs that Vedran set out for us. Desa looked much better than I remembered her during the war, almost radiant, with her hair freshly dyed blond and a T-shirt so declaratively pink as to announce her good cheer.

"That's good—I'm looking for a boyfriend," she shot back, when I complimented her appearance. She laughs, then says more seriously, "I used to be a weak person, but I'm getting stronger."

Desa seems happily oblivious to the difficulties of living in Sarajevo. She attends services at both the Serb Orthodox church, the faith of her childhood, and the Catholic church, the faith of her late husband.

"It's all normal."

Vedran, the introspective boy who curled in a corner nursing his wounds, is now a tall, striking man with a jagged lightning bolt of a scar like Harry Potter's that runs from his mostly bald skull to piercing blue eyes.

Although he has been through numerous operations to remove the shrapnel from the 1992 mortar attack in their backyard, he still suffers from headaches and epileptic seizures. He has nevertheless recovered to the point where he was able to complete college and graduate school in Sarajevo, getting a degree in psychology.

Vedran is more sensitive to the nuance of ethnic tensions, especially in the workplace, where jobs are often allocated by nationality. His job over the summer was with the government ministry overseeing disabled veterans. "In my contract, it says I'm employed as a non-Bosniak person," said Vedran. "That's how it is. When you apply for a job, you fill out a form and state your nationality."

The system had its genesis in Communist times and was reinstated after the war in a misguided attempt to achieve ethnic balance. In the Dayton peace agreement, it applied to elected political offices, namely the tripartite presidency—in which a Muslim, a Serb, and a Croat share power. It has been expanded since to include military, police, and other civil service jobs. Departments have to be filled with X number of Muslims, Y number of Croats, and Z number of Serbs. Known as the "national key," the system is dysfunctional and discriminatory, widely ridiculed, and subject to legal challenges.

Jakob Finci, the head of the Jewish community, who evacuated thousands of people during the war, is suing the government along with Roma activist Dervo Sejdić on the grounds that the national key deprives them of their political rights; neither Serb, Croat, nor Muslim, they are officially listed as "others" and cannot run for the presidency. The European Court of Human Rights ruled in Finci and Sejdić's favor in 2009.

It's not just Jews and Romas who are cast out by the system. By far the biggest population of "others" are the tens of thousands of Sarajevans born to mixed marriages. In 1990, before the breakup of Yugoslavia, 13 percent of marriages were mixed, and in Sarajevo, the figure was above 30 percent. Nermin is among those who refused to be categorized. Rather than choose between his Muslim father and Catholic mother, he listed himself as "other." He and his girlfriend, also the child of a mixed marriage, picked the name Darian for their infant son, which isn't associated with any of the three ethnic groups.

Others pick an identity for reasons pragmatic rather than religious. There are never quite enough Serbs and Croats to fill the positions since the quotas are based on a census taken in 1991, back when Muslims were only 50 percent of the population. If you're a half Muslim, do you declare yourself Muslim to enjoy the confidence of being in the majority, or do you choose to be a minority, a Serb or a Croat, for the affirmative action that will help you get a job? And, of course, the preference for Serbs and Croats builds ethnic resentment.

"When they open a new job and a Bosnian Croat or Bosnian Serb gets it, you can overhear people talking about it. They'll say, 'Do you see that guy? He's a Serb.'"

Vedran isn't ostracized. After all, he has the bona fides, having lost his father and almost his own life for the Bosnian cause, but it doesn't make him like it any better. "You can physically feel the divisions," he says.

The most famous Serb on Logavina Street, maybe the most famous Serb in all Sarajevo, is Jovan Divjak, the retired general from the Yugoslav National Army who is lionized for defending the city in the Bosnian Army. His war service has always rankled the nationalist Serbs, who consider him a traitor to the race. They exacted their revenge by charging him with war crimes. The allegations stem from a shooting incident on May 2, 1992, in the chaotic early days of the war, when somebody fired on a Yugoslav National Army convoy that had been given safe passage by the Bosnian government to exit Sarajevo. Most of the soldiers in the convoy were Serbs. (Divjak has said in an interview that eight people were killed; the Serbs at times have claimed up to forty-two.)

No matter that nobody ever figured out who fired on the convoy; no matter that a videotape of the incident showed Divjak, one of the Bosnian officers on the scene, trying to avert the bloodshed, yelling "Don't shoot!" No matter that the International Criminal Tribunal for the former Yugoslavia had already investigated the incident at the Serbs' request and concluded there was no case against Divjak or other Bosnian officials; Serbia issued an indictment and filed an arrest warrant with Interpol. Divjak was arrested March 3, 2011, at the Vienna airport.

I knew Divjak was in Austria when I visited Sarajevo, but I wondered if anybody was at his apartment toward the bottom of Logavina. It is in an undistinguished mid-rise with mossy green paint peeling off gray cement, built during the Yugoslav period for military families. Divjak's name was on the mailbox. Along with a photographer and a Bosnian journalist who was helping me, I made my way up the dim stairwell to knock on the door. My knuckle had barely grazed the wood when the door swung open and a strong arm yanked me inside. It was his wife, Vera, a large woman with her hair cut in a silver bob and pale blue cat's-eye glasses.

"You've come at the right time. He's on the phone," said Vera, passing the telephone on so we could talk to him.

Divjak had been released from prison, but was staying in an apartment in Vienna lent to him by a patriotic Bosnian. The Austrian government had already decided that the charges against him were bogus and that they wouldn't extradite him to Serbia, but the paperwork hadn't been cleared for him to leave the country. He was expecting to return to Sarajevo any day now. "I thought this would be over in a few days, and it's five months now, and I'm still here," Divjak told us on the phone.

After we hung up, Vera ushered us into the living room. One wall was covered floor to ceiling with bookcases—I spotted the book the general had written in French after the war, *Sarajevo, Mon Amour*. Elsewhere, the eggshell-blue walls were barely visible under the closely spaced artworks, mostly expressionist paintings from the Yugoslav period. Photographs of Tito were scattered about the apartment. Vera went into the kitchen and brought out slices of baklava she had made a week earlier anticipating her husband's homecoming, urging us to finish it off since it was getting stale. Although his release looked imminent—in fact, he came home to a hero's welcome shortly after I left Sarajevo—Vera was agitated and angry.

"It was a terrible thing they did to Jovan. He was put in a jail cell for nine days with thieves and drug addicts," she said. She fretted about health issues—his and her own, since both were in their seventies—and about the injustice of it all. She believed Serbia had indicted her husband in an attempt to muddle the questions of wartime guilt and to appease nationalist sentiment.

Vera was clearly proud of her husband, but I wondered, was it worth it? To be an ethnic Serb and symbol of tolerance in Sarajevo gave them a heavy burden. "His parents are buried in Serbia. He cannot go to visit their graves. I'm afraid they'd kill him if he went. I'm afraid even here in Sarajevo somebody could come after him." In fact, the family is under police protection. I'd noticed the policeman standing outside their apartment.

There was the loneliness, too. Vera was heading to the hospital later that evening for a minor operation and said she would get a taxi and go on her own because there was nobody to take her. Her sons left during the war and never returned. Their next-door neighbors in the building, mostly Yugoslav National Army families from Belgrade like themselves, were long gone. But no, Vera never considered leaving.

"At the hospital the other day, there was another patient who was the wife of a former Yugoslav National Army officer. They'd moved to Novi Sad [in northern Serbia], but she said she realized that living in Sarajevo is better.

"The other Serbs, too, they should come back. Living together in Sarajevo is the best solution," said Vera. Besides, her husband would never go to join their children in the United States. "Jovan? To America? You'll never get him out of Sarajevo except in a coffin."

After Divjak, the biggest celebrity on Logavina Street is Tarik Kaljanac, the younger son of Ekrem and Minka Kaljanac. I remembered him very fondly as an impish toddler who would sneak sips from our beer bottles and prance around the living room pretending to shoot Chetniks on television. He was a true child of war, raised on powdered milk and his mother's war recipes cobbled together from humanitarian aid. They must have been more nutritious than anybody imagined because Tarik is now six feet two, two hundred pounds, a bodybuilder and model for Calvin Klein underwear among other famous brands.

Minka and Ekrem's apartment, more than any other on Logavina Street, looked like a time capsule from the war years. The warped wooden stairs groaned as we walked up to the second floor. The plaster in the stairwell was crumbling where they'd crudely patched the damage from a mortar shell that had crashed through the roof. Inside, though, the door opened into their cheerful kitchen, lemon yellow with white lace curtains, wooden knickknacks, and a kettle on the stove that sang.

Now that the boys were big, Minka and Ekrem had given them the apartment's one bedroom and moved their own bed into what had been the living room, leaving the kitchen as the common space. We sat on the L-shaped sofas piled with pillows around a low wooden kitchen table.

It didn't take much prompting for Minka to show off some of Tarik's photo spreads. With a shy, almost sheepish smile, she laid them on the kitchen table. On the cover of *Men's Style*,

there was Tarik striking a sultry pose in an embroidered bro-
cade jacket; in another photo spread he was banker-like in
horn-rimmed glasses and a linen suit; in yet another he wore a
tuxedo, his wrist turned just so to display a Louis Vuitton
wristwatch.

They explained how it happened. Son Haris, who is now
twenty-seven and like many of the people I knew as children
during the war proficient in English, interpreted for his parents. Tarik had torn a ligament skiing and had to give up playing soccer. With nothing else to do, he started lifting weights at
the gym, toning his body. One of his buddies had been planning to enter an international male modeling pageant in the
Dominican Republic, as Bosnia's representative, but was unable to get the time off from work and suggested Tarik take his
place. To raise $3,000 for the plane ticket, Tarik sold his car.

Minka jumped up to retrieve from the bedroom the plexi-
glass trophy. Mr. Universe Model 2010. A photo showed Tarik
with the trophy draped with the blue-and-yellow Bosnian flag.

"We were really proud," Minka said.

Winning first place in the pageant opened doors. Tarik was
one of the few contestants who didn't already have an agent,
but he was quickly signed up and landed a job with a modeling
agency based in Singapore.

I got to meet Tarik a few days later visiting his parents for
the summer. As in his photos, he has toffee-colored silky hair,
dark brown eyes, and a chiseled jawline underneath carefully
cultivated stubble, though he was less glamorously attired in
gym shorts and a blue Italia soccer shirt. He was lounging
around at home because he was jetlagged, one eye red from a
minor case of conjunctivitis, and he didn't want to go downtown just yet, where he risked being photographed not looking

his best. Vanity, perhaps? Tarik didn't seem to take himself all that seriously.

Picking himself up off the couch, he demonstrated the various poses he had to strike modeling underwear.

"One assignment I had to model 160 pair of underwear in 16 hours." He laughed. "To be honest, I do it just for the money. I work, work, work all the time," said Tarik.

For a kid from a working-class Bosnian family to be traveling the world didn't strike Tarik as particularly glamorous or enviable. He had just finished a three-month stint in Seoul, where he didn't do any sightseeing, and rarely went out to eat or drink with the other models with whom he was sharing an apartment.

His plan was to save up as much as possible while he had his looks and then come back to Sarajevo and buy a new place for the family to live. One reason their building was in such disrepair was that the rights to the property, which was formerly state-owned, were still in limbo two decades after the fall of Communism. "If I was one of those rich, famous models, I'd take them with me when I travel," he said. During his holiday, he would spend most of his time with the family and fast for Ramadan, which in 2011 coincided with the month of August. He wasn't such a devout Muslim, Tarik said. "It's a good way to lose weight."

I saw more of Tarik's modeling biographies, which talked about his passion for sports, especially soccer. None of them mentioned the war in Bosnia. Tarik said he avoided telling people he met in the modeling business about his early childhood under siege for fear it would be a downer.

"If you talk to people about your country in war, it's like, Oh my God, this guy is part of a sad story. I don't want people to look at me in that way. They'd maybe think you are aggressive: You fight among yourselves. I say the war is twenty years ago. Sometimes I say it was thirty years ago—they don't know. They think I'm a normal guy."

"Normal" seemed to be the family's favorite word—*normalno*, in Bosnian. They kept stressing the situation was *normal* in Sarajevo. Relations between ethnic groups were more or less *normal*. The economy was lousy, but that was to be expected. *Normal.*

As best I could tell from a few visits, the family seemed happy, happier perhaps than any of the others I met on the street. Minka looked better than when I'd known her before, having fixed her teeth after the war. Ekrem had gotten paunchy and lost most of his hair, but not his sense of humor. He'd become chairman of a volunteer organization, War Invalids of the Old City, and traveled around Bosnia frequently in his official capacity. He told me about a trip to Srebrenica, where he'd attended a memorial service for the eight thousand who died and met a survivor who'd hidden for days in the river to avoid being killed. The story struck him with fresh horror.

Ekrem still did electrical work, sometimes doing installations on new houses on the other side of Sarajevo, and he often worked with Serbs. Minka was not as comfortable crossing over. In 2010, she went to see a back specialist from Belgrade who was working out of a hospital in Eastern Sarajevo.

"I was in the waiting room and they called my name, Kaljanac, Jasmina, and I thought I'd die," says Minka, referring to her full name, which is distinctly Muslim. "I felt like everybody was looking at me like I had 'Muslim' written across my forehead. I wanted to get in quickly before anything happened."

Minka laughs at herself now, and says she is, as she puts it, "learning to be more flexible." In everyday life, they rarely talk about the war.

"It's not that we've forgotten about the war. We just don't talk about it as much," said Ekrem.

I asked Tarik and Haris, who was already eight when the war started and in a better position to remember, whether they were traumatized by the experience of seeing neighbors killed, their father losing his fingertips. They both emphatically answered no.

Minka jumped back into the conversation. She had kept the boys in the basement as much as possible during the war to shelter them not just from the mortar shells but also from the fear and anger. "I didn't want them to hate anybody for who they were. To my children, everybody is a good guy unless something happens to prove otherwise," she said in her soft, shy voice. She wanted them to be normal.

Of the people on Logavina Street, most more or less confirmed almost two decades later my earlier expectations of what they would become.

The dentist Esad Taljanović spent some time in the United States with his brother, but didn't like it any better than he had the glimpses he saw on his brother's videotapes during the war. He still lives in the mustard-yellow house just up from the school, although he teaches dentistry now, rather than practicing. His son, he told me, went to journalism school, but after graduating decided to become a dentist.

Kasema Telalagić is working as hard as during the war, with a daytime job in a state ophthalmology hospital and a nighttime job in a private optometry clinic. Her daughter, Dženana, is a soft-spoken university student majoring in English. Fuad Kasumagić still runs jewelry shops in the Turkish market. Some of the older people I knew on Logavina had passed away, among them Alija Žiga, the imam of the mosque. Milutin Đurđevac died a few years after the war, and his wife, Cvijeta, moved out to live closer to her children. Sead Vranić also passed away a few years after the war. To the very end he refused all offers to rent out his spectacular Austro-Hungarian mansion as an embassy.

Mladen Marković, who disappeared from Sarajevo in 1995, had moved to Australia as the neighbors suspected. He was working as a civil engineer in the building industry. He and his wife, Veronika, had another child, a daughter. Mladen e-mailed to say that his wife was homesick for Sarajevo, but that he was not.

"Australia is my home, my present and future," he said. He could not explain to me how and why he had left Sarajevo without saying good-bye to anybody on Logavina Street. At the time, he wrote, "I was in two separate worlds, one real, war, killings, sufferings and second, my past and future family life with Veronika and Boris. That's how my poetry started which kept me going day by day. Many of my poems were more predictions for the future than poetry: everything was completely fulfilled."

At the top of Logavina Street, the old orphanage looks as ominous as ever, a brooding hulk of a building overlooking the cemetery. It is used as a depository for the Historical Archive of Sarajevo. The refugees who used to live there have gone back to their hometowns or found new housing in Sarajevo.

Mirza and Selma Kapić eventually were able to recover their childhood house in Derventa, among 580,000 Bosnians who have done so, according to figures by the UN High Commissioner for Refugees. In the partition, Derventa ended up in the Republika Srpska. A key annex of the Dayton agreement gave all refugees and displaced persons the right to return to their original homes, but it was 1998 before the family got up the nerve to visit. Lana Lačević, whose mother owned a share of the house as well, said they discovered that a Serb family who had left a town in the Federation was living in it.

"We stood outside the house. They were screaming at us: 'You pieces of shit, Muslims,'" Lana recalled.

They did eventually recover the rights to the house in 2006. By that time, Mirza and Selma's parents, who had spent their final years pining for Derventa, had both passed away. The house was completely destroyed, even the plumbing and electrical fixtures stripped. Mirza and Selma renovated one bedroom and a bathroom so they would have a place to go on weekends. Somehow they don't get there very often. Lana and Maša are both doctors like their mother, and Lana, who married Delila's ex-boyfriend, Haris, also has a young son. Selma works for a trading company. Mirza has a car dealership and recently opened a café.

Nowadays, when they visit the house, they don't have any difficulties with the Serb neighbors, but at the same time they don't have too many friends there either. "Most old people returned to Derventa. Not so many young people. More might have come back, but there are no jobs," said Mirza.

True to her word, Delila Lačević moved to America and never came back, except for one brief visit. The year after she arrived in the States, a Bosnian activist introduced her to a young academic who looked like an all-American football player and spoke like a college professor. He was interested in Eastern Europe and remembered Delila from an interview she'd given ABC Television. They were married on a brilliant July day in 1997 on the sloping lawn of his parents' lakeside home in northern Michigan. Delila became a U.S. citizen in 2006. She's kept her maiden name in honor of her parents, and many of her Bosnian traditions as well. "I gave up pork and swearing for the month of Ramadan," she said. Delila has been back to Sarajevo only once, in 2007, when she promised to show her husband and mother-in-law around for two weeks. They left after five days. She couldn't even take the sight of the gravestone she and Berin had purchased for their parents—topped with a Turkish fez in the traditional Bosnian Muslim style. After a decade without cigarettes, she started chain-smoking again. "I can't forget. I can't forgive. I can't get over it. I don't want to stare at it," Delila told me about her trip. She didn't want to stick around Sarajevo feeling sorry for herself. "Shit happens. Kids in Srebrenica are still waiting for their dads' body parts. At least I know where my parents are buried."

Delila and her husband now live in Austin, Texas. She is a retail executive. Berin was a college football star for Purdue University and is now working in medical sales. They speak to each other in English.

EPILOGUE

THE ANGRIEST PERSON I MET on Logavina Street, Harun Išerić, was two years old when the war ended. Whatever authentic experiences he had of the siege were lost to the amnesia of early childhood. His parents, especially his father, who had served in the army, never talked about the war. What Harun knew came mostly from his voracious reading on the Internet, which perhaps explains why his anger sounded so fresh and unprocessed. In his mind, the war happened yesterday.

Harun's family had moved to Logavina in 2004, renovating the top floor of a small apartment house around the corner from the imam Alija Žiga, an old family friend. From the bunk bed Harun shared with a younger brother, he could see through the window into the cemetery, could clearly see the graves of Delila's parents.

Not yet eighteen when we met, Harun was athletically built with a closely trimmed beard, which he cultivated to make his pink-cheeked baby face look older. He usually wore the same blue tracksuit. On the crown of his head was a small strip of scalp without hair, a scar from where he'd been grazed by a sniper's bullet as a baby. "My mother told me I was so close to death. The bullet only just passed over my head."

Harun was obsessed with the war and had found a natural outlet as a tour guide, lecturing foreign tourists about the horrors that had befallen Sarajevo. The company he worked for operated out of a storefront near the Princip Bridge, named for the Archduke Franz Ferdinand's assassin Gavrilo Princip, and it specialized in war locales—the library, the market, Sniper Alley, and the tunnel under the airport that had been used to sneak supplies in and people out during the siege. Although Harun was still in high school, his English was excellent and his passion for history unquestionable. He landed the job by simply walking into the office and asking about the position. He was hired on the spot.

It was a good business. Foreign tourists were nearly as obsessed with the war as Harun—after all, it was the most notable thing that had happened in Sarajevo since the assassination in 1914—and the tour was often crowded. The day I took it, Harun crammed twelve people into an eight-seat Volkswagen. The roads around the city are one-way, so we first drove east along the Miljacka River past the national library, which was enveloped in scaffolding for repairs not yet complete, then looped around the Baščaršija to head back westward out of town.

Along the way, Harun pointed out the sights in a sonorous Slavic baritone that didn't need a microphone. "The library was five days burning. Two million books. *Auf Wiedersehen*; destroyed. Burning the books was evidence that fascism didn't die in Europe in 1945, fascism lives." Then, driving by a monument for children killed in war: "One thousand six hundred children were murdered by Serbian fascists in the heart of Europe at the end of the twentieth century."

When we passed the former UN headquarters, Harun's words were even angrier. "The UN didn't do anything. They were eating hamburgers while I was eating pigeons. They drank water while I licked the rain. They played Ping-Pong while I was playing roulette with my life." Harun had no inhibitions about lecturing people twice his age about genocide and fascism. He liberally appropriated sound bites from the Holocaust. "I can forgive but I cannot forget. To forget is the biggest sin."

In Harun's opinion, the Bosnian government deliberately downplayed the war, putting reconciliation ahead of justice. "In the schools, they teach nothing about the war or genocide. The schools should go to Omarska, Visegrad, Srebrenica, just like we must organize trips to Auschwitz." There were plaques at the sites of the major mortar attacks—the brewery where Delila's parents were killed, the open-air market, and the monument to children—but there was no memorial or monument to the experience of the siege as a whole. The closest thing to a war museum is the tunnel under the airport, where tourists can crawl underground and see videos about the war.

The lack of education about the war, Harun said, had left the population unprepared if there is another conflict with the Serbs. "They wanted to make a greater Serbia during World War I, World War II, through the last war. They are still dreaming of greater Serbia," said Harun.

Although still in high school, Harun was clear about his future plans. He wants to be a politician, and is already active in the Muslim-nationalist party founded by the late president Izetbegović, the Party of Democratic Action. He and his family are devout Muslims; one of his uncles trained as an imam in Pakistan, and most of his family have made the hajj to Mecca.

"Every Muslim has a dream to live in a united Muslim union, like Europe, stretching from Bosnia to Indonesia, with our brothers from Palestine, Chechnya, Somalia, China," said Harun. "We will not be slaves to the Serbian people."

Angry young men. Angry young Muslims. Harun's rhetoric conjures up the worst fears of many Bosnians. Radical Islam is the bogeyman that Republika Srpska's nationalist politicians use to justify the existence of their mini-state, which they say is needed to protect Christians against the tyranny of the Muslim majority. At the time of the Bosnian war, few people knew the name of Osama bin Laden or Al-Qaeda; in the years since September 11, Serb and Croat nationalists have been more successful at playing the "Muslim peril" card. "Their ultimate goal," warned Republika Srpska president Milorad Dodik in an editorial in *The Washington Times* in 2007, referring to the Bosnian government, is a Bosnia "in which one group, Bosniak—and one religion, Islam—will gain unquestionable supremacy." When I visited Pale over the summer, stopping at an association of retired Serb soldiers in its offices across the street from the Orthodox cathedral where Radovan Karadžić's daughter was married, the association's head, Mihajlo Paradina, told me, "The biggest danger for Bosnia is an Ayatollah Khomeini."

In Sarajevo, people are fixated on headscarves. Bosnians and visitors sit in cafés and nervously count the women with covered heads as though scarves per square mile were some pseudo-scientific measure of Islamization. (My personal count suggests there are fewer today than at the end of the war, but others disagree.)

New investment increasingly comes from the Middle East, perhaps as a result of Europe's financial crisis. The Bristol

Hotel, the fanciest in Sarajevo, where Desa Stanić worked as a bartender before the war, now serves no alcohol—the decision of the Saudi-based Al Shiddi Group, which renovated and re-opened the hotel in April 2010. The hip new BBI Centar off Maršala Tita, the most modern shopping mall in the city with its only authorized Apple dealership, is also dry, having been developed by a consortium of Islamic banks from the United Arab Emirates. Many of the flights into Sarajevo come through Istanbul, reaffirming Sarajevo's historic ties with Turkey. Wary of offending Muslim sensibilities, organizers of the Sarajevo Film Festival moved the dates in 2010 and 2011 so that it would not coincide with the start of Ramadan.

Harun rejects the idea of creeping Islamization. If anything, he says, people are becoming less devout. "The mosques were full during the war—now they are half-empty." Even among devout Muslims like himself, he says there is little support for a state governed by Islamic law. "The country here has never been officially Muslim. This is a country of Serbs, Catholics, Muslims, Jews."

Whether or not Sarajevo is becoming a Muslim city, there is no doubt that it is populated largely by people who happen to be Muslim. Muslims make up about 90 percent of the population in Sarajevo today, a majority that causes discomfort for the remaining Serbs and Croats, not to speak of the Bosnian Muslims themselves. The Bosnian government has worked hard to keep radical Islam out of the country. Over the past few years, they have been trying to deport hundreds of Arab fighters (the "mujaheddin") who came during the war and stayed on, often marrying Bosnian women and becoming Bosnian citizens. But getting Serbs and Croats to come back to Sarajevo is a more difficult proposition.

This is true not only in Sarajevo, but throughout Bosnia.

Population patterns show that Bosnians after the war moved to towns and neighborhoods with their own kind, the ethnic fault lines congealing. Although displaced people were largely allowed to recover their homes in keeping with the Dayton pact, they often sold or exchanged their property, or, like the Kapić and Lačević cousins, use it only as a vacation home. A critical report in 2005 by the Helsinki Committee for Human Rights in Bosnia and Herzegovinia, established by a group of Sarajevo lawyers, stated that in all Bosnian municipalities except Tuzla, the majority ethnic group now constituted more than 90 percent of the population. Their conclusion was that the Serbs had succeeded in their strategy of ethnic cleansing. People increasingly live in ethnically pure enclaves.[1]

"People are afraid if we do a census, it will show the real percentages on the ground," said Peđa Kojović, a member of the Bosnian parliament. With his shoulder-length blond hair he still looks like a cameraman for Reuters, the job he held during the war. He left after the war for New York and moved back in 2008 to start a new political party with two friends—Oscar-winning filmmaker Danis Tanović and theater director Dino Mustafić. The idea was to get politically apathetic young, educated Bosnians to get involved again in building a multicultural society. The party, Naša Stranka, has embraced a grab bag of odd causes—gay rights, a bill that would make it a crime to deny the Srebrenica massacre took place (modeled on similar laws about Holocaust denial), and even, in the name of free speech, the rights of Serbs from the other side to have a memorial ceremony for war dead in Sarajevo.

"After the war, there was a spirit of a new beginning. That's gone now. People can't see the way out. They've lost interest in politics," said Kojović. "Every day I'm on the verge of packing up my things and going back to New York."

.   .   .

Could there be another war? It is the question I'm asked most
often about Bosnia and one that I ask many of the people I meet
there. Unfortunately, I haven't heard an unequivocal no. More
often I hear "I hope that will not be." Thus answered Haris
Mulahasanović, Lana's husband. He works for the Bosnian military, which by law is made up of Muslims, ethnic Serbs, and
Croats. Although they work together, most of the Serbs, even if
they are from Sarajevo, now live in rented apartments in suburbs like Pale and Lukavica in the Republika Srpska. During
lunchtime and after hours, people keep to themselves. "When
we have a break, Serbs drink with Serbs, Muslims with Muslims. Sometimes the situation is dangerous."

Events that might lead to another war are easy to imagine:
if, say, the Republika Srpska tried to secede from Bosnia. The
Republika Srpska has its own government and a hard-line
president, Milorad Dodik, who uses every opportunity to
make clear he does not want to be part of Bosnia. In 2011, he
threatened a referendum to withdraw from the Bosnian judi-
cial system, which he claimed was biased against Serbs. Widely
considered a dress rehearsal for a vote to secede from Bosnia
entirely, the referendum was called off under heavy pressure
from the United States and European Union. Had it taken
place, said the International Crisis Group in a report in October, it could have brought Bosnia to the brink of war. The think
tank further warned, "If its Serb leaders continue driving every
conflict with Sarajevo to the brink, as they have done repeatedly to date, they risk disaster. The agility of leaders and the
population's patience need only fail once to ignite serious violence."

The lousy economy doesn't help. Although the same mal-
aise afflicts most of Europe, especially the lack of good jobs for

recent graduates, Bosnians tend to blame the war—it was better, they say, under Yugoslavia. They call this phenomenon—of
looking back to better times—*Yugonostalgia*. These views only
encourage Bosnians to blame whoever was on the other side.
Underemployed young people have plenty of time to read incendiary websites that hype the dangers of Islamic radicalism
or of Serb nationalism, keeping alive the hatred.

There are some positive developments in the region, mostly
emanating from Belgrade. Slobodan Milošević was toppled by
popular demonstrations in 2000 and died in 2006 in The
Hague, where he was standing trial before the International
Criminal Tribunal for the Former Yugoslavia. Boris Tadić,
Serbia's president since 2004, is a pro-European liberal who
has tried to steer his people away from the belligerent nationalism that was the undoing of Yugoslavia. On May 26, 2011,
Serbia arrested sixty-nine-year-old Ratko Mladić, who had
been living under an assumed name with relatives. "We have
ended a difficult period of our history and removed the stain
from the face of Serbia and the members of our nation wherever they live," Tadić said in announcing the arrest.

Tadić was born in Sarajevo and has come several times as
president; a formal state visit to the city in July 2011 raised
expectations of better relations. The year before, Tadić had
made a tearful pilgrimage to Srebrenica for the fifteenth anniversary of the massacre, July 11, 2010, kneeling at the memorial for victims. (Unfortunately, Tadić has been less conciliatory
when it comes to Kosovo, which declared its independence in
2009 and has been recognized by the United States and European Union, but not by Serbia.)

Bosnia's current leaders are mostly Social Democrats, who

inched ahead of the ethnic parties in the general elections in 2010. At Sarajevo's City Hall, I was ushered in to meet Mayor Alija Behmen, who told me enthusiastically about the various initiatives he hoped would reintegrate Serbs into the city. Working together, he and the mayor of Pale ("a very nice fellow," said Behmen), had begun a $40 million project to restore the cable car from Sarajevo to Mount Trebević. An even more ambitious proposal would extend Sarajevo's trams to Pale to make it easier for the estimated ten thousand people per day who commute to the city. "Multiethnicity is the sine qua non of civilization," said Behmen, a genial man with white wispy hair and pouches under his eyes that reminded me of Frank Morgan playing the Wizard of Oz. "I know everything is still not in the best order, but we are going in the right direction."

Unfortunately, it's hard to get things done in Bosnia. The multilayered structure of the Bosnian government almost guarantees paralysis. After the October 2010 elections, it took fifteen months for the Social Democrats to get a coalition government approved. "The reform of public administration is essential," said Behmen. "Each official has two assistants and each assistant has two assistants and so you have this big pyramid." With the benefit of hindsight the Dayton pact has been judged a great success insofar as it stopped the war, but it was in essence a cease-fire agreement, not a plan for a functional government.

Bosnia faced an almost-farcical predicament in spring of 2011, when the Fédération Internationale de Football Association (FIFA) threatened to ban it from competition because there were three presidents of the Bosnian football association instead of just one as required by FIFA. The Bosnian Serb president, Milorad Dodik, put up a fuss, telling reporters he was "against having one president of anything in Bosnia, even a beekeepers' association." Although a compromise was reached, it underscored Bosnia's dilemma: If it barely qualified for international soccer competitions, how could it possibly dream of joining the European Union?

If Bosnia were to join, as it hopes to do, it would have to do a census and face up to the facts on the ground. The national key in which everybody has to peg themselves as a Serb, Croat, or Muslim would be eliminated. Just about everybody agrees it is an absurd system that keeps alive ethnic divisions, but getting rid of it is not so simple because the Serb nationalist parties would likely object, since they'd stand to lose some of the jobs allocated strictly for Serbs. "It is a trivial problem, but hard to fix," sighed Behmen.

Nowadays, even to talk about multiethnicity sounds naïve and passé, a bit, well, 1990s. In an influential essay in *Foreign Affairs* in 2008, political scientist Jerry Z. Muller argued that ethnic nationalism, although despised by liberal intellectuals, is part of human nature and integral to the creation of stable, modern nation-states: "Making and keeping peace between groups that have come to hate and fear one another is likely to require costly ongoing military missions. . . . Partition may thus be the most humane lasting solution to such intense communal conflicts," Muller wrote in the essay "Us and Them."[2] While I was in Sarajevo, people were talking about the horrific July 22 attack in Oslo in which an anti-Muslim extremist murdered seventy-seven people, nodding sadly as though to say, See how difficult it is for a multiethnic society to be peaceful. If it could happen in Norway, how can we in Bosnia expect peace?

.   .   .

Multiethnicity is, like democracy, complicated. It is an irony that the Republika Srpska today is doing somewhat better economically and politically than the rest of Bosnia; it is easier to govern. The ethnic mix that once allowed Sarajevans to boast they lived in the "Jerusalem of Europe"—a city of Muslims and Catholics and Orthodox and Jews—continues to make their life difficult. Sarajevans don't have any choice in this matter. Where else do people like the Džinos live but in Sarajevo? Whether or not it is the intellectual fashion, multiethnicity was handed to them by their history and geography. Multiethnicity, tolerance, diversity—these were values that brought Susan Sontag and Bono and foreign correspondents to Bosnia during the war and what ultimately drew the Clinton administration to intervene. Bosnia's very creation as an independent state was to establish a neutral space in the wreckage of Yugoslavia where residents did not have to be Serb, Croat, or Muslim. One wants to believe that that's still worth saving.

ACKNOWLEDGMENTS

So MANY RESIDENTS on Logavina Street gave generously of their time and insight, but none more so than Jela and Zijo Džino, who were my hosts on so many trips to Sarajevo. Members of the Kaljanac and Lačević families also pitched in as guides and translators and friends.

This project was first conceived at *The Philadelphia Inquirer* and many fine editors worked with me—Fran Dauth, Max King, Don Kimelman, Robert Rosenthal, Nancy Szokan, Lois Wark, and David Zucchino, as well as foreign desk staffers Lisa Karoly and John Brumfield, and *Inquirer* writers Jane Von Bergen and Carrie Rickey.

In Sarajevo, Amela Filipović first helped me pick Logavina Street. Among the journalists I worked with in Sarajevo in the 1990s who offered insight, outrage, companionship, rides in their bulletproof cars, were Joe Brand, Emma Daly, Tom Gjelten, John Pomfret, Kurt Schork, Samantha Power, David Rieff, Clay Scott, Ed Serotta, and Stacy Sullivan. Tracy Wilkinson of the *Los Angeles Times* has been involved with the project almost from its inception to the present.

Finally, this book is dedicated to my dear friend and fellow traveler Elizabeth Neuffer, the most committed journalist I've known, who lost her own life covering the war in Iraq.

This book would not have been republished without my agent, Flip Brophy, and editors, Julie Grau in New York and Bella Lacey in London, as well as Laura Van der Veer. On my most recent trip to Sarajevo, Julie Talen shot video and acted as a sounding board; Zdravko Ljubas offered interpretation and analysis. Others who deserve thanks for bringing this book to fruition include Mark Bartolini, David Berreby, Ann Dalporto, Gladys Demick, Nicholas Demick, Gady Epstein, Molly Fowler, Terri Jentz, Nomi Morris, Evan Osnos, Catherine Peterson, Ben Rauch, Dave Schmerler, Isabel Schmerler, Margaret Scott, Laura Silber, and Dorothy Wickenden.

SOURCES

Bass, Gary Jonathan. *Stay the Hand of Vengeance: The Politics of War Crimes Tribunals.* Princeton, NJ: Princeton University Press, 2000.

Gjelten, Tom. *Sarajevo Daily: A City and Its Newspaper Under Siege.* New York: HarperCollins, 1995.

Glenny, Misha. *The Fall of Yugoslavia: The Third Balkan War.* London: Penguin Books, 1992.

Kaplan, Robert D. *Balkan Ghosts: A Journey Through History.* New York: St. Martin's Press, 1993.

Maas, Peter. *Love Thy Neighbor: A Story of War.* New York: Alfred A. Knopf, 1996.

Malcolm, Noel. *Bosnia: A Short History.* London: Macmillan, 1994.

Mousavizadeh, Nader, ed. *The Black Book of Bosnia: The Consequences of Appeasement.* New York: Basic Books, 1996.

Neuffer, Elizabeth. *The Key to My Neighbor's House: Seeking Justice in Bosnia and Rwanda.* New York: Picador, 2001.

Power, Samantha. *Breakdown in the Balkans: A Chronicle of Events, January, 1989 to May, 1993.* New York: Carnegie Endowment for International Peace, 1993.

———. *A Problem from Hell: America and the Age of Genocide.* New York: HarperPerennial, 2002.

Prstojevic, Miroslav. *Sarajevo: Ranjeni Grad.* Ljubljana: DAG Grafika, 1993.

Rieff, David. *Slaughterhouse: Bosnia and the Failure of the West.* New York: Simon & Schuster, 1995.

Rohde, David. *Endgame: The Betrayal and Fall of Srebrenica, Europe's Worst Massacre Since World War II.* Boulder, CO: Westview Press, 1997.

Silber, Laura, and Allan Little. *The Death of Yugoslavia.* London: Penguin, 1995.

Stewart, Rory, and Gerald Knaus. *Can Intervention Work?* NewYork: W. W. Norton, 2011.

Thompson, Mark. *A Paper House: The Ending of Yugoslavia.* London: Vintage Books, 1992.

Toal, Gerard, and Carl T. Dahlman. *Bosnia Remade: Ethnic Cleansing and Its Reversal.* New York: Oxford University Press, 2011.

Vuillamy, Ed. *Seasons in Hell: Understanding Bosnia's War.* London: Simon & Schuster, 1994.

NOTES

Preface

1. Susan Sontag, "A Lament for Bosnia," *The Nation*, December 25, 1995.
2. Stewart and Knaus, *Can Intervention Work?* p. 101. The Clinton speech is also quoted here, p. xii.

Introduction

1. Primo Levi, *Survival in Auschwitz* (New York: Touchstone Books, 1995), p. 17.

1: Denial

1. Izetbegović quoted in Gjelten, *Sarajevo Daily*, p. 85.
2. Karadžić speech quoted in Silber and Little, *Death of Yugoslavia*, p. 237. "You want to take Bosnia-Herzegovina down the same highway of hell and suffering that Slovenia and Croatia are traveling. Do not think that you will not lead Bosnia-Herzegovina into hell, and do not think that you will not perhaps lead the Muslim people into annihilation, because the Muslims cannot defend themselves if there is war—How will you prevent everyone from being killed in Bosnia-Herzegovina?"
3. Izetbegović quoted in Rieff, *Slaughterhouse*, p. 131.

2: Orphans of War

1. Sign quoted in Gjelten, *Sarajevo Daily*, p. 37. Writer Anna Husarska of the *New Republic* was given a list of restrictions imposed on non-Serbs in Celinac, near Banja Luka. Muslims and Croats were forbidden to

meet in cafés, swim in the rivers, drive or travel by car, or contact relatives outside Celinac. In Mousavizadeh, *Black Book of Bosnia*, p. 75.

3: A Death in the Family
1. Prstojević, *Sarajevo*, p. 117.
2. The Mladić tape was broadcast most recently in the BBC series *The Death of Yugoslavia*.

5: Serbs, Croats, and Muslims
1. Gjelten, *Sarajevo Daily*, p. 137.
2. Malcolm, *Bosnia: A Short History*, p. 192. According to Malcolm, 75,000 Bosnian Muslims are thought to have died in World War II, 8.1 percent of their total population.

9: Awakening
1. Rumors circulated through diplomatic circles after the market shelling of a secret UN report that blamed the Bosnian government. Charles Lane dealt with the issue in *The New Republic*, June 20, 1994, p. 25. He concluded that there was no evidence of the Bosnian Muslims bombing themselves.

10: Betrayal
1. Clinton's quote is taken from a selection of statements by the president on Bosnia, as compiled by Hanna Rosin in *The New Republic*, August 7, 1995, p. 14.
2. Boutros Boutros-Ghali quoted in Power, *Breakdown in the Balkans*, p. 74.

11: Escape
1. Mladić quoted in *The New York Times*, June 27, 1995.
2. The best estimates put the number of deaths from Srebrenica at 8,000. The massacre is examined extensively in several books published since the end of the war. See Rohde, *Endgame*, and Neuffer, *The Key to My Neighbor's House*.

Epilogue
1. The Helsinki Committee report is quoted by Toal and Dahlman, *Bosnia Remade: Ethnic Cleansing and Its Reversal*, p. 298.
2. Jerry Z. Muller, "Us and Them: The Enduring Power of Ethnic Nationalism," *Foreign Affairs*, March/April 2008.

© JINNA PARK

BARBARA DEMICK is the author of *Eat the Buddha: Life and Death in a Tibetan Town; Nothing to Envy: Ordinary Lives in North Korea,* a finalist for the National Book Award and the National Book Critics Circle Award; and *Logavina Street: Life and Death in a Sarajevo Neighborhood.* She was a reporter with the *Los Angeles Times* and headed the paper's bureaus in Beijing and Seoul. She was also a correspondent for *The Philadelphia Inquirer* out of the Balkans and Middle East.

Demick grew up in New Jersey and graduated from Yale College. Her work has won many awards, including the Samuel Johnson Prize (now the Baillie Gifford Prize) for nonfiction in the United Kingdom, the Overseas Press Club's human rights reporting award, the George Polk Award, the Robert F. Kennedy Journalism Award, and Stanford University's Shorenstein Journalism Award for Asia coverage. She was a press fellow at the Council on Foreign Relations, a Bagehot fellow in business journalism at Columbia University, and a visiting professor of journalism at Princeton University. She lives in New York City.

From bestselling author
BARBARA DEMICK

BY THE AUTHOR OF THE NATIONAL BOOK AWARD FINALIST
NOTHING TO ENVY

EAT THE BUDDHA

LIFE AND DEATH
IN A TIBETAN TOWN

BARBARA DEMICK

A gripping portrait of modern Tibet told through the lives of its people, from the author of National Book Award finalist *Nothing to Envy*

"You simply cannot understand China
without reading Barbara Demick on Tibet."

—EVAN OSNOS, author of *Age of Ambition*

RANDOM
HOUSE

RandomHouseBooks.com